全国高等院校翻译专业规划教材

国学典籍英译教程

A Textbook for English Translation of Chinese Classics

主　编　李照国

副主编　丁大刚　刘　霁

编　委　（以姓氏笔画为序）
　　　　丁大刚　刘　霁　李志强
　　　　李照国　金　辉　谈剑明

策　划　汤定军

苏州大学出版社

图书在版编目(CIP)数据

国学典籍英译教程/李照国主编. —苏州：苏州大学出版社，2012.8（2024.1重印）
全国高等院校翻译专业规划教材
ISBN 978-7-5672-0235-1

Ⅰ.①国… Ⅱ.①李… Ⅲ.①国学-英语-翻译-高等学校-教材 Ⅳ.①H315.9

中国版本图书馆 CIP 数据核字（2012）第 197592 号

书　　名：	国学典籍英译教程
	A Textbook for English Translation of Chinese Classics
作　　者：	李照国　主编
责任编辑：	汤定军
策划编辑：	汤定军
装帧设计：	刘　俊
出版发行：	苏州大学出版社（Soochow University Press）
社　　址：	苏州市十梓街1号　邮编：215006
印　　装：	广东虎彩云印刷有限公司
网　　址：	www.sudapress.com
E - mail：	tangdingjun@suda.edu.cn
邮购热线：	0512-67480030
销售热线：	0512-65225020
开　　本：	787mm×960mm　1/16　印张：15　字数：271 千
版　　次：	2012 年 8 月第 1 版
印　　次：	2024 年 1 月第 2 次印装
书　　号：	ISBN 978-7-5672-0235-1
定　　价：	48.00 元

凡购本社图书发现印装错误，请与本社联系调换。服务热线:0512-65225020

前言 PREFACE

  为了给外语专业的研究生和本科生讲授中国古典文化以完善其知识结构，我们从2007年起组建了教学团队，开始为学生开设"国学典籍英译"课程。在教学中，我们本着翻译搭台、文化唱戏的原则，努力向学生展示中华文化的精气神韵和独特魅力，为中华文化的弘扬开辟一条学科交融、中西合璧、多法并举的蹊径。

  中华文化千古一系，万古一脉，是世界民族文化之林中绝无仅有之一例。在过去数千年的历史发展过程中，中华大地虽历经改朝换代之乱，中华民族虽频遭内忧外患之苦，但中华文化却历经沧桑而始终绵延不断，成为世界文明发展史上独一无二之奇迹。作为中国人，我们当为此而自豪和骄傲。然而，自20世纪初社会变革以来，特别是自"文革"浩劫以来，万古不灭的中华文化却在中国大地日渐萎缩，以至于今日的中国青年学子知西学者甚多，而解国学者甚少，奉西学者甚众，而行中学者甚寡。要改变这一现状，就必须加大国学教育的力度，通过教学旨在使学子们了解中华文化、感悟中华文化、体验中华文化，最终使其能自觉地实践中华文化、探索中华文化、弘扬中华文化。

  中华文化自初创之时起，便不断而深刻地影响着周边部族和地区，并逐步传扬海外，推动了世界文明的发展。从先秦时期对外族的感化，到汉唐时期对东南亚地区的影响，并通过这些地域而辐射全球，中华文化在过去几千年中可谓惠及东方、感应世界。近年来，随着我国综合国力的不断增强，中华文化已经逐步走出国门，为提升我国的国际软实力和国际竞争力发挥了无可替代的作用。为了弘扬祖国传统文化以适应全球战略发展的需要，国家也采取了许多积极措施鼓励开展对中国传统文化的学习和研究，以推进其国际化和全球化的历史进程。

国学典籍英译教程

要使中华文化走向世界、惠及万国，就必须通过翻译铺路搭桥。从某种意义上说，翻译是中华文化走向世界的必经之路。由于历史的原因，中华文化西译的研究和教学一直是我国外语教学和翻译教学的一个薄弱环节。由于教育的缺失，在目前的中国外语界和翻译界，较为系统地了解和掌握中华传统文化并能较为贴切地将其翻译成西方语言的学人愈来愈少。青年学子中具有中华文化功底和翻译能力的人更是屈指可数。要想有效地改变这一现状，就必须在外语院校开展中华文化的教育普及和翻译教学，使学生有机会领悟中华文化的形质，感悟中华文化西传的理法，掌握中华文化翻译的原理。

经过五年多的实践和探索，我们在教学中取得了一定的进展，教学团队先后成功申请到国家社科基金项目2项、教育部人文社科项目1项、国家中医药管理局特别项目2项、全国翻译专业硕士研究生指导委员会规划项目1项、上海市教委科技创新项目2项、上海市教委重点课程建设项目1项、上海市卫生局规划项目1项。同时我们还编写出版了多部学术著作，发表了一系列研究论文，参与了国家中医药管理局和全国科技名词审定委员会主持的中医国家标准英文版的研制以及世界卫生组织、世界标准化组织、世界中医药学会联合会等国际学术组织开展的有关中医药名词术语英译国际标准化的研究工程。

本教材就是我们五年来教学实践和科研探索的初步总结，旨在进一步规范和深化"国学典籍英译"的学科建设和教学开展，不足之处敬请指正。本教材"绪论"及第九课和第十课由李照国编写；第一课、第二课、第三课、第四课、第五课、第八课、第十课、第十六课由丁大刚编写；第六课和第七课由李志强编写；第十一课、第十三课、第十四课、第十五课、第十七课由刘霁编写；第十二课由谈剑明编写。全书由李照国、金辉统稿。

编　者
2012 年 6 月 20 日

目 录 CONTENTS

绪论 …………………………………………………………………… (1)

第一课　《大学》 ……………………………………………………… (26)

第二课　《中庸》 ……………………………………………………… (33)

第三课　《论语》 ……………………………………………………… (40)

第四课　《孟子》 ……………………………………………………… (48)

第五课　《荀子》 ……………………………………………………… (56)

第六课　《老子》 ……………………………………………………… (64)

第七课　《庄子》 ……………………………………………………… (81)

第八课　《孙子兵法》 ………………………………………………… (94)

第九课　《易经》 ……………………………………………………… (106)

第十课　《诗经》 ……………………………………………………… (117)

第十一课　《史记》 …………………………………………………… (129)

第十二课　唐诗宋词 …………………………………………………… (139)

第十三课　《世说新语》 ……………………………………………… (154)

第十四课　《聊斋志异》 ……………………………………………… (161)

第十五课　晚明小品 …………………………………………………… (169)

第十六课　《水浒传》 ………………………………………………… (178)

第十七课　《红楼梦》 ………………………………………………… (191)

第十八课　《黄帝内经》 ……………………………………………… (202)

绪 论

> 典籍是记录古代文化传承、学术研究和社会发展的重要文献，是开启民族文明的源泉，是孕育民族文化的沃土，是历练民族精神的熔炉，是引领民族发展的航标。
>
> 自从盘古开天、三皇化物、五帝立国以来，华夏文明历千秋而不断，经万代而不绝，成为世界文明史上绝无仅有的奇观。成就这一奇迹的因由，无疑是多方面的。但中华古籍千古一脉的传承、传播和传扬，无疑是铸就这一历史奇观的重要因素。
>
> 从上古三坟五典到儒家四书五经，从诸子百家学说到历代诗书文论，中国古典文献承上启下，推动着中华文明从远古走向现代，从现代走向未来。

第一节 国学典籍的对外传播与翻译

自汉唐以降，随着中华民族的繁衍发展和中华古国的繁荣富强，华夏文明逐步走出国门，传入朝鲜、日本、越南等周边国家和地区，开启了东南亚国家和地区文明的先河。而作为华夏文明的重要载体，中国的典籍文献也先后传入这些国家和地区，并以华文华语在其域传播弘扬，逐步形成了以中国文化为共有基础的汉文化圈。

在引导周边国家和地区文化发展与繁荣的同时,有关中华文明及其重要典籍的信息也随着陆地和海洋丝绸之路的开辟,逐渐传扬到了亚洲之外的世界各地。特别是明代以来,西洋传教士和中国商船不断来往于东西之间,彼此间的直接交流日渐频繁。正是在这一历史背景下,华夏文明的典籍开始被译成西方语言而传入泰西诸国。在当今的西方各国语言中,孔子和孟子的名讳被称为 Confucius 和 Mencius,此一译法即是当年来华传教士的杰作。

当时来华的传教士所翻译的中国文化典籍主要是儒家四书五经,如《尚书》、《诗经》、《论语》等。很多来华的传教士都曾参与了中国典籍的翻译和传介,比较著名的有利玛窦(Matthieu Ricci,意大利人,1599 年来华)、金尼阁(Nicola Trigault,法国人,1611 年来华)、郭纳爵(Ignatius de Costa,葡萄牙人,1634 年来华)、柏应理(Philippe Couplet,比利时人,1658 年来华)、殷铎泽(Prospero Intorceta,意大利人,1659 年来华)、卫方济(François Noël,比利时人,1687 年来华)、宋君荣(Antoine Ganbil,法国人,1721 年来华)、蒋友仁(Michel Benoist,法国人,1744 年来华)。(黄鸣奋,1997:2)

需要说明的是,早期西方传教士翻译中国典籍时基本上都是采用的拉丁语或法语。例如,金尼阁所翻译的儒家五经,采用的即是拉丁语,1626 年刊印于杭州。这也是我国典籍最早的西译本。

在译介中国典籍的同时,传教士们还翻译了一些中国文学和戏剧作品,开启了中国文学在西方传播的先河。例如,法国人马若瑟(J. H. Marie de Bremare,1698 年来华)不仅节译了《尚书》和《诗经》,而且还翻译了元代纪君祥的杂剧《赵氏孤儿》。再如,英国传教士李提摩太(T. Richard,1870 年来华)曾将《西游记》以"天国行"之名翻译成英语,成为《西游记》在西方最早的英译文本。(黄鸣奋,1997:2)

近代以来,特别是清末民国初之后,中西方的交流更加频繁,更多的中国典籍被翻译或重译成西方语言,为西方汉学的兴起奠定了文献基础。此一时期翻译中国典籍的人士不再是清一色的西方学者,一些学贯中西的中国学人也积极参与其中。其中最为著名的中国学者,便是辜鸿铭先生。他在 19 世纪末先后将《论语》、《中庸》等儒家重要典籍翻译成英文,先后于 1898 年和 1906 年在上海由别发洋行出版发行。由于他学识渊博、中西汇通,故而能较为准确地在译文中再现原文的精神主旨,从而修正了许多先前译者的不足。正如他自己在《英译〈论语〉序》中所指出的那样:

自从理雅各博士开始发表关于"中国经典"翻译的最初部分(指先在英文刊物上发表

的部分,不是指成书出版的 Chinese Classics——译者注),迄今已 40 年了。现在,任何人,哪怕是对中国语言一窍不通的人,只要反复耐心地翻阅理雅各博士的译文,都将禁不住感到它多么令人不满意。因为理雅各博士开始从事这项工作的时候,他的文学训练还很不足,完全缺乏评判能力和文学感知力。他自始至终都表明他只不过是个大汉学家,也就是说,只是一个对中国经书具有死知识的博学的权威而已。我们遗憾地得知这位大汉学家最近刚刚去世,但为了工整地纪念他,必须指出,尽管他的工作尽了力所能及的努力,是完全严谨的,但他却没能克服其极其僵硬和狭隘的头脑之限制,这是他的性情气质造成的。(黄兴涛,1996:345)

　　辜鸿铭先生对理雅各所译《论语》的评价,深刻地反映了西方学者理解和翻译中国古典文集时的不足和缺憾。在辜鸿铭所处的那个时代,那些翻译中国典籍的西方学者对于中国文化的感悟、对于中国语言的学习、对于中国典籍的研读还是相当深刻和精细的,而且所取的态度也是极其认真负责的,翻译时也"尽了力所能及的努力"。尽管如此,由于中国文化、语言和典籍千古一脉的传承和汇通,形成了其独特的形神气韵,而这种形神气韵又是异域人士无法明了和彻悟的,所以那些西方汉学家们尽管对于中国的语言和文化"学识渊博",但却"只是对中国经书具有死知识的博学",因此在解读和翻译中国古籍时"完全缺乏评判力和文学感知力"。这使得他们对中国典籍的理解常常显得较为浅薄,对中国典籍的翻译往往按字释义,时有南辕北辙之误。

　　中国古籍是中华文明、文化和文识的载体,每一个概念,每一个词语,甚至于每一个字,都有着深刻的内涵和寓意,解之不当,必然"误解作者"、"误达读者",影响西方人对中华文化的准确了解。正因为如此,学界不少人士很早便开始对这一问题进行比较研究,试图正本清源,校正中国典籍对外翻译的思路和方向。自辜鸿铭先生之后,中国的很多学者,如钱钟书、林语堂等,都曾从中西文化比较入手对中国文化的翻译问题进行了研究和探讨,提出了不少意见和建议。

　　目前在国内外,仍然有不少的学者在从事中国典籍的英语翻译研究。全国典籍英译研讨会迄今已经召开了五届,出版了三辑《典籍英译研究》论集。以汪榕培教授为代表的一批典籍翻译专家和学者,在中国典籍英译的理论研究和实践探索方面作了许多扎实细致的工作,有力地推动了这一领域的学术发展和人才培养。中国新闻出版总署为了促进中国文化的对外交流和发展,20 世纪末组织海内外学者、译家,开始了《汉英对照大中华文库》的翻译工作,目前已经出版了 72 种中国文化典籍,极大地推动了中国典籍的英译及其理论研究。

由于中国古典文化本身的深奥玄妙,再加上半个多世纪以来对之漠视和弃置,中国文化典籍在中国本土已日渐淡出历史舞台和文化殿堂,使得一般中国学人对本民族的传统文化日显隔膜。而以这样隔膜的状态去审视英译的中国典籍,其真伪之辨、虚实之鉴、表里之别,便时有亥豕之讹、鱼鲁之误。这也在很大程度上制约了学界对中国典籍英译问题的深入研究。钱钟书先生曾对当时热衷于谈论中西文化比较却对中西文化缺少起码了解的现象极为厌恶,他说:

有些人连中文、西文都不懂,谈得上什么比较?戈培尔说过,有人和我谈文化,我就拔出手枪来。现在要是有人和我谈中西文化比较,如果我有手枪的话,我也一定要拔出来!(李照国,2007:55)

今天我们在研究中国文化翻译问题时,钱先生的愤怒仍然具有深刻的现实意义。他警示我们,在研究中国典籍的英语翻译时,对中国传统文化的精神实质,要了解深入、感悟透彻、把握准确;对相关典籍的翻译研究,要做到明确历史、谙熟内容、了悟主旨。只有这样,才能洞悉有关典籍所涉理论、体系、概念甚或字词的基本内涵和实际寓意,才能明辨是非、透析真伪、详察虚实,才能真正做到"跨越两极",并且彻悟"理在其中"的意义。

第二节 国学典籍英译理法

20世纪70年代末,随着赤县神州的春潮涌起,一股源自华夏古国的激流冲破了层层牢笼的羁绊,汹涌澎湃,激荡寰宇。封闭的东方古国终于开启了闭锁的国门。东西风潮由此而开始交会、交流和交融。

随着中西方文化交流的不断开展,中国传统文化典籍,如儒家经典、诸子之学、百家之论,已经先后被翻译为多种文字在海内外出版发行。这对于加强中西方文化交流,提高海外读者对中国文化的了解,促进中华传统文化在世界各地的传播和发展,无疑发挥了积极作用。

但由于译者,无论是西方译者还是中国译者,对中国文化的精神、中国语言的演变和诸子学说的传承之了解和把握,或偏于表,或偏于狭,使得一些基本概念的理解和翻译与原文颇为相异。下面试根据语言、文化和翻译的基本原理对其加以探讨，以期抛砖引玉，引起学界对这一问题的关注。

一、 词义辨析与典籍翻译

望文生义如同"秀才识字认半边"一样，自然不能一概加以否定，因为在很多情况下望文所生之义其实并非谬见，正如很多汉字是可以通过"认半边"而加以正确解读一样。因此，中国古人就有"望而知之谓之神"之说。但"望"虽可以"知之"，却并非万能之法，亦非万全之策。凡事若总以一法应之，必然有不应之时，自然有难应之处。

国学典籍翻译中存在的种种问题即有望文生义之过。从现有译本来看，很多问题的存在实际上都是由于译者对原文未加仔细审读而引发的。此类现象在国学典籍的翻译中可谓比比皆是、屡见不鲜。

由于历史的发展和文字的演变，古今字义时有变异，我们在解读和翻译古典文集时须慎加注意。我们现在使用的很多字古今并无变化，但其内涵已发生了部分变异或完全变异。这就提醒我们，在整理、注解和翻译古典文献时，一定要在思维上回归到有关典籍成书的那个时代，根据古人的思想观念和认识问题的方式来解读古人的著作，不能一味地按照今人的认识来解析古人的思想，不然，就会犯指鹿为马、张冠李戴的错误。

国内某出版社出版的一本英文版的《论语》，就有不少类似的情况。例如，《论语·述而》篇说：

子曰：自行束脩以上，吾未尝无诲焉。

孔子的意思是说，带上一束干肉来拜他为师的人，他没有不教的道理。按古语的意思，这句话中的"束脩"指的是一束干肉。这是古代拜师的最低礼物。孔子虽然贵为圣人，但毕竟不是不食人间烟火的神仙，因此办学也是要收取学费的。所以 Arthur Waley 在其翻译的《论语》(*The Analects of Confucius*)中，将这句话译为：

The Master said, From the very poorest upwards—beginning even with the man who could bring up no better present than a bundle of dried flesh—none has ever come to me without receiving instruction.

国学大师辜鸿铭更将其解释性地意译为：

Confucius remarked, "In teaching men, I make no difference between the rich and the poor. I have taught men who could just afford to bring me the barest presentation gift in the same way as I have taught others."

但在某出版社出版的英文版《论语》(Analects of Confucius)中,这句话的翻译却另有主张:Confucius said, "I never refuse to teach those fifteen-year old children who are reaching adolescence."

译者将"束脩"理解成"束发修饰",因为古代男子15岁左右即束发为髻,开始接受教育。译者其实也意识到了"束脩"作为学生拜师所交纳礼物的传统解读,但在具体翻译时,还是另辟蹊径,自立一说。这样的解读是否符合历史事实呢?很值得商榷。

苏洵在《心术》一文中说:"为将之道,当先治心。"为译之道,其实亦在于治心。惟有心治,才能定静安虑,译而有得。《文心雕龙·原道》篇有"仰观吐曜,俯察含章"之句,至为精妙。译者在从译之时,若亦能具有仰观天象、俯视地理、六仪在胸、往今熟谙之境界,则译事本末自在胸中。

考古学家和人类学家研究发现,炎黄子孙身体上有三项区别于世界其他民族的特有生理印记:一是铲形门牙(即上颌两颗中门齿的两边缘翻卷成棱形,中间低凹),我国绝大多数人都具有这一特征,而白种人和黑种人中具有这一特征的人却只有8.4%和11.6%。二是青斑(即新生儿的尾骶部或其他部位常有淡灰色或青灰色斑块,一般一二岁时褪去),我国新生儿(尤其是东北地区的新生儿)几乎都有这种特征,而白种人和黑种人的新生儿却都没有这一特征。三是内眦褶(即眼的内角处,由上眼睑微微下伸,遮掩泪阜而呈一小小皮褶,旧称"蒙古褶"),我国大部分人有这种内眦褶,而外国人则无。这三项印记是中国人区别于外国人的基本生理特征。一个中国人,无论他在异国他乡漂泊了多长时间,无论他从服装到语言洋化到了何种程度,岁月的无情都无法消除其作为中国人的最基本的标记。因为在他身上,始终循环着华夏民族的气血,永远激荡着炎黄圣祖的基因。

今天我们在对外翻译介绍国学典籍的时候,应该充分了解其源流实质及其异于异域文化的基本特征,并在译文中努力保持这些独特的语言和文化标记,这样才能在跨文化交流中始终保持中华文化固有的色彩和形质。中国文化区别于其他地域文化的特征就是中国文化特有的标记,如果这些标记在译文中被人为地剔除了或忽略了,那么译者所传述的大概已不能算是中国文化了,充其量是侠客茶余饭后的海上奇谈了。

二、关联性思维与典籍翻译

若用一个词来概括中国文字与意趣之间的关联性,那就是"意境"。人们往往将中文的"意境"理解为 context,这自然是 sweeping generation and oversimplification。

中文的"意境"当然包括 context,但却远远高于 context。从某种意义上讲,任何一个文本都有 context,但并不是任何一篇文字都有"意境"。换句话说,只有文辞优美、寓意深刻、仪态万千、出神入化之作,方有"意境"。而文辞粗俗、空洞无物、拖沓不经之文,是谈不上什么"意境"的。

汉高祖刘邦的《大风歌》"大风起兮云飞扬,威加海内兮归故乡,安得猛士兮守四方"自然是意境独具之传世佳作。而北洋军阀张宗昌的模仿之作"大炮开兮轰他娘,威加海内兮回家乡,数英雄兮张宗昌"除了一股匪气之外,却无任何"郁郁乎文哉"之意境可言。

阅读和理解古典文集时,除了从字词上对其详加分析外,还须从其意境入手去感悟其文趣要旨。而要了悟其意境、感受其文趣,就必须以关联性的思维去认识和感验有关概念或话语,切勿孤立地看待字词句的关系,切忌将部分与整体割裂开来,否则就会见点不见面、见木不见林,其结果便是凭空想象、随意诠释。

孔子在评论《诗经》的时候说过一句话:《诗》三百,一言以蔽之,曰:"思无邪"。Arthur Waley 将其译作:

The Master said, If out of the three hundred *Songs* I had to take one phrase to cover all my teaching, I would say "Let there be no evil in your thoughts".

这样的释义与原文之意自然有些风马牛不相及了。相比较而言,辜鸿铭先生对这句话的理解就比较准确,翻译得也比较贴切。他的译文是:

Confucius remarked, "*The Book of Ballads, Songs and Psalms* contains three hundred pieces. The moral of them all may be summed up in one sentence:'Have no evil thoughts.'"

菲律宾人丘文明、丘文郊、丘文星、丘文祁昆仲(大约是一门华裔)在其所编译的《论语英译今译》(*The Confucian Bible Book: Analects English and Modern Chinese Versions*)一书中,对此句也作了较为准确的解读和翻译:

The Master said, "The Book of Songs contains (some) three hundred pieces. Their subject matter may be covered in one saying: 'Think no evil!'"

同样一句话,不同的译者翻译,自然有不同的译法,但基本意思却不能走样太过。像上面这个例子,就是由于译者对原文的理解不当而导致了原文意思在译文中的变异。

古人为文,谨慎有加,一字一词,精雕细琢,无有废言。翻译时,须得仔细斟酌,以明文意,不可随意着笔,恣意旁释。孔子一生矢志不移地追求真理,谈到自己的这一志向时,他说:"朝闻道,夕死可矣。"Arthur Waley 将其译为:

The Master said, In the morning, hear the Way; in the evening, die content.

与原文相较,译文似乎尚为对应,但仔细推敲,则不免似是而非。将"道"译作 Way,很值得推敲。"道"在中国古籍及诸子论著中涉及颇多,其内涵极为丰富,其外延亦极为宽广,译作 Way 显然过于轻浅。而"闻道"译作 hear the Way,则更觉虚无缥缈。这里的"闻"实际上是"懂得了"的意思。

相比较而言,辜鸿铭先生对孔子这句话的翻译,就比较符合原文之意:

Confucius remarked, "When a man has learnt wisdom in the morning, he may be content to die in the evening before the sun sets."

但辜氏的这个译文似乎也有值得商榷之处。其实孔子所说的"朝闻道,夕死可矣"是自我激励之辞,并非是对他人的说教。因此,将其译作"When a man has learnt wisdom"云云,听起来似乎是教主训导信众的腔调,而非圣人自勉之辞。另外,"to die in the evening before the sun sets"亦即有怪异之处,既是 in the evening,又加上 before the sun sets,似有画蛇添足之嫌,因为 evening 就是指从日落至就寝这段时间。

而菲律宾丘氏昆仲将孔子的这句名言则作了如下这般翻译:

The Master said, "When one hears about the Way in the morning, one may die in the evening."

孔子的"朝闻道,夕死可矣"表达的是对真理的无限渴望和追求,只要找到了真理,就是死了也是值得的。然而,丘氏昆仲的这个译文似乎将"闻道"和"夕死"之间设立了一种因果关系,即一个人若早上"闻"了"道",则晚上就会死去。这与孔子追求真理的精神似乎颇为隔膜。

以上两则例子均由译界大家和学界高士所译,尚且有些许瑕疵,更何况一般译者!

能否使译文在风格、内涵、用词等方面做到与原文滴水不漏地完全对应呢?这实在是不大可能办到的。正如冯友兰先生所言,任何形式的翻译,在一定意义上都是对原文某种形式的注解,所以很难与原文实现完全的对应。

比如说《老子》全书只有五千字,但翻译成英文时所用之词往往数倍于原文。为何译文比原文用词甚多?解释之故也。冯友兰先生在谈到这一问题时说:

我们如果把《老子》书中提到的概念列举出来,重述一遍,可能用上五万字,或五十万字,它可能帮助读者了解《老子》一书的含义,但它本身将成为另一本书,而永不可能代替《老子》的原著。

郭象是《庄子》一书的著名注释家。他的注释本身是道家的一本重要古典文献,他的论述比《庄子》一书清晰得多。但是,《庄子》原书富于提示,而他的注释本则明晰具体。两者之中到底哪个更好呢?《大慧普觉禅师语录》卷二十二说:"曾见郭象注庄子,识者云,却是庄子注郭象。"这话说得极有意思,很值得仔细品味。谈到哲学的翻译问题时,冯友兰先生说:

任何人如果不能用原文阅读某种哲学著作,要想完全理解原著,的确会有困难。这是由于语言的障碍。中国哲学著作由于他们的提示性质,语言的困难就更大。中国哲学家的言论和著作中的种种提示,很难翻译。当它被翻译成外文时,它由提示变成一种明确的陈述;失去了提示的性质,就失去了原著的味道。(冯友兰,2006:11)

从这个意义上讲,任何形式的翻译,说到底,都只是对原文的某种解释。当我们把《老子》书中的一句话译成白话文或外文时,我们是按照自己的理解或今人的观点来阐述其含义的。事实上,译文通常只能表述《老子》一个概念、一个词语或一句话的一层含义,而原文却可能包含着数层含义。就表述形式而言,《老子》的原文是提示性质的,译文则不可能做到这一点。于是,原文中的丰富含义在翻译过程中就可能被丢失。

清代毛宗岗父子修订《三国演义》时,选取明人杨慎(1488—1559)晚年所著之《历代史略词话》中的《说秦汉》第三段《临江仙》冠于《三国演义》回目之前,作为卷首词。这首《临江仙》怀古伤今,感慨兴亡,意境清空。借助《三国演义》恢弘悲壮的历史画卷,该词传遍大江南北,妇孺皆知,成为中国诗词中的不朽名篇。

许渊冲教授对杨词的翻译至为精妙,意境壮阔,颇具原作之神韵。试比较杨之原作与许之译作:

原作	译文
滚滚长江东逝水,	Wave on wave the long River rolls away;
浪花淘尽英雄。	Gone are all heroes with its spray on spray.
是非成败转头空。	Success or failure, right or wrong, all turn out vain;
青山依旧在,	Only green mountains still remain
几度夕阳红。	To see the setting sun's departing ray.
白发渔樵江渚上,	The white-haired fishermen sail on the stream with ease,
惯看秋月春风。	Accustomed to the autumn moon and vernal breeze.
一壶浊酒喜相逢:	A pot of wine in hand, they talk as they please.
古今多少事,	How many things before and after
都付笑谈中。	All melt into gossip and laughter.

许教授的译文在形式上与原作几近同一,内涵亦颇为相望。当然,将中国古典诗词翻译成英文,完全对应其实是很难做到的。在一篇杂感中,我们曾对此作了这样的概括:"就像一株花草,在空谷幽岭中,飘逸俊清,宛若云气初凝。一旦移栽他处,喧嚣聒噪,俗流灌注,转眼便神丧气消,清灵全无。翻译亦如移栽花草一样,境变而神易,在所难免矣。"虽然在所难免,但译者下笔从译之时,仍当采取一切可行之法,曲径向幽,曲中求直,将潜在的异化之势降到最低。

《老子》第二章说:

故有无相生,难易相成,长短相形,高下相倾,音声相和,前后相随。

Authur Waley 将其译作:

For truly Being and Not-being grow out of one another;

Difficult and easy complete one another.

Long and short test one another;

High and low determine one another.

Pitch and mode give harmony to one another;

Front and back give sequence to one another.

国内一译家则将其译作：

Hence Being the Nothingness in exist in opposition;

The difficult and the easy complement each other;

The long and the short manifest themselves by comparison;

The high and the low are inclined as well as opposed to each other;

The consonants and vowels harmonize with each other;

The front and the back follow each other.

和原文的表现形式与内容比较起来，两则译文虽然在一定程度上阐释了原文之意，但原文所富含的提示风格却没有能够转换到译文之中。就表现形式而言，原文是提示性的，而译文却是解释性的；就内涵而言，原文是幽深的，而译文却是直白的。

冯友兰先生关于哲学翻译问题的见解可谓精辟之至。其他方面的翻译又何尝不是如此！当我们知道了翻译的性质其实就是对原文另一种形式的注解时，便会明白译文和原文的关系，便会清楚原文的无可替代性与译文的相对局限性。当然对原文的理解必须立足客观实际，要历史地考察，而不能现实地分析。因为语言和文字都深深地打上了时代的烙印，脱离了特定的历史背景，很难准确把握原文的主旨精神。胡适先生 1916 年 12 月发表在《留美学生季报》冬季四号上的《论诗偶记》一文对此曾作了颇为精辟的论述，至今读来，仍不失其现实意义。现摘其一节，以明其理：

时代不同，则语言文字亦随之而变。其变也，非有意于变而变也，不得不变耳。《易》曰："穷则变。变则通，通则久。"此明于世变史事者之言也。穴居野处者，变而为上栋下宇；茹毛饮血者，变而为烹调肴馔；结绳变为书契。皆进化之迹野。文字亦时时变耳。往往有同一意思而以时代不同之故，遂有不同之说法。

三、文理辨证与典籍翻译

翻译典籍，常用的方法无非直译与意译而已。意译注重释义，且便于发挥，故常为一般译者所倚重。而采用直译之法所译之文句,因其与原文形象甚为相似,故亦时为译人所用,且常常可收便捷传递信息之效。

直译虽不失为一种便捷的传译之法,但用之不慎便生对号入座之误,使译文显得生搬硬套。就传译之法而言,对号入座式的翻译,其实已不能算是直译,而是鲁迅先生所斥之死译。死译之法人皆知之,但往往不易避之。

孔夫子晚年对自己的一生曾经作过这样的总结:

吾十有五而志乎学,三十而立,四十而不惑,五十而知天命,六十而耳顺,七十而从心所欲不逾矩。

孔子的这段"自我鉴定",大凡读书之人,无不了然于心。然而,将其置于译人笔下时,其意却往往难以明了。明人梦醒龙在《古今谭概·无术部第六》讲了这样一则笑话:

魏博节度使韩简,性粗质,每对文士,不晓其说,心常耻之。乃召一士人讲《论语》,至《为政篇》。明日喜谓同官曰:"近方知:古人禀质瘦弱,年至三十,方能行立。"

意思是说,唐代有个名为魏博的藩镇,其节度使韩简是个大字不识的粗鲁人,每次与读书人在一起时,总是听不懂他们在讲什么,心里常常感到羞愧。于是便请了一位先生给自己讲《论语》,一直讲到《为政篇》。第二天,韩简高兴地对同僚们说:"近来方才知道,古人体质瘦弱,到了三十岁才能站起来走路。"

这位封疆大吏对"三十而立"的曲解,自然是滑稽可笑的。那么在译人的笔下,"三十而立"又是如何解读的呢?

Arthur Waley 将孔子这段自述翻译为:

The Master said, At fifteen I set my heart upon learning. At thirty, I had planted my feet firm upon the ground. At forty, I no longer suffered from perplexities. At fifty, I knew what were the biddings of Heaven. At sixty, I heard them with docile ears. At seventy, I could follow the dictates of my own heart; for what I desired no longer overstepped the boundaries of right.

"三十而立"是"I had planted my feet firm upon the ground"吗?"知天命"是"I knew what were the biddings of Heaven"吗?"耳顺"是"I heard them with docile ears"吗?恐怕

不能这样照猫画虎地理解和翻译。

相对地讲,辜鸿铭先生的翻译还是比较接近原文之意的,也可以作为孔子"自我鉴定"的一个注脚。辜先生的译文是:

Confucius remarked, "At fifteen I had made up my mind to give myself up to serious studies. At thirty I had formed my opinions and judgment. At forty I had no more doubts. At fifty I understood the truth of religion. At sixty I could understand whatever I heard without exertion. At seventy I could follow whatever my heart desired without transgressing the law."

辜先生的译文,总体上尚属达意,但也有个别地方需要进一步推敲。比如,先生将"知天命"译作"understood the truth of religion."此处将"天"译作religion,就很值得商榷。所谓"知天命",更多的是指对自然规律的掌握和顺从。

在丘氏昆仲所译的《论语》中,孔子的这个"自我鉴定"被译为:

The Master said, "At fifteen I resolved to study seriously. At thirty I became established. At forty I was free of doubts. At fifty I knew Destiny. At sixty the ears functioned smoothly. At seventy I could follow my heart's desire and not step out-of-bounds".

译文后附有如下注解:

Read "the ear functioned smoothly" as "I understand everything heard".

尽管作了这样的注解,"耳顺"的意思还是没有完全揭示出来。所谓"耳顺",不仅仅指能理解所听到的(正如丘氏昆仲译文之后所注解的那样),而且——其实最重要的——是指能听进去不同的意见。所谓"忠言逆耳",说的就是听不进不同意见和批评意见。所谓"耳顺",就是正反两方面的意见都能听得进去。

有些汉字初看起来很是相像,有些甚至完全一样,但阅读时稍有"眼花",便无从正解原文。这种"走眼"的情况,圣明的古人也难以幸免。这是因为古代没有印刷技术,书籍全靠手抄。手抄之时,总有讹误错漏。而且先秦典籍本来是用古文字所撰写,后来改用隶书抄写,有些形似之字便不免抄错。如此以讹传讹,传至今日,读者便难解其意了。

《论语·乡党》中有这样一段记载:

色斯举矣,翔而后集。曰:"山梁雌雉,时哉时哉!"子路共之,三嗅而作。

这段记述大约是《论语》中最难解读之处，所以自汉以来注家都不免牵强附会，难以明了其意。有些注家干脆不加注解，承认自己无法理解其意。历代注家尚且如此困惑难解，译人自然就更难下笔度传。从目前流行的几种译本来看，译者可谓蹊径独劈、千秋各具，却很难把握文之真意。

Arthur Waley 的译文如下：

(The gentleman) rises and goes at the first sign, and does not "settle till he has hovered". (A song) says：

The hen-pheasant of the hill-bridge,

Knows how to bide its time, to bide its time!

When Tzu-lu made it an offering,

It sniffed three times before it rose.

这个译文，自然，猜测的成分最大。将"雉"误以为人，所以便有了所谓的(the gentleman) rises and goes at the first sign, and does not "settle till he has hovered"这一奇解。"山梁雌雉，时哉时哉！"有注家说是孔子之叹，有注家说是子路之叹，还有注家说是他人之叹。总之，这是感叹"山梁雌雉"机敏异常，见危而飞，时机把握恰到好处。Arthur Waley 将其理解为一首歌谣，亦属个人猜测。而"子路共之，三嗅而作"本来是描述子路对"山梁雌雉"及时起飞的一种反应和表示，译文也纳入到所谓"Song"的内容之中，显属不妥。而且将其译作"When Tzu-lu made it an offering, It sniffed three times before it rose."则更属误解。这里的"共"其实是"拱手"之意，即 wave hands。而"嗅"照字面译作 sniff，亦属望文生义。

辜鸿铭先生将这段文字谨慎地翻译如下：

As they turned to look at it, it instantly rose and, hovering about, it settled again. Somebody said, "Ah! Pheasant on the hill! Ah! Pheasant on the hill! You know the times! You know the times!" Confucius' disciple, the intrepid Chung Yu, conned it over three times; then, suddenly understanding the meaning of the remark, made an exclamation, rose and went away.

译文后，辜先生特意加了这样一条注解：

Chinese commentators give up the passage in this section, confessing they cannot understand its meaning. Sir Chaloner Alabaster, however, has discovered a very good explanation of this passage which unfortunately we cannot exactly remember. We here make a guess of his explanation from memory.

"三嗅而作",本来是说"雌雉"嘎嘎叫了三声(三只是表示多,并非真的指"三"这个具体数字)而飞走了。观辜先生的译文,这一连串的动作似乎是子路发出的。

比较来说,新加坡丘氏昆仲的译文似乎比较切合实际一些。以下便是他们的翻译:

Seeing a change in (the observer's) countenance, birds take off and fly around before regrouping. The Master said, "She-pheasants on the bridge by the hill! They do what is timely! They do what is timely!" Zi Lu joined his hands in salute, causing them to puff three times and fly off.

译文之后同样附有这样一条说明:

Scholars have various interpretations of this section, but they all agree that Confucius was essentially referring to the relaxed life of the birds while humans have to continue struggling against the disorderly conditions existing during their lifetime.

丘氏昆仲的译文也含有猜测的成分,但却基本猜对了。如将"色斯举矣,翔而后集"译作 Seeing a change in (the observer's) countenance, birds take off and fly around before regrouping,至少隐含了"见危而飞"这样一层意思,这就基本反映了原文之意,所以是可取的。将"子路共之"译作 Zi Lu joined his hands in salute,也基本说明了问题。将"三嗅而作"译作 causing them to puff three times and fly off 虽说有些勉强,但还基本表达了"鸟已飞走"之意。至于将"嗅"译作 to puff three times,已属不易解析了。

这段话之所以难理解,其实就难在两个字上,"色"与"嗅"。近有中国学者商承祚,对此作了较为切合实际的分析,提出了自己的见解,似乎还是比较可取的。他认为,"色"当是"危","嗅"当为"嘎"。这是古人在传抄过程中笔误所致。商先生的解释听起来还是有道理的。因为古文"危"与"色"、"嘎"与"嗅"字形大同小异,而古时之文又刻在竹简或木简之上,翻阅时简册的不断摩擦致使某些笔画模糊,传抄者一时"走眼",就很可能造成笔误。

弄清了"色"与"嗅"的本来意义之后,理解《论语》中的这段文字就比较简单了。

近代中国大学问家王国维先生曾说,六艺之中,《诗经》和《尚书》最难读懂。他研读《尚书》,大约有一半不能理解;研读《诗经》,大约十分之一二不能理解。这或许是他的谦虚之辞。但我想,他讲的也许是实情。大师读古书尚且如此,我等于国学早已隔膜之人,又当何如呢?

前年季羡林先生在谈到《大中华文库》的翻译问题时,曾感叹能承担此任者寥寥。这其实道出了目前中国学界的现实。虽然说在译界不是人人都有机会或兴趣从事古典文化的翻译,但是对中国传统文化的隔膜终究会影响我们对中国文化和语言的解读和辨析。即便是从事一般文本的翻译,也会遇到这样和那样的类似问题。前两年连战和宋楚瑜来大陆访问,有关接待人员连连口误,即再明白不过地说明了这一点。

况且,中国文化千万年一脉相承,即便目前古今完全断层,但今日之白话亦是由古汉语发展、延伸和通俗而来,其中常用词语、典故和俗语仍然古今一脉地延承了下来。对中国传统文化的隔膜必然影响我们对日常用语的解读和释义。对此,作为译人,我们是万万不可掉以轻心的。

元丰三年(1080)苏轼被贬黄州,寓居定惠院,夜填《卜算子》,述词家之寂寞彷徨,道人生之无可奈何:

缺月挂疏桐,漏断人初静。谁见幽人独往来,缥缈孤鸿影。
惊起却回头,有恨无人省。拣尽寒枝不肯栖,寂寞沙洲冷。

仔细品味苏词,不独悟得"人间"冷暖几何,亦可明得译人同等寂寞。词首所重笔着意之"缺"、"疏"、"漏"、"断"四字,点破词家幽独凄苦心境。然此四字若用以解析译事,记述译人面对原语与译语之感验,似乎亦独具意趣。

译事之中,何以有"缺"、"疏"、"漏"、"断"之缺憾?这与两种语言、两种文化之不同形质,自然有根本之关联。同时,与译人之心境、意识和参悟,亦有绝大关系。

老子的《道德经》有如下一句:

知不知上不知知病

古人撰文,不加标点,全靠读者自行断句,这给后人的阅读理解造成了一定的不便。在翻译这句话时,几位译者便根据自己的理解和分析,作出了不同的断句,于是便形成了意义不尽相同的译文：

Carus 将其断句为：知不知，上。不知知，病。所以翻译为：

To know the unknowable, that is elevating.

Not to know the knowable, that is sickness.

Arthus Waley 则将其断句为：知不知，上。不知，知，病。所以翻译为：

To know when one does not know is best.

To think one knows when one does not know is a dire disease.

Lionel Giles 则断句为：知，不知，上。不知，知，病。所以翻译为：

To know, but to be as though not knowing, is the height of wisdom.

Not to know, and yet to affect knowledge, is a vice.

吴经熊则断句为：(以)知(为)不知，上。(以)不知(为)知，病。所以翻译为：

To regard knowledge as no-knowledge is best.

To regard no-knowledge as knowledge is sickness.

究竟谁的翻译符合老子的原意，恐怕一时很难定夺。因为这几位译者的断句，皆可自圆其说，译文自然别样。这是翻译古典文化时译者不得不时时面对的一个怪圈。若处理不当，则不但作茧自缚，而且误传信息、误导读者，从而导致原文信息在译入语中被"熵化"、"耗散"和"重构"。

这种现象的出现有时亦与译者所选取之行文方式及语言风格有一定的内在联系。如在白话文一统天下的今天，若译者因某种需要而采用稍有古色的语言风格从事翻译，则不免在读者中引起信息的某种变异和重构。因为今时之中国读者大多对古文已恍若隔世，很难准确把握其文词句法，自然难以解析文意，只能猜测想象。

第三节　国学典籍英译方要

在对外翻译中国传统文化特别是国学典籍的时候，要做到"信"、"达"、"雅"，其实是极难的。从某种意义上说，这样理想的境界实际上是可望而不可即的。个中缘由，洞若观火，不辩自明。从国学典籍对外翻译的历史和现状来看，能勉强做到一个"信"字，并使译文较为畅达，已颇为不易了。

在对外翻译国学典籍时，译者首要解决的问题是理解正确。只要理解正确，即便译文不够雅致，也还基本能传达原文之意。如果理解错误，即便译文雅致非常，也只能熵化和耗散原文信息。而译者要准确理解原文之意，就需要对诸多因素进行梳理，以揭示其背后所隐藏的种种玄机和暗喻。在这个过程中，任何微小的疏忽都可能"误解作者，误达读者"。

那么，国学典籍对外翻译中究竟涉及哪些因素呢？到底该如何梳理和协调这些因素以便客观准确地理解原文之意呢？从目前的发展来看，国学典籍翻译中至少涉及传变、源流、常异、虚实、表里和古今六大关系。明确了这六大关系，对于我们较为客观地把握国学典籍翻译的理法方要至为重要。

▶▶ 一、传变关系

国学典籍的成书年代一般都比较久远，传说中的"三坟五典"据说是三皇五帝时期的典籍，《尚书》据传是三代时期流传下来的历史文献，而流传至今的诸子学说和百家之论则基本形成于春秋战国到秦汉时期。这些典籍上承远古圣王之说，中继先贤哲人之论，下传黎民百姓之声，具有鲜明的历史继承性、时代开创性和未来预见性。

然而，由于历史的演变、思想的发展和时代的需要，不同历史时期的人们对这些典籍的解释和阐发都深深地打上了时代的烙印。有时为了时运之济，人们甚至对这些传颂千古的典籍进行有意的篡改或别解。这种情况的出现导致了后世对同一经典、同一概念的不同见解。今天我们在翻译这些经典时，在理解相关概念和学说时，就需要正本清源，明确其原始内涵和历史演变，以便能客观准确地把握其旨、理解其意。

在学习诸子百家时，笔者常常为后人对先贤思想的误读和衍化而惋惜。"文革"在批判孔子时,一种很流行的说法是孔子提倡"读书做官",其根据是孔子曾经说过的"学而优则仕"。这实在是对孔夫子历史性的误会,因为"学而优则仕"只是孔夫子所讲之话的后半句,其前半句是"仕而优则学"。"仕而优则学,学而优则仕"讲的是"读书做官"吗?当然不是。孔子的意思是说,"做官的人有空闲的话应该去学习,而读书人有空闲的话也应该去做做管理工作"。这里的"优"其实不是"优秀"的意思,而是指"空闲"。例如,苏洵在《心术》中提出国君应该奖励兵士,加强国防。他说:"丰犒而优游之,所以养其力。"(牛宝彤,1983)意思是说,要犒劳奖励兵士,使他们悠闲自在地生活。这里的"优"即"悠闲"之意,而不是"优秀"。(李照国,2006:112)

再如《大学》中的"大学之道,在明明德,在新民"中的"新民",原作"亲民",宋朝朱熹以为此处存在烂简现象,即"新民"因烂简而变为"亲民",因此改"亲民"为"新民"。自此以来,诸多版本均改"亲民"为"新民"。朱氏之说似乎有理,但恐与当时政务之需有些关系。其实"亲民"、"新民"内涵与意境截然不同。"亲民"含有"仁者爱人"之意,而"新民"则含有"上智下愚"之喻。前者强调的是和谐,后者则强调的是教化。从孔孟的一贯思想来看,"亲民"似乎更合乎他们的道德要求。(李照国,2007:227)

所以,在翻译古典文献时,我们不得不对有关典籍基本概念的流传解释与其原始内涵的关系有所了解,以便尊重历史,从实而译。笔者在翻译《黄帝内经》(以下简称"《内经》》")时之所以提出"与时俱退"之原则,就是为了尊重历史事实,按照历史的本来面目来诠释相关典籍的思想和观点。

▶▶ 二、源流关系

枝叶繁茂的参天大树,其势源于一根;波澜壮阔的民族文化,其流源于一宗;博大精深的古典学说,其质源于一本。明晰这些道理,对于我们理解和翻译国学典籍,可谓至关重要。

以《内经》为例,其学说虽然奠定了中国医药学的理论基础和实践规范,但其基本理论的来源却是诸子之学和百家之论。因此要完整准确地理解《内经》的基本思想,就必须了解相关的诸子之学。如《内经》的"阴阳"学说,即来源于阴阳家,其"五行"学说则源于方士,其物候学说则源于农家,其天人关系学说则源于星相家,其用药之法则源于兵家。

因此,要了解一种学说的本旨精神,就必须了解其源流关系。源是流赖以形成和发展的源泉和动力,而流则是对源的发展和补充。二者之间的关系是母与子的关系,是相互依托但又彼此分异的关系。所以我们在理解源的本旨问题时,可以借鉴流的寓意,但不能完全以流释源,否则就可能犯以标释本的错误。

《内经》中有"命门"一说,如《灵枢》"根结"篇说:"太阳根于至阴,结于命门。命门者,目也。"这里明确说明,"命门"指的是眼睛。但在《难经》"三十六难"谈到命门时却说:"肾两者,非皆肾也。其左者为肾,右为命门。"由于《难经》的这一发挥,便衍生了后世所谓的"命门"学说,但同时也使"命门"这一概念的寓意大为改变。今天国医所谈到的"命门",大多指的是《难经》所谓的"命门",而不是《内经》的"命门"。所以我们在翻译《内经》和《难经》时,便需明辨"命门"在二者之中的传承和发展关系,不可等同视之。也就是说,翻译《内经》的"命门"时需循其源,而翻译《难经》的"命门"时,则需顺其流。

三、常异关系

常异关系是典籍解读中时常遇到的棘手问题。所谓"常",指的是一般情况;所谓"异",则指的是特殊情况。在典籍的诠释方面,"常"与"异"关系的表现是多方面的,既有常理与时喻之用,也有正体与异体之别。

所谓常理,就是指常见之理,即 general reference。所谓时喻,指的是权宜之用,即 temporary reference。在国学典籍中,基本概念总是有其基本的寓意和常规用法,但在特定情况下因修辞、文理和表达的需要,又会发生一定的变化。这种变化的产生主要是为了更好地论述某一特定内容。所谓正体与异体,则指的是汉字常规与变异的书写方式。这种情况在国学典籍中普遍存在,稍有疏忽便有毫厘之差、千里之谬。

如《内经》中的"气",指的是构成世界万物的本原,常音译为 Qi 或 qi。但在"四气五味"中,"气"则指的是药物"升降沉浮"的四种特性。国外译者一般按"气"的常规用语对其进行释义,故将"四气"译作 four qi。这自然是望文生义之作,因为这里的"气"已经变"常"为"异"了,应从实而译为 property 或 nature。

再如《内经》中的"阴阳",指的是事物内部正反两个方面,所以常音译为 yin and yang。但在《素问》第 1 章"阴阳合,故能有子"一句中,"阴阳"却指的是男女。所谓"阴阳合",则指的是 sexual intercourse,因此不能按"阴阳"的常规之意译作 combination of yin and yang。

又如《内经》中的"父"与"母",其基本含义是人父人母,即 father and mother。但也常常因表达和修辞之需而指代别物。如在《素问》第 5 章"阴阳者,天地之道也,万物之纲纪,变化之父母,生杀之本始,神明之府也"中,"父母"则指的是事物变化的根源,故当译作 cause 或 origin,而不宜直接译作 parents。在《素问》第 52 章"鬲肓之上,中有父母"一句中,"父母"却指的是心肺,因为心属阳为父,肺属阴为母。所以这里的"父母"也不宜直接译为 parents,而应译作 liver and lung;如果需要对其深层寓意加以解释,似可将其译作 liver, which pertains to yang and acts as a father, and lung, which pertains to yin and serves as a mother。

像这样的常异之变,在典籍中时常出现,翻译时务必审慎,以明其常法和异用。至于典籍中字体的正与异,亦颇为常见。如《论语》开篇说"学而时习之,不亦说乎!有朋自远方来,不亦乐乎!"这里的"说"和"乐"均读 yuè,是"悦"的意思,属于假借,也可谓"悦"之异形。这种情况在《内经》中也时常出现。如《灵枢》第 12 章有"其藏之坚脆,府之大小"之说,其中的"藏"和"府"就是"脏"和"腑"的假借形式。除假借之外,《内经》中还有不少的异体字的存在。如《素问》第 12 章有"其民嗜酸而食胕",其中的"胕"就是"腐"的异体字。所以在翻译诸如《内经》这样的典籍时,辨其字之正异也是正确理解和表达的重要前提。

四、虚实关系

所谓虚实关系,指的是典籍叙述中的比兴关系。中国古人在思辨和论辩时,常常喜欢采用比喻和提示之法,而不是直接点破主题。所以我们在读《庄子》、《韩非子》等典籍时,就常常遇到各种各样的寓言和故事。这些寓言和故事的作用就是帮助和引导读者理解作者所要阐发的道理或所要论证的要点,而不是作者所要论述的核心。

这就如同民歌中的起兴手法一样,目的是为了引起人们对下文内容的关注。如陕北民歌《翻身道情》开首的歌词是这样的:"一道道山来,一道道水,咱们中央红军到陕北。"句首的"一道道山来,一道道水"就是起兴,就像《刘三姐》对歌中开口必然是"哎……"一样,也是为了起兴。句末的"咱们中央红军到陕北"才是要歌唱的主要内容。

《论语》开篇"学而时习之,不亦说乎!有朋自远方来,不亦乐乎!人不知而不愠,不亦君子乎!"中,也同样存在着比兴的问题。中国古人在进行论辩的时候,总是喜欢将最重要的内容放在最后,前面的相关论述则发挥着比兴的作用。在这段话中,孔子由"学而时习之,不亦说乎"的学习精神和"有朋自远方来,不亦乐乎"的友朋关爱而引申出了君子自我修养中一个至关重要的方面,那就是"人不知而不愠"。正因为能在"人不知"的时候"而不愠",才使孔子虽政治上终生不得其志而能泰然处之,并因此而成就了他的千古圣人的事业。

除上面提到的比兴手法之外,《内经》等典籍中还有一种称为偏义复词的修辞手法。这是汉语里特有的一种构词现象。如《史记·仓公传》有"生子不生男,缓急无可使者"一句,其中的"缓急"意义相反,但这里只取"急"的意思,不取"缓"之意。再如《出师表》"宫中府中,俱为一体,陟罚臧否,不宜异同"一句中,"异同"只取"异"意而不取"同"意。

在解读以这种修辞手法所表达的相关概念时,就必须仔细体味其虚实之喻,以防误解原意。这种修辞手法的具体表现就是一个词由意义相反的两个字所构成,但该词的含义却不是两个字意义之和,而是只取其一。我们生活中常说的"是非"一词就是这样,如在"搬弄是非"这个俗语中,实际上只强调的是"非",而不是"是"。

中国古典文集中有不少这样的偏义复词,常见的有"逆从"、"死生"、"虚实"等。如在《素问》第1篇"辩列星辰,逆从阴阳"(to differentiate the arrangement of constellations and to follow the law of yin and yang)中,"逆从"只表示"从"(follow),而不表示"逆"(deviate from)。再如《素问》第21章中,黄帝问岐伯:"决死生奈何?"其中的"死生"究竟指的是"死"还是"生"呢?根据偏义复词的修辞格,这里的"死生"只取"死"而不取"生"。这从岐伯的回答也可以看出,岐伯回答说:"形盛脉细,少气不足以息者危,形瘦脉大,胸中多气者死。"

▶▶ 五、表里关系

所谓表里关系,指的是有关典籍基本概念、论述方式和行文风格与其所承载的内容之间的关系。套用现在语言学界使用的一个术语,就是表层与深层之间的关系。对于谙熟国学典籍行文特点和古汉语修辞风格的学人来说,这一点并不难理解,也不难判别。但对于不甚了解这些问题的人来说,要理解这一点却是困难的,因此也就无法正确判断其能指与所指。

海外人士翻译国学典籍时所引发的种种问题,很大程度上都与其对古汉语字词间的表里关系缺乏足够的认识有着直接的关系。汉语字性和词性及其用法非常灵活,其意也常常随之而发生变化。如果认识不到汉语词语的这种用法的灵活性,便很难准确把握其要义。下面试举中医典籍中的几个常见字加以说明。

1. 前:"前"一般用以表示方位或次第。但在"前大后小,即头痛目眩;前小后大,即胸满短气"(《伤寒论》)中,"前"不再指方位或次第,而是指脉的寸部;在"伤寒哕而腹满,视其前后,知何部不利"(《伤寒论》)中,"前"指的是小便;在"发汗则声乱咽嘶,舌萎声不前"(《医宗金鉴》)中,"前"则指的是提高。

2. 荣:"荣"一般用以表示茂盛或荣耀。但在"刺必中其荣"(《素问》)中,"荣"则指的是穴位,即五腧穴中的"荥"穴;在"荣卫不和,五脏不通"(《素问》)中,"荣"则指的是"营气";在"故脉弗荣,则筋急"(《灵枢》)中,"荣"指的是"营养";在"阴气太盛则阳气不能荣也"(《灵枢》)中,"荣"指的是"运行";在"风寒气郁于皮毛,致血不荣于肌表"(《外科正宗》)中,"荣"指的是"显现"。

3. 亡:"亡"的一般意义是死亡或逃跑。但在"小便与汗,皆亡津液"(《脾胃论》)中,"亡"指的是"消耗";在"有亡,忧知于色"(《素问》)中,"亡"指的是"失意";在"不知此道,失经绝理,亡言妄期,此谓失道"(《素问》)中,"亡"指的是"乱说"。

有时要了解一个词的含义,还须弄清楚它的原始内涵,然后再根据有关典籍的基本精神来判断该词在某一句话中的实际意义。比如《内经》等中医学经典中有"地道"一词,其一般含义是具体的,但在实际应用中却有多种引申,须得仔细审辨。《黄帝内经素问集注》说:"地道,下部之脉道也。"也就是说,"地道"指的是人体下部之"脉道"。中医将人体分为天地两部:上半身为天,属阳;下半身为地,属阴,因而有"天道"、"地道"之说。但在具体的语境中,"地道"的实际所指仍须仔细辨析。如在"天癸竭,地道不通,故形坏而无子"(《素问》)中,"地道不通"指的是"绝经"(menopause);在"今地道不通如此,非独燥胜,直是火胜矣"(《世补斋医书》)中,"地道不通"则指的是"大便不通"(constipation);在"大黄通地道,又解巴豆毒"(《医宗金鉴》)中,"通地道"指的是"通利大便"。

由以上各例可以看出,要准确理解国学典籍中概念的具体所指,但望其形有时是很难判断的,只有结合其表里关系及上下文趣对其慎加分析,才有可能明了其意。

六、古今关系

今人解读和翻译国学典籍时,在先入为主观念的影响下,很容易以今释古,把今作古,其结果是完全按照今人的思维方式解读古人的思想和观念。中国有文字记载的历史可以按甲骨文追溯到殷商时期,有明确纪年的历史则可以追溯到公元前841年的西周共和时期。但从那时到现在,中华民族的历史、文化和语言都发生了巨大的变化。同一个字、同一个词、同一个概念在不同的历史时期则完全可能有不同的含义和用法。对此我们必须要有充分的认识，不能一味地按照今人的思想去理解古人的观念。

如《内经》中有"百姓"一词，但该词与我们今天所讲的"百姓"是不是一回事呢？对此我们还须慎加分析，绝不可随意妄断。在《内经》中，我们可以看到这样一些话语："百姓闻之，以为残贼"、"使百姓昭著，上下和亲"、"余子万民，养百姓"、"百姓人民皆欲顺其志也"等。在这些话语中，"百姓"与"人民"及"万民"同时使用。难道它们具有同样的意思吗？特别是在"余子万民，养百姓"（这里的"子"是动词，是爱护的意思）这句话中，"万民"和"百姓"显然是两个不同的概念。它们的区别究竟在哪里呢？

要了解这个问题，就必须沿着历史的长河逆流而上，追本求源，探询这几个概念的本始之意。根据历史文献的记载，古代的时候只有贵族才能有姓，普通民众则只有名而没有姓。可能到了春秋战国晚期，随着社会变革的兴起和传统观念的崩溃，普通民众开始像贵族一样拥有姓了。所以当黄帝说："余子万民，养百姓"的时候，他所谓的"百姓"实际上指的是百官，他所谓的"万民"、"人民"，才是我们今天意义上的"百姓"。明白了这一点，我们在翻译"养百姓"时才不会按今天的观念将其译作 support the people。

在《内经》中，还有一个听起来挺时髦的概念——"美眉"。如《灵枢》中便有"美眉者，足太阳之脉气血多"、"美眉者，太阳多血"等说法。前些年"美眉"一词极为流行，用以指美貌年轻的女子。如果有人将《灵枢》这两句话里的"美眉"理解为 beautiful girl，自然是典型的以今释古、张冠李戴了。但这样的例子在目前的国学典籍翻译中，却并不罕见。如《素问》第 32 章有"其刺而反者，三周而已"一句，有人将其译为"If the treating is in an adverse way, the disease will last for three weeks"（吴连胜，吴奇，1999）。此处的"三周"之"周"究竟是什么意思，我们暂且不去探讨，仅从将其译作 week 这一做法来看，即可判明其属误译无疑。因为 week 是一个欧洲概念，传入中国也不过百年左右，何以会出现在成书于秦汉之际的《内经》之中呢？

关于"三周"这一概念，历来认识不一。如《类经》第 15 卷第 44 注说："三周者，谓三遇所胜之日而后已。"唐人王冰注解说："三周，谓三周于三阴三阳之脉状也。"《素问经注节解》注释说："三周，言重复也。"高士宗则解释说："三周，三日也。"综观各家之注解，似乎《类经》之说较为实际。作为一般译者，很难判断"三周"究竟所指为何。遇到这样的情况，比较稳妥的做法是结合诸家之论，对"三周"进行解释性翻译。Veith 氏在翻译这句话时，即按照《类经》的说法进行了解释性翻译，基本还是可取的。她的译文如下：

If the disease is treated at the opposite region [from where it arose], it takes three cycles of the celestial stems to cure it.

翻译国学典籍的时候,最容易导致的错误便是以今释古。如果译人在下笔之时能充分把握相关概念和词语的时代原貌与历史演变,便可明了其古时之义与今时之喻。当然,要做到这一点是非常不易的。这不仅要求译人有高度的责任感,而且要有扎实的古典文化功底和系统的专业知识。

第一课

《大 学》

▶▶ 一、内容简介

《大学》原为《礼记》中的一篇,相传为曾参(前505—前436)所撰,为唐人韩愈、李翱所极力推崇。宋代程颐、程颢兄弟对其进行了系统整理和深入研究,使其初具独立成经的地位。二程说:"《大学》,孔氏之遗书,而初学入德之门也。于今可见古人为学次第者,独赖此篇之存,而《论》、《孟》次之。学者由是而学焉,则庶乎其不差矣。"

朱熹又祖述二程之说,将《大学》从《礼记》中分离出来,重加编排补正,撰写提要,详加注解,定名《大学章句》,使其最终独立成书。不但成书,而且位居"经"列,与《中庸》、《论语》、《孟子》并称为"四书",成为儒家经典体系的一个重要组成部分。自宋代程、朱确立《大学》经学地位以来,其文句思想广为流传。

孙中山赞之曰:"中国政治哲学,谓其为最有系统之学,无论国外任何政治哲学都未见到,都未说出,为中国独有之宝贝。"其所论述之三纲、八目,对于人生之目的以及为达此目的所必须采取的步骤与方法,深入浅出,至精至微,发乎于远古,推及于素行,诚为珍贵。《大学》虽尊为"四书"之首,内容却极为简洁,通篇只有两百余字。虽不及现代诸家明师煌煌大论之一段,然其所阐述之至理大法,穷天地之常道、极六合之明晦,从天子以至庶民,无不以其为本。

"明明德"、"亲(新)民"、"止于至善"为《大学》之"三纲"。《大学》认为,人生来就具有高尚的德操,即"明德",亦即"人之初,性本善"也。入世以后,"明德"逐步为尘欲所泯,故需接受"大学之道"的教育,使之重新发现其"明德",力行"仁者爱人"之思想,达到尽善尽美的精神境界。"格物"、"致知"、"诚意"、"正心"、"修身"、"齐家"、"治国"、"平天下"为《大学》之"八目"。在这"八目"中,"格物"、"致知"为探索求知,"诚意"、"正心"、"修身"是精修身心,"齐家"、"治国"、"平天下"为人生之目的。

二、翻译传播

英语世界《大学》最早转译自柏应理(Philippe Couplet)编纂的 Confucius Sinarum Philosophus(《中国哲学家孔子》,中文书名为《西文四书直解》)的法文节译本 La Morale de Confucius(Amsterdam,1688),于1691年在伦敦出版,转译者不详。其全书译名为《中国哲学家孔子的道德箴言——孔子活跃于我们的救世主耶稣基督到来的500年前,本书是该国知识遗产的精华》(The Morals of Confucius, A Chinese Philosopher, who flourished above Five hundred Years before the Coming of our Lord and Saviour Jesus Christ, Being one of the Choicest Pieces of Learning Remaining of that Nation)。

早期《大学》较为完善的英译本有1812年伦敦会传教士马礼逊(Robert Morrison)的译文,收录他的《中国通俗文学译文集》(Horae Sinicae: Translations from the Popular Literature of the Chinese);还有1814年浸信会传教士马士曼父子(Joshua Marshman,John C. Marshman)合作的译文,收录乔舒亚·马士曼编写的《中国言法》,作为附录以供练习之用;以及1828年,高大卫(David Collie)在马六甲翻译出版的《四书》(The Chinese Classical Work Commonly Called The Four Books)。

在这些早期的英文译本中,尤其值得注意的是马士曼父子的译文。它采用汉英对照、译注同行的形式,为汉语典籍翻译开创了一个体例上的典范,被理雅各(James Legge)于1861—1872年翻译出版的《中国经典》(The Chinese Classics)所继承。理雅各的《大学》译本,无论在思想上还是在语言表达上,都是19世纪乃至今天的一个典范之作。

这些传教士的译本大都采取了直译的策略,目的是向英国人介绍中国的文化和语言,以期更好地为他们在中国传教服务,因此在他们评论性的注释中常常否认《大学》所阐释的理念或把《大学》所阐释的意旨导向基督教的教义。

20世纪,《大学》的译本主要有庞德(Ezra Pound)1928年的译本(Ta Hio, The Great Learning of Confucius)和1945年的译本。庞德1928年的译本从鲍狄埃的法文译本转译而来,当时没有引起太多关注。1947年,庞德将1945年的新译本与《中庸》的译本合订出版(Confucius: The Unwobbling Pivot & The Great Digest)。庞德的这个新译本采取了析字法,译得颇有趣味,也很有中国诗意,尤其是他对《大学》引证《诗经》诗句的翻译。

1938年,林语堂在《孔子的智慧》(The Wisdom of Confucius)一书中也完整地翻译了《大学》的全文。总体上讲,林语堂的翻译较为自由,容易为西方普通读者所接受。

修中诚(E. R. Hughes)翻译的《大学》和《中庸》合订本(The Great Learning and The Mean-in-Action),1942年在伦敦出版。德效骞(Homer H. Dubs)说他的译文简明易读,"特别的好"(unusually good)。(Dubs,1944:220)

20世纪《大学》的译本还有陈荣捷(Wing-Tsit Chan)、缪勒(A. Charles Muller)、何祚康等的译本。较之19世纪的译本,这些译本少了许多"欧洲文化中心论"的痕迹,基本上都较为客观地再现了《大学》的基本思想。2003年,普林斯顿大学的东亚学教授浦安迪(Andrew Plaks)翻译了《大学》和《中庸》的合订本,作为企鹅经典(Penguin Classics)出版发行,书名为 Ta Hsueh and Chung Yung: The Highest Order of Cultivation and On the Practice of the Mean,这是《大学》较新的译本。浦安迪教授把"大学"译为 the highest order of cultivation,一定意义上揭示了其基本内涵。

三、翻译对比

- 原文:

大学之道,在明明德,在亲民,在止于至善。

知止而后有定,定而后能静,静而后能安,安而后能虑,虑而后能得。

物有本末,事有终始,知所先后,则近道矣。

古之欲明明德于天下者,先治其国;欲治其国者,先齐其家;欲齐其家者,先修其身;欲修其身者,先正其心;欲正其心者,先诚其意;欲诚其意者,先致其知;致知在格物。

物格而后知至,知至而后意诚,意诚而后心正,心正而后身修,身修而后家齐,家齐而后国治,国治而后天下平。

自天子以至于庶人,壹是皆以修身为本。其本乱而末治者,否矣。其所厚者薄,而其所薄者厚,未之有也。

理雅各译文:

What the great learning teaches, is—to illustrate illustrious virtue; to renovate the people; and to rest in the highest excellence.

The point where to rest being known, the object of pursuit is then determined; and, that being determined, a calm unperturbedness may be attained. To that calmness there will succeed a tranquil repose. In that repose there may be careful deliberation, and that deliberation will be followed by the attainment of the desired end.

Things have their root and their completion. Affairs have their end and their beginning. To know what is first and what is last will lead near to what is taught in the Great Learning.

The ancients who wished to illustrate illustrious virtue throughout the empire, first ordered well their own States. Wishing to order well their States, they first regulated their families. Wishing to regulate their families, they first cultivated their persons. Wishing to cultivate their persons, they first rectified their hearts. Wishing to rectify their hearts, they first sought to be sincere in their thoughts. Wishing to be sincere in their thoughts, they first extended to the utmost their knowledge. Such extension of knowledge lay in the investigation of things.

Things being investigated, knowledge became complete. Their knowledge being complete, their thoughts were sincere. Their thoughts being sincere, their hearts were then rectified. Their hearts being rectified, their persons were cultivated. Their persons being cultivated, their families were regulated. Their families being regulated, their states were rightly governed. Their states being rightly governed, the whole kingdom was made tranquil and happy.

From the emperor down to the mass of the people, all must consider the cultivation of the person the root of everything besides.

It cannot be, when the root is neglected, that what should spring from it will be well ordered. It never has been the case that what was of great importance has been slightly cared for, and, at the same time, that what was of slight importance has been greatly cared for.

<u>林语堂译文：</u>

The principles of the higher education consist in preserving man's clear character, in giving new life to the people, and in dwelling (or resting) in perfection, or the ultimate good.

Only after knowing the goal of perfection where one should dwell, can one have a definite purpose in life. Only after having a definite purpose in life can one achieve calmness of mind. Only after having achieved calmness of mind, can one have peaceful repose. Only after having peaceful repose can one begin to think. Only after one has learned to think, can one achieve knowledge.

There are a foundation and a superstructure in the constitution of things, and a beginning and end in the course of events. Therefore to know the proper sequence or relative order of things is the beginning of wisdom.

The ancients who wished to preserve the fresh or clear character of the people of the world, would first set about ordering their national life. Those who wished to order their national life, would first set about regulating their family life. Those who wished to regulate their family life would set about cultivating their personal life. Those who wished to cultivate their personal lives, would first set about setting their hearts right. Those who wished to set their hearts right would first set about making their wills sincere. Those who wished to make their wills sincere would first set about achieving true knowledge. The achieving of true knowledge depended upon the investigation of things.

When things are investigated, then true knowledge is achieved; when true knowledge is achieved, then the will becomes sincere; when the will is sincere, then the heart is set right (or then the mind sees right); when the heart is set right, then the personal life is cultivated; when the personal life is cultivated, then the family life is regulated; when the family life is regulated, then the national life is orderly; and when the national life is orderly, then there is peace in this world.

From the emperor down to the common men, all must regard the cultivation of the personal life as the root or foundation. There is never an orderly upshot or superstructure when the root or foundation is disorderly. There is never yet a tree whose trunk is slim and slender and whose top branches are thick and heavy. This is called "to know the root or foundation of things".

▶▶ 四、翻译赏析

"大学"一词现在较为通行的译法是理雅各的 the great learning。汉代郑玄在《礼记注》中说："大学者以其记博学可以为政也。"从这个意义上讲，"大学"颇似现在培养治理安邦之才的大学，所以林语堂把它译为 higher education。但这种归化的译法与原文的内涵其实并不完全一致。

《礼记·学记》说："比年入学，中年考校。一年视离经辨志，三年视敬业乐群，五年视博习亲师，七年视论学取友，谓之小成。九年知类通达，强立而不反，谓之大成。夫然后足以化民易俗,近者说服而远者怀之,此大学之道也。"由此可见,古时的"大学"学习时限约为九年,主要为教育王子、贵族子弟而设,主要内容为修身、治国、安邦、平天下。朱熹说:"大学者,大人之学也。"由此可见,理雅各将"大学"译为 the great learning 还是较为可取的。

"道"在中国古籍及诸子论著中涉及颇多,其内涵极为丰富,外延也甚为宽广,译作 path,course,或通常的 way,都显得过于表化。"大学之道"中"道"的基本含义是道理、原理、原则、纲领,含有人生观、世界观、政治主张、思想体系等。所谓"大学之道",即大学所阐发的基本思想或基本原理,林语堂将其译为 principles,较为符合原文之意。理雅各则将"道"略而不译,将《大学》第一纲译为 what the great learning teaches, is to—illustrate illustrious virtue。

"明明德"中前一个"明"字是动词,有使动的意味,即"使彰明",也就是发扬、弘扬的意思;后一个"明"是形容词,有"光明"、"灵明"之意。"明德",也就是光明正大之德。"明明德",就是彰显人所固有的美德。理雅各译之为 to illustrate illustrious virtue,林语堂译之为 preserving man's clear character,皆可传达原作之意。

《大学》的第二条纲领"亲民",程颐改作"新民",朱熹从之,并解释说"新者,革其旧之谓也"。多数译者以朱熹《大学章句》为底本,改"亲民"为"新民",并将其译为 to renovate the people(理雅各),giving new life to the people(林语堂),making new people(修中诚),但也有倾向于王阳明之解释的,取儒家一贯思想"仁者爱人"之意,将其译为 loving the people(陈荣捷,缪勒)。

《大学》的第三条纲领"止于至善",理雅各将其译为 to rest in the highest excellence,林语堂将其译为 dwelling (or resting) in perfection, or the ultimate good,虽属直译,但也较为符合原文之意。

五、课后练习

(一) 思考题

1. 《大学》的"三纲"和"八目"分别指什么?
2. "物有本末,事有终始"中的"本"、"末"、"终"、"始"分别指什么?
3. 如何理解"大学"?

(二) 翻译题

1. 大学,孔氏之遗书,而初学入德之门也。

2. 苟日新,日日新,又日新。

3. 富润屋,德润身,心广体胖。

4. 财聚则民散,财散则民聚。

5. 生财有大道:生之者众,食之者寡,为之者疾,用之者舒,则财恒足矣。

参考读物

Chan, Wing-Tsit. *A Source Book of Chinese Philosophy* [M]. Princeton:Princeton University Press, 1969.

Collie, David. Trans. *The Chinese Classical Work Commonly Called The Four Books* [M]. Malacca, Malaysia:Printed at the Mission Press, 1828.

Dubs, Homer H. Review of The Great Learning & The Mean-In-Action [J]. *The Philosophical Review*, 1944(2).

Hughes, E. R. Trans. *The Great Learning and The Mean-in-Action* [M]. London:J. M. Dent and Sons, 1942.

Legge, J. Trans. *The Chinese Classics* (Vol. I) [M]. Hong Kong:At the Author's; London:Trübner & Co., 1861.

Lin, Yutang. *The Wisdom of Confucius* [M]. New York:The Modern Library, 1938.

Marshman, J. *Elements of Chinese Grammar, with a Preliminary Dissertation on the Characters, and the Colloquial Medium of the Chinese, and an Appendix Containing the Ta-Hyoh of Confucius with a Translation* [M]. Serampore, India:Printed at the Mission Press, 1814.

Morrison, R. Trans. *Horae Sinicae: Translations from the Popular Literature of the Chinese* [M]. London:Printed for Black and Parry, 1812.

何祚康. 大学中庸:汉英对照[M]. 北京:华语教育出版社,1996.

李照国. 译海心悟——中国古典文化翻译别论[M]. 上海:上海中医药大学出版社,2007.

南怀瑾. 原本大学微言[M]. 上海:复旦大学出版社,2003.

王辉. 析字法与庞德的《大学》译本[J]. 翻译季刊(香港),2005(4).

第二课

《中庸》

▶▶ 一、内容简介

　　《中庸》原为《礼记》中的一篇。《中庸》一书的作者据传是孔子的孙子子思。《史记·孔子世家》有"孔子生鲤,字伯鱼,伯鱼生伋,字子思。年六十二,子思作《中庸》"之言。

　　自汉以来,《中庸》一直受到学者关注。北宋程颢、程颐对《中庸》极为尊崇,程颐说它是"孔门传授心法……其味无穷,皆实学也。善读者玩索而有得焉,则终身用之,有不能尽者矣"。南宋朱熹把《中庸》和《大学》独立成篇,与《论语》、《孟子》并列为"四书",作《中庸章句》。

　　宋、元以后,《中庸》成为法定的教科书和科举考试的必读书,对古代教育产生了极大的影响。林语堂(1998:109)说:"生活的最高类型终究是《中庸》的作者,孔子的孙儿,子思所倡导的甜蜜理性的生活。古今与人类生活问题有关的哲学,还不曾有一个发现比这种学说更深奥的真理。"(The highest type of life after all is the life of sweet reasonableness as taught by Confucius' grandson, Tsesse, author of *The Golden Mean*. No philosophy, ancient or modern, dealing with the problems of human life has yet discovered a more profound truth than this doctrine.)

　　《中庸》一书言天命性道,论人与宇宙之关系,说理至精,论道至微。其中心思想则是儒学中的中庸之道,其主旨在于修养人性,通过自我修养、自我教育,把自己培养成为具有理想人格的理想人物。《中庸》在结构上虽不如《大学》那样明晰,但其构思极其精巧。首章"天命之谓性,率性之谓道,修道之谓教"为全书的纲要,提出了命、性、道、教的重要哲学命题。

▶▶ 二、翻译传播

　　《中庸》的对外传播与翻译经历了差不多与《大学》相同的过程。最早将《中庸》一书翻译成拉丁文并刊印的是殷铎泽(Prospero Intorceta)，书名为《中国政治道德科学》(*Sinarum Scientia Politico-Moralis*)，出版时间为1667年。《中庸》完整的英译本迟至1828年才由高大卫译出，而且还没有引起太多的关注。1861年理雅各推出了《中国经典》(*The Chinese Classics*)第一卷，其中包括《大学》、《中庸》、《论语》的翻译。理雅各把《中庸》翻译为 *The Doctrine of the Mean*。理雅各译本问世后，受到西方读者的好评，被奉为汉学经典译本。

　　由于不满理雅各翻译的中国经典，辜鸿铭翻译了儒家经典中的《大学》(未曾出版)、《中庸》和《论语》，其中《中庸》译本1906年由上海别发洋行出版，书名为 *The Universal Order, or Conduct of Life*(普遍秩序或人生之道)。辜鸿铭翻译的《中庸》旨在"阐明中国人的道德责任感，正是这种责任感形成了中国文明体制下的人类行为和社会秩序的基础"(Ku, 1906: x)。他翻译《中庸》的最终目的是"希望欧美人，尤其是在华的欧美人，能更好地理解'道'，加强道德责任感，在对待中国和中国人时，放弃欧洲那种'坚船利炮'和'武力威慑'的文明，而代之以'道'；无论是个人还是民族，在同中国人的交往中，遵从道德责任感"(Ku, 1906: xi-xii)。

　　辜鸿铭翻译《中庸》的原则是"在彻悟其中的意义之后，不仅译出原文的'质'(matter)，而且要再现原作的'形'(manner)。"但他也坦言此非易事，"然而，要再现古代圣哲之文，即文学上称之为'style'的东西，就必须努力使自己具备同圣哲一样的性情和心境——这对于生活在现代'文明进步'的世界的人们并非易事"(Ku, 1906: ii)。辜鸿铭在翻译策略上基本上采用了"归化"的译法，这从他的《中庸》英译副标题 A Confucian Catechism 即可窥得一斑。这个副标题回译为中文就是"儒家教理问答"。辜鸿铭把《中庸》放在了等同于基督教经典的地位，他这样做是要方便西方读者理解和接受儒家的道德理念。

　　《中庸》的另一译本是1938年林语堂《孔子的智慧》中的译本。从某种意义上说，林语堂《孔子的智慧》中的《中庸》并非完全由他本人所译，而是对辜鸿铭的译文进行了"增补、删减、替换某些字词或句子，使其更切合原作"(Lin, 1938: 102)。

　　20世纪《中庸》的译本还有修中诚译本、庞德译本、陈荣捷译本、何祚康译本、缪勒译本。21世纪之初，安乐哲、郝大维(Roger Ames, David Hall)从哲学的角度用过程语言翻译了《中庸》，译名为 *Focusing the Familiar: A Translation and Philosophical Interpretation of the*

Zhongyong；另一个译本是普林斯顿大学教授浦安迪的译本。

三、翻译对比

- 原文一：

天命之谓性，率性之谓道，修道之谓教。道也者，不可须臾离也，可离非道也。是故君子戒慎乎其所不睹，恐惧乎其所不闻。莫见乎隐，莫显乎微，故君子慎其独也。喜怒哀乐之未发，谓之中；发而皆中节，谓之和。中也者，天下之大本也；和也者，天下之达道也。致中和，天地位焉，万物育焉。

理雅各译文：

What Heaven has conferred is called THE NATURE; an accordance with this nature is called THE PATH of duty; the regulation of this path is called INSTRUCTION.

The path may not be left for an instant. If it could be left, it would not be the path. On this account, the superior man does not wait till he sees things, to be cautious, nor till he hears things, to be apprehensive.

There is nothing more visible than what is secret, and nothing more manifest than what is minute. Therefore, the superior man is watchful over himself, when he is alone.

While there are no stirrings of pleasure, anger, sorrow, or joy, the mind may be said to be in the state of EQUILIBRIUM. When those feelings have been stirred, and they act in their due degree, there ensues what may be called the state of HARMONY. This EQUILIBRIUM is the great root from which grow all the human actings in the world, and this HARMONY is the universal path which they all should pursue.

Let the states of equilibrium and harmony exist in perfection, and a happy order will prevail throughout heaven and earth, and all things will be nourished and flourish.

辜鸿铭译文：

The ordinance of God is what we call the law of our being (性). To fulfill the law of our being is what we call the moral law (道). The moral law when reduced to a system is what we call religion (教). The moral law is a law from whose operation we cannot for one instant in our existence escape. A law from which we may escape is not the moral law. Wherefore it is that the moral man (君子) watches diligently over what his eyes cannot see and is in fear and awe of what his ears cannot hear.

There is nothing more evident than what cannot be seen by the eyes and nothing more palpable than what cannot be perceived by the senses. Wherefore the moral man watches diligently over his secret thoughts.

When the passions, such as joy, anger, grief and pleasure, have not awakened, that is our true self (中) or moral being. When these passions awaken and each and all attain due measure and degree, that is the moral order (和). Our true self or moral being is the great reality(大本 lit. great root) of existence, and moral order is the universal law (达道) in the world.

When true moral being and moral order are realised, the universe then becomes a cosmos and all things attain their full growth and development.

- 原文二:

诚者,天之道也;诚之者,人之道也。诚者,不勉而中,不思而得,从容中道,圣人也。诚之者,择善而固执之者也。

博学之,审问之,慎思之,明辨之,笃行之。有弗学,学之弗能弗措也;有弗问,问之弗知弗措也;有弗思,思之弗得弗措也;有弗辨,辨之弗明弗措也;有弗行,行之弗笃弗措也。人一能之,己百之;人十能之,己千之。果能此道矣,虽愚必明,虽柔必强。

修中诚译文:

It is the characteristic of Heaven to be the real. It is the characteristic of man to be coming-to-be-real. (For a man) to be real [i.e. to have achieved realness] is to hit the Mean without effort, to have it without thinking of it, entirely naturally to be centred in the Way. This is to be a sage. To be coming-to-be-real is to choose the good and hold fast to it. This involves learning all about the good, asking about it, thinking it over carefully, getting it clear by contrast, and faithfully putting it into practice. If there is any part about which he has not learnt or asked questions, which he has not thought over and got clear by contrast, or which he has not put into practice, he sets to work to learn and ask and think and get clear and put into practice. If he does not get the required result, he still does not give up working. When he sees other men succeeding by one effort, or it may be a hundred, he is prepared to add a hundredfold to his own effort. The man who can last this course, although he is stupid, will come to understand; although he is weak, will become strong.

浦安迪译文：

A perfect state of integral wholeness can only be attributed to the Way of Heaven; the process of making oneself whole is, however, within the province of the Way of Man. "Integral Wholeness" means a state of centred balance requiring no striving, complete attainment requiring no mental effort. To strike the mean with absolute effortlessness is the mark of none but those of perfect cultivation. The process of "making oneself whole", by contrast, requires choosing the good and holding fast to it with all one's strength.

Study it extensively,

question its meaning precisely,

ponder it with full vigilance,

scrutinize its distinctions with clarity of vision,

practice it in all earnestness.

If there should remain that which has not been studied, or that has been studied but has not yet led to full mastery, do not desist!

Should there remain that which has not been questioned, or that has been questioned but has not yet led to full comprehension, do not desist!

Should there remain that which has not been pondered, or that has been pondered but has not yet led to a complete grasp, do not desist!

Should there remain that which has not been scrutinized, or that has been scrutinized but has not yet led to clear distinction, do not desist!

Should there remain that which has not been put into practice, or that has been practiced but not in full earnestness, do not desist!

What other men may master in a single try, you yourself must strive to attain with efforts increased a hundredfold;

and what others may master in ten tries, you must strive to attain a thousand times over.

For, one whose efforts reach fruition in the mastery of this path,

be he of limited intellectual capacity, he will gain clear understanding;

and be he of weak disposition, he will enjoy great strength.

四、翻译赏析

在"原文一"的翻译中,辜鸿铭的译文无论从内容还是语言上都实现了他翻译《中庸》的目的,即向西方彰显中国的道德文明。特别是对一些关键术语的翻译,均将其纳入 moral 的范畴,如将"道"译作 the moral law,将"君子"译作 moral man,将"中"译作 our true self, or moral being,将"和"译作 moral order。其他一些术语的翻译也有其特别的用意,如将"天"译为 God,将"教"译为 religion,即以西方术语解释儒家概念。

相比较而言,理雅各的翻译似乎较为接近原文之意。例如,他把"中"译为 equilibrium,将"和"译为 harmony,一定意义上还是较为接近原文之意的。但由于中国语言的多义性,很多基本概念的实际内涵往往很难再现于译文。如理雅各把"道"译作 the path of duty,即难以传达"道"的丰富内涵,而且 duty 一词尤其让人觉得与上下文不够协调。同样,理雅各把"教"译作 instruction 亦显表浅。《中庸》里的"教"应是"教化"之意,译作 moral instruction 或 education 似乎更为贴切。

从译文风格来看,理雅各的译文似有维多利亚时代的古板,辜鸿铭的译文则显得较为生动。此外,辜鸿铭把"天地位焉"译为 the universe then becomes a cosmos,别有深意,值得玩味。

在"原文二"中,子思从天道、人道两方面立言:天道就是诚,人道就是追求诚,而追求诚的途径是学问。浦安迪主要采取了解释性翻译,在译文中增加了一些文内注解。为了使译文表达更加明晰,这原本是一种常用的翻译方法。但对于言简意赅的中国经籍而言,这种文内注解的方法容易使不懂中文的读者把他的文内解释理解成原文固有的内容,从而造成"衍文"现象的出现。例如,他把"择善而固执之"译为 choosing the good and holding fast to it with all one's strength,其中 with all one's strength 是原文中所没有的。根据译者的注释,这层意思是他根据《中庸》第六章和第八章的内容推演而来的:"固"是一个不断权衡的过程。而且译出这层意思也与前一句保持了句法和内容的对称。

发表于1942年的修中诚译文可谓对理雅各、辜鸿铭译文的改进,较理雅各译文有更多阐释的成分,但没有辜鸿铭译文那么自由,可以说是一个"中和"的译本。虽然他的译文内也有注解,但他都用方括号把它们与正文区别了开来,很容易被读者所识别。

另外,这两个译文在关键术语的处理方面都很有特色。由于修中诚认为《大学》、《中庸》是古代儒家典籍中最为形而上的,因此他在翻译《中庸》的某些核心概念时用了西方形而上的哲学术语。例如,"诚"一般都译作 sincere 或 sincerity,而辜中诚则用了形而上的术语 real 或 realness(实在)来翻译。此外,他把此选段中的"道"译作 characteristic,也是独具一格。

五、课后练习

(一)思考题

1. 何谓"中庸"?
2. 《中庸》的基本精神是什么?
3. 如何理解《中庸》的为学之道?

(二)翻译题

1. 不偏之谓中,不易之谓庸。中者,天下之正道;庸者,天下之定理。

2. 道之不行也,我知之矣:知者过之,愚者不及也。道之不明也,我知之矣:贤者过之,不肖者不及也。人莫不饮食也,鲜能知味也。

3. 在上位不陵下,在下位不援上;正己而不求于人,则无怨;上不怨天,下不尤人。故君子居易以俟命,小人行险以侥幸。

4. 好学近乎知,力行近乎仁,知耻近乎勇。知斯三者,则知所以修身;知所以修身,则知所以治人;知所以治人,则知所以治天下国家矣。

5. 博学之,审问之,慎思之,明辨之,笃行之。有弗学,学之弗能弗措也;有弗问,问之弗知弗措也;有弗思,思之弗得弗措也;有弗辨,辨之弗明弗措也;有弗行,行之弗笃弗措也。人一能之,己百之;人十能之,己千之。果能此道矣,虽愚必明,虽柔必强。

参考读物

Ku, Hung-Ming. Trans. *The Universal Order, or Conduct of Life* [M]. Shanghai: Shanghai Mercury, Ltd., 1906.

Plaks, Andrew. Trans. *Ta Hsueh and Chung Yung: The Highest Order of Cultivation and On the Practice of the Mean* [M]. London: Penguin Classics, 2003.

林语堂. 生活的艺术[M]. 北京:外语教学与研究出版社,1998.

冯友兰. 中国哲学简史(英汉对照)[M]. 天津:天津社会科学院出版社,2007.

第三课

《论 语》

▶▶ 一、内容简介

《论语》乃儒家经典之一,由孔门弟子及其再传弟子编撰而成,成书于战国初期,是记录孔子主要弟子及其再传弟子关于孔子言行的一部书,它以语录体和对话文体为主,共四十卷,为汉语文章的典范。《论语》的语言简洁精炼,含义深刻,其中的许多言论至今仍被世人视为至理。

"论"是论纂的意思,"语"是话语。作为一部优秀的语录体散文集,它以言简意赅、含蓄隽永的语言记述了孔子的言论。《论语》中所记孔子循循善诱的教诲之言,或简单应答,点到即止,或启发论辩,侃侃而谈,或富于变化,娓娓动人。

《论语》又善于通过神情语态的描写,展示人物形象。孔子是《论语》描述的中心,"夫子风采,溢于格言"(《文心雕龙·征圣》);书中不仅有关于他的仪态举止的静态描写,而且有关于他的个性气质的传神刻画。此外,围绕孔子这一中心,《论语》还成功地刻画了一些孔门弟子的形象,如子路的率直鲁莽、颜回的温雅贤良、子贡的聪颖善辩、曾皙的潇洒脱俗等,都称得上个性鲜明,能给人留下深刻印象。孔子因材施教,对于不同的对象,考虑其不同的素质、优点和缺点、进德修业的具体情况,给予不同的教诲,表现了诲人不倦的可贵精神。

因秦始皇焚书坑儒,到西汉时期仅有口头传授及从孔子住宅夹壁中所得的本子,计有:鲁人口头传授的《鲁论语》20篇,齐人口头传授的《齐论语》22篇,从孔子住宅夹壁中发现的《古论语》21篇。现存《论语》20篇,492章,其中记录孔子与弟子及时人谈论之语的444章,记录孔门弟子相互谈论之语的48章。

孔子生于公元前551年9月28日(农历八月二十七),卒于公元前479年4月11日(农历二月十一),姓孔,名丘,字仲尼,鲁国陬邑(今中国山东省曲阜市南辛镇)人,祖上为宋国(今河南商丘)贵族。他是中国春秋末期的思想家、教育家、儒家思想的创始人。孔子集华夏上古文化之大成,被后世尊为孔圣人、至圣、至圣先师、万世师表。孔子和儒家思想对中国和朝鲜半岛、日本、越南等地区有深远的影响。

▶▶ 二、翻译传播

《论语》在英语世界的传播最早源于1691年转译自法语的 The Morals of Confucius: A Chinese Philosopher (《中国哲学家孔子的道德》)。它是当时西方人心目中孔子形象的基础。但这是一个很不完善的节译本。例如,"益者三友,损者三友。友直,友谅,友多闻,益矣。友便辟,友善柔,友便佞,损矣"被译为"We have three Friends that are Useful to us, a Sincere Friend, a Faithful Friend, a Friend that Hears every Thing, that Examines what is told him, and that Speaks little. But we have three also whose Friendship is pernicious, a Hypocrite, a Flatterer, and a great Talker"。

1809年,马士曼翻译出版了《论语》上卷译文,书名为 The Works of Confucius: Containing the Original Text, with a Translation。马士曼翻译《论语》的主要目的是"向国人揭示汉语的特点,为研究中国文学和古文,最终向中国介绍西方的科学,特别是向中国介绍《圣经》开辟道路"(Marshman, 1809: xxxiv-xxxv)。为此,他采用"尽量直译"的方法,甚至使译文与原文在词序和句法上保持对应。即使如此,他认为也"无法真正揭示汉语和中国文学的魅力"。因而,他采用了中英文对照的形式,并加上注释和汉字解析。但就马士曼的译文来看,他的目的恐怕是很难达到的。例如,他把"知者乐水,仁者乐山;知者动,仁者静;知者乐,仁者寿",译为"Knowledge produces pleasure clear as water; complete virtue, happiness solid as a mountain; knowledge pervades all things; virtue is tranquil and happy; knowledge is delight; virtue is long life"。读者若看了这样的译文,恐怕难以领略中国圣哲的智慧,也难以学得中国文学之精妙。1828年,高大卫翻译的《四书》出版,其中有《论语》的完整译文。这是《论语》的第一个英文全译本。1861年,理雅各的《论语》译本(Confucian Analects)成为后来《论语》众多译本的参照本。之后《论语》的翻译有1895年出版的威廉·詹宁斯(William Jennings)的译本(The Confucius Analects: A Translation, with Annotations and an Introduction to the Chinese Master)以及1898年出版的辜鸿铭的译本(The

Discourses and Sayings of Confucius)。

到了 20 世纪,《论语》的英译更是异彩纷呈。1907 年英国汉学家翟林奈(Lionel Giles)出版了他的译本(*The Sayings of Confucius: A New Translation of the Greater Part of the Confucius Analects*)。他的译本的一个显著特点是对《论语》的章节内容按主题重新分类,这使得孔子的言论更具系统性。1910 年英国传教士苏慧廉(William Edward Soothill)出版了他的译本(*The Analects of Confucius*)。1938 年英国汉学家韦利(Arthur Waley)出版了他的译本(*The Analects of Confucius*)。韦利的译本是公认的高水平译本,很受西方读者欢迎。除了《论语》,韦利还翻译有《道德经》、《诗经》以及许多诗歌。闻一多曾称赞韦氏的译文"在字句的结构和音节的调度上,韦利是最讲究的"。

1950 年,美国诗人庞德(Ezra Pound)依据当代石刻本翻译的《论语》(*The Analects*)刊登于《哈德逊评论》(*Hudson Review*)上。其译本主观发挥较多,多有创造。庞德之后,《论语》较受读者关注的译本有香港中文大学教授刘殿爵(D. C. Lau)1979 年出版的译本(*The Analects*)、英国汉学家道森(Raymond Dawson)1993 年出版的译本(*Confucius: The Analects*)、澳大利亚籍比利时汉学家李克曼(原名 Pierre Ryckmans,英文名 Simon Leys)1997 年出版的译本(*The Analects of Confucius*)、美籍华人黄治中(Chichuang Huang)1997 年出版的译本(*The Analects of Confucius*)、安乐哲(Roger T. Ames)和罗思文(Henry Rosemont)1998 年出版的译本(*The Analects of Confucius: A Philosophical Translation*)。安乐哲和罗思文的译本从哲学角度阐释儒家思想,强调中西哲学的差异,在对儒家核心概念的处理方面独具一格。例如,他们把"仁"译为 authoritative conduct,把"君子"译为 an exemplary person。此外,美国汉学家亨顿(David Hinton)1998 年出版了他的译本(*The Analects of Confucius*),面向普通读者,注重通俗和流畅,可读性高。

在 21 世纪的前十年中,《论语》又有了一些新的译本。其中有美国当代汉学家森舸澜(Edward G. Slingerland)2003 年出版的译本。这是一个纯学术的译本,文后附有大量的评注,推荐了大量的参考文献。还有华兹生(Burton Watson)2007 年出版的译本。华兹生的译本文笔清晰、行文简洁、语言优美。2010 年,我国著名翻译家林戊荪推出了《论语》的最新译本(*Getting to Know Confucius: A New Translation of The Analects*),这是我国翻译家推出的最新《论语》译本。

三、翻译对比

- 原文一：

子曰："学而时习之,不亦说乎?有朋自远方来,不亦乐乎?人不知而不愠,不亦君子乎?"(《学而》)

理雅各译文：

The Master said, "Is it not pleasant to learn with a constant perseverance and application? Is it not delightful to have friends coming from distant quarters? Is he not a man of complete virtue, who feels no discomposure though men may take no note of him?"

刘殿爵译文：

The Master said, "Is it not a pleasure, having learned something, to try it out at due intervals? Is it not a joy to have friends come from afar? Is it not gentlemanly not to take offence when others fail to appreciate your abilities?"

- 原文二：

子曰："君子食无求饱,居无求安;敏于事而慎于言;就有道而正焉,可谓好学也已。"(《学而》)

理雅各译文：

The Master said, "He who aims to be a man of complete virtue in his food does not seek to gratify his appetite, nor in his dwelling place does he seek the appliances of ease; he is earnest in what he is doing, and careful in his speech; he frequents the company of men of principle that he may be rectified—such a person may be said indeed to love to learn."

林戊荪译文：

The Master said, "The man of honor seeks neither a full belly nor a comfortable house. He is quick in action, but cautious with his words. He corrects his own mistakes by learning from those who know the Way. He can thus be regarded as studious."

- 原文三：

子曰："吾十有五而志于学,三十而立,四十而不惑,五十而知天命,六十而耳顺,七十而从心所欲,不逾矩。"(《为政》)

理雅各译文：

The Master said, "At fifteen, I had my mind bent on learning. At thirty, I stood firm. At forty, I had no doubts. At fifty, I knew the decrees of Heaven. At sixty, my ear was an obedient organ for the reception of truth. At seventy, I could follow what my heart desired, without transgressing what was right."

辜鸿铭译文：

Confucius remarked, "At fifteen I had made up my mind to give myself up to serious studies. At thirty I had formed my opinions and judgment. At forty I had no more doubts. At fifty I understood the truth in religion. At sixty I could understand whatever I heard without exertion. At seventy I could follow whatever my heart desired without transgressing the law."

- 原文四：

子曰："朝闻道，夕死可矣。"(《里仁》)

辜鸿铭译文：

Confucius remarked, "When a man has learnt wisdom in the morning, he may be content to die in the evening before the sun sets."

苏慧廉译文：

The Master said, "He who heard the Truth in the morning might die content in the evening."

- 原文五：

子曰："贤哉，回也！一箪食，一瓢饮，在陋巷，人不堪其忧，回也不改其乐。贤哉，回也！"(《雍也》)

理雅各译文：

The Master said, "Admirable indeed was the virtue of Hui! With a single bamboo dish of rice, a single gourd dish of drink, and living in his mean narrow lane, while others could not have endured the distress, he did not allow his joy to be affected by it. Admirable indeed was the virtue of Hui!"

辜鸿铭译文：

Confucius remarked of his disciple, the favourite Yen Hui, saying, "How much heroism is in that man! Living on one single meal a day, with water for his drink, and living in the lowest hovels of the city—no man could have stood such hardships, yet he—he did not lose his cheerfulness. How much heroism is in that man!"

- 原文六：

子曰："夫仁者,己欲立而立人,己欲达而达人。能近取譬,可谓仁之方也已。"(《雍也》)

辜鸿铭译文：

Confucius remarked, "A moral man in forming his character forms the character of others; in enlightening himself he enlightens others. It is a good method in attaining a moral life, if one is able to consider how one would see things and act if placed in the position of others."

安乐哲译文：

The Master said, "Authoritative persons establish others in seeking to establish themselves and promote others in seeking to get there themselves. Correlating one's conduct with those near at hand can be said to be the method of becoming an authoritative person."

- 原文七：

子曰："管仲相桓公,霸诸侯,一匡天下,民到于今受其赐。微管仲,吾其被发左衽矣！岂若匹夫匹妇之为谅也,自经于沟渎而莫之知也！"(《宪问》)

辜鸿铭译文：

Confucius remarked, "Kuan Chung as Prime Minister enabled the prince, his master, to exercise Imperialism and give it peace. Down to the present day the people are enjoying the benefits due to his great services. But for Kuan Chung we should now be living like savages. He was certainly not like your faithful lover and his sweetheart among the common people, who, in order to prove their constancy, go and drown themselves in a ditch, nobody taking any notice of them."

理雅各译文：

The Master said, "Kwan Chung acted as prime minister to the Duke Hwan, made him leader of all the princes, and united and rectified the whole kingdom. Down to the present day, the people enjoy the gifts which he conferred. But for Kwan Chung, we should now be wearing our hair unbound, and the lappets of our coats buttoning on the left side. Will you require from him the small fidelity of common men and common women, who would commit suicide in a stream or ditch, no one knowing anything about them?"

四、翻译赏析

《论语》开篇即论学，可见孔子对学之重视。正如清人梁清远在《雕丘杂录·采荣录》一书所言："《论语》一书，首言为学，即曰'悦'，曰'乐'，曰'君子'，此圣人最善诱人处。"

两个译本行文风格基本相同，都保留了原文反问的语气。但若译为"To study and frequently practice what has been learnt, is that not a pleasure?"也许更吻合原文的行文结构。至于"习"字的解释，自汉至清，向来不一。何晏认为"习"乃反复诵习，但在朱熹看来，"习"则为实践之义。清儒则兼取复习与实习之义。显然，理雅各的译文 constant perseverance and application 较好地体现了"习"字的温习、应用之义。

孔子自述其一生坚持学习与道德修养的进程，从"十有五而志于学"到"三十而立"，再到"从心所欲不逾矩"，是学问和道德修养日臻完美的过程。理雅各将"立"译为 stand firm，有坚定立场之意，似与原文之意不甚吻合。何晏《论语注疏》释"立"为"有所成"，故而英译为 established 较为恰当。

《论语》中的"道"字虽不同于《老子》之"道"，但语义也是很丰富的。何晏《论语注疏》中说"言将至死不闻世之有道也"，其中的"世之有道"，即《季氏》篇所云"天下有道"。根据孔子所处时代及其政治活动和理想，此解最合经意。辜鸿铭将其译为 wisdom，似嫌不足，但却有其特别用意。苏慧廉用西方哲学术语 truth 译"道"，似乎没什么不妥，因为孔子所说的"道"似乎涵盖了天地与人世所有的真理。但苏慧译文的句型结构似乎与原文有出入。原文含有条件之意，"早上闻道，即便夕间死去也可"，表明孔子对当时之世道日衰、礼乐崩坏的无奈。

▶▶ 五、课后练习

（一）思考题

1.《论语》是怎样的一部经典？
2.《论语》最早是如何传播到西方的？
3. 孔子在世界文化史上的地位和影响是怎样的？

（二）翻译题

1. 吾日三省吾身,为人谋而不忠乎？与朋友交而不信乎？传不习乎？
2. 宰予昼寝。子曰:"朽木不可雕也,粪土之墙不可圬也;于予与何诛？"子曰:"始吾于人也,听其言而信其行;今吾于人也,听其言而观其行。于予与改是。"
3. 颜渊问仁。子曰:"克己复礼为仁。一日克己复礼,天下归仁焉。为仁由己,而由人乎哉？"颜渊曰:"请问其目？"子曰:"非礼勿视,非礼勿听,非礼勿言,非礼勿动。"
4. 子曰:"后生可畏,焉知来者之不如今也？四十、五十而无闻焉,亦不足畏也已。"
5. 不患无位,患所以立;不患莫己知,求为可知也。

参考读物

Ku, Hung-Ming. Trans. *The Discourses and Sayings of Confucius*［M］. Shanghai：Kelly and Walsh, Limited, 1898.

Lau, D. C. Trans. *Confucius: The Analects*［M］. New York：Penguin Classics, 1979.

Soothill, William Edward. Trans. *The Analects of Confucius*［M］. Shanghai：The Presbyterian Mission Press, 1910.

安乐哲,罗思文.《论语》的哲学诠释［M］.北京:中国社会科学出版社,2003.

辜鸿铭著,黄兴涛等译. 辜鸿铭文集［M］.海口:海南出版社,1996.

金学勤.《论语》英译之跨文化阐释——以理雅各、辜鸿铭为例［M］.成都:四川大学出版社,2009.

林戊荪. 论语新译:汉英对照［M］. 北京:外文出版社,2010.

钱穆. 论语新解［M］. 北京:三联书店,2007.

钱穆. 四书释义［M］. 北京:九州出版社,2010.

第四课

《孟子》

▶▶ 一、内容简介

《孟子》七篇主要记录孟子的言论,由孟子及其弟子共同编写而成。该书反映了孟子对儒家学说的继承与发展,表现了其人性善的思想和仁政的政治主张。

孟子(约前372—前289),名轲,字子舆,邹国(今山东省邹县东南)人,有人认为邹国是鲁国的附属国,故也有人说孟子是鲁国人。孟子是战国时期伟大的思想家、政治家、教育家,是孔子之孙孔伋的再传弟子,继承孔子的思想,被尊称为亚圣。著有《孟子》一书,属语录体散文集。孟子继承并发扬了孔子的思想。在政治上主张法先王、行仁政;在学说上推崇孔子,攻击杨朱、墨翟。孟子提倡仁政,提出"民贵君轻"的民本思想。孟子曾游历于齐、宋、滕、魏、鲁等诸国,企图推行自己的政治主张,前后历时二十多年。最后他退居讲学,和他的学生一起"序《诗》、《书》,述仲尼之意,作《孟子》七篇"。

《孟子》语言平实浅近,精练准确,善用比喻,长于论辩,感情激越。可以说,先秦散文发展到《孟子》已经相当成熟,对后世散文影响颇深。唐宋古文大家韩愈、苏洵、苏轼的散文也都有得益于《孟子》。南宋时朱熹将《孟子》与《论语》、《大学》、《中庸》合在一起称"四书"。《孟子》是"四书"中篇幅最大的一部,有35000多字。

▶▶ 二、翻译传播

早在19世纪的时候,《孟子》便翻译传播到了西方世界。其译者包括来华的传教士、西方的汉学家和中国的学者。传教士的译本包括1828年出版的高大卫译本,这是《孟子》最早的完整英译本;1861年出版的理雅各译本,这是《孟子》较为完善的英译本,至今仍被视作标准译本；1882年出版的由哈钦森（Arthur B. Hutchinson）翻译自花之安（Ernst Faber）德译本的英译本，书名为 The Mind Of Mencius: Or, Political Economy Founded Upon Moral Philosophy: A Systematic Digest Of The Doctrines Of The Chinese Philosopher Mencius。这些传教士翻译《孟子》是为其在中国传教服务的，正如花之安在其序言中所说："孟子比任何其他中国作者更适合用来向中国人解释基督教的教义。"（Faber, 1882: x）他们在翻译方法上基本都采用直译，都声称尽量忠实于原文。

西方汉学家的译本主要有赖发洛（Leonard Arthur Lyall）1932年出版的译本 Mencius（London: Longmans, Green and Co., 1932），其译文以直译为主，用语简洁明快，注释较少，适合普通读者阅读（但他对某些关键术语的处理引起一些汉学家的批评，如他把"仁"译作 love，把"德"译作 mind）；魏鲁男（James R. Ware）1960年出版的译本 The Sayings of Mencius（New York: The New American Library of World Literature, 1960），这是一个相当简洁的译本，除了引言中对孟子及同时代的其他诸子有所介绍外，没有任何注释，译文也不甚忠实于原作，尤其是对于某些关键术语的处理甚为标新立异（例如，把"天"译作 Sky，把"道"译作 process，把"仁"译作 manhood-at-its-best）；杜百胜（W. A. C. H. Dobson）1963年出版的译本 Mencius: A New Translation Arranged and Annotated for the General Reader（Toronto: University of Toronto Press, 1963），他采取意译法或解释翻译法，译文虽然晓畅，但恐怕会误达读者（他把《孟子》的内容重新调整为 Mencius at Various Royal Courts, Public Life, Disciples, Philosophical Rivals, Comments on the Times, Teachings, Maxims，但这样的安排并不为学者所认同，而且对读者理解孟子的思想帮助也不是很大）；戴维·亨顿（David Hinton）1998年出版的译本 Mencius（Washington, D. C.: Counterpoint, 1998），这是一个针对普通读者的译本，行文简练，全文几乎没有任何注释；万百安（Bryan W. Van Norden）2008年出版的译本 Mengzi: With Selections from Traditional Commentaries（Indianapolis and Cambridge, Mass.: Hackett, 2008），这是继刘殿爵译本之后又一个优秀的译本，具有很高的可读性，译文中穿插翻译了许多朱熹的注解和译者的观点，增加了它的学术性；艾琳·布鲁姆（Irene Bloom）2009年出版的译本 Mencius（New York: Columbia University Press, 2009），这是一个较为简略的译本，译文只有168页。

中国学者的译本主要有刘殿爵（D. C. Lau）的译本 Mencius（Baltimore: Penguin Books, 1970），Mencius: A Bilingual Edition（Revised edition. Hong Kong: Chinese University Press, 2003），其译文在西方有很高的评价；赵甄陶等的译本《孟子：汉英对照》（湖南人民

出版社1999年出版),其译文在准确性方面值得肯定。

除了以上提到的全译本之外,还有一些节译本,其中较为著名的有翟林奈(Lionel Giles)的译本 The Book of Mencius（abridged）（The Wisdom of the East Series；London：John Murray, 1942)。

▶▶▶ 三、翻译对比

● 原文一：

孟子曰:"人皆有不忍人之心。先王有不忍人之心,斯有不忍人之政矣。以不忍人之心,行不忍人之政,治天下可运之掌上。所以谓人皆有不忍人之心者,今人乍见孺子将入于井,皆有怵惕恻隐之心。非所以内交于孺子之父母也,非所以要誉于乡党朋友也,非恶其声而然也。由是观之,无恻隐之心,非人也;无羞恶之心,非人也;无辞让之心,非人也;无是非之心,非人也。恻隐之心,仁之端也;羞恶之心,义之端也;辞让之心,礼之端也;是非之心,智之端也。人之有是四端也,犹其有四体也。有是四端而自谓不能者,自贼者也;谓其君不能者,贼其君者也。凡有四端于我者,知皆扩而充之矣,若火之始然,泉之始达。苟能充之,足以保四海;苟不充之,不足以事父母。"(《公孙丑上》)

理雅各译文：

Mencius said, "All men have a mind which cannot bear to see the sufferings of others.

"The ancient kings had this commiserating mind, and they, as a matter of course, had likewise a commiserating government. When with a commiserating mind was practised a commiserating government, to rule the kingdom was as easy a matter as to make anything go round in the palm.

"When I say that all men have a mind which cannot bear to see the sufferings of others, my meaning may be illustrated thus: even now days, if men suddenly see a child about to fall into a well, they will without exception experience a feeling of alarm and distress. They will feel so, not as a ground on which they may gain the favour of the child's parents, nor as a ground on which they may seek the praise of their neighbours and friends, nor from a dislike to the reputation of having been unmoved by such a thing.

"From this case we may perceive that the feeling of commiseration is essential to man, that the feeling of shame and dislike is essential to man, that the feeling of modesty and complaisance is essential to man, and that the feeling of approving and disapproving is essential to man.

"The feeling of commiseration is the principle of benevolence. The feeling of shame and dislike is the principle of righteousness. The feeling of modesty and complaisance is the principle of propriety. The feeling of approving and disapproving is the principle of knowledge.

"Men have these four principles just as they have their four limbs. When men, having these four principles, yet say of themselves that they cannot develop them, they play the thief with themselves, and he who says of his prince that he cannot develop them plays the thief with his prince.

"Since all men have these four principles in themselves, let them know to give them all their development and completion, and the issue will be like that of fire which has begun to burn, or that of a spring which has begun to find vent. Let them have their complete development, and they will suffice to love and protect all within the four seas. Let them be denied that development, and they will not suffice for a man to serve his parents with."

刘殿爵译文：

Mencius said, "No man is devoid of a heart sensitive to the suffering of others. Such a sensitive heart was possessed by the Former Kings and this manifested itself in compassionate government. With such a sensitive heart behind compassionate government, it was as easy to rule the Empire as rolling it on your palm.

"My reason for saying that no man is devoid of a heart sensitive to the suffering of others is this. Suppose a man were, all of a sudden, to see a young child on the verge of falling into a well. He would certainly be moved to compassion, not because he wanted to get in the good graces of the parents, nor because he wished to win the praise of his fellow villagers or friends, nor yet because he disliked the cry of the child. From this it can be seen that whoever is devoid of the heart of compassion is not human, whoever is devoid of the heart of shame is not human, whoever is devoid of the heart of courtesy and modesty is not human, and whoever is devoid of the heart of right and wrong is not human. The heart of compassion is the germ of benevolence; the heart of shame, of dutifulness; the heart of courtesy and modesty, of observance of the rites; the heart of right and wrong, of wisdom. Man has these four germs just as he has four limbs. For a man possessing these four germs to deny his own potentialities is for him to cripple himself; for him to deny the potentialities of his prince is for him to cripple his prince. If a man is able to develop all these four germs that he possesses; it will be like a fire starting up or a spring coming through. When these are fully developed, he can take under his protection the whole realm within the Four Seas, but if he fails to develop them, he will not be able even to serve his parents.

- 原文二：

曰："不为者与不能者之形何以异？"

曰："挟太山以超北海，语人曰'我不能'，是诚不能也。为长者折枝，语人曰'我不能'，是不为也，非不能也。故王之不王，非挟太山以超北海之类也；王之不王，是折枝之类也。"（《梁惠王上》）

赵甄陶译文：

The king asked, "What is the difference in outward appearance between not being willing to do a thing and not being able to do it?"

Mencius replied, "If you were asked to jump over the North Sea with Mount Tai under your arm, you say to people, 'I am not able to do it.' That is a real case of not being able to. If asked to break a twig for an elder, you say to people, 'I am not able to do it.' That is a case of not being willing to do it, rather than a case of not being able to. Therefore, Your Majesty's failure to win the unification of the world is not a case of jumping over the North Sea with Mount Tai under your arm. Your Majesty's failure to win the unification of the world is a case of breaking a twig."

布鲁姆译文：

The king asked, "How can one distinguish between 'not doing something' and 'not being able to do it'?"

Mencius said, "If it were a matter of taking Mount Tai under one's arm and jumping over the North Sea with it, and one were to tell people, 'I am unable to do it', this would truly be a case of being unable to do it. If it is a matter of bowing respectfully to an elder, and one tells people, 'I am unable to do it', this is a case of not doing it rather than a case of being unable to do it. And so the king's failure to be a true king is not in the category of taking Mount Tai under one's arm and jumping over the North Sea with it; his failure to be a true king is in the category of not bowing respectfully to an elder."

- 原文三：

孟子谓齐宣王曰："王之臣有托其妻子于其友，而之楚游者。比其反也，则冻馁其妻子，则如之何？"王曰："弃之。"曰："士师不能治士，则如之何？"王曰："已之。"曰："四境之内不治，则如之何？"王顾左右而言他。(《梁惠王下》)

亨顿译文：

Mencius said to Emperor Hsüan of Ch'i, "Suppose one of your ministers entrusts his family to the care of a friend and then leaves on a journey to Ch'u. When he returns, he finds that the friend abandoned his family to hunger and cold. What should be done?" "End the friendship," replied the emperor. "And if a chief judge can't govern his court—what should be done?" "Turn him out," pronounced the emperor. "And if someone can't govern this land stretching out to the four borderlands—what then?" The emperor suddenly turned to his attendants and spoke of other things.

刘殿爵译文：

Mencius said to King Hsüan of Ch'i, "Suppose a subject of your Majesty's, having entrusted his wife and children to the care of a friend, were to go on a trip to Ch'u, only to find, upon his return, that his friend had allowed his wife and children to suffer cold and hunger, then what should he do about it?"

"Break with his friend."

"If the Marshal of the Guards was unable to keep his guards in order, then what should be done about it?"

"Remove him from office."

"If the whole realm within the four borders was ill-governed, then what should be done about it?"

The King turned to his attendants and changed the subject.

四、翻译赏析

对"原文一"的翻译，刘殿爵的译文语言通俗流畅，但将"非恶其声而然也"译为 nor yet because disliked the cry of the child，则显得比较表浅。汉代赵岐《孟子注疏》将其解释为"非恶有不仁之声名",即担心自己留下不好的名声,揭示了孟子的本意。故理雅各的译文 nor from a dislike to the reputation of having been unmoved by such a thing 较为符合原文之意。

理雅各以 principle 译"端",取的是 principle 作"根源,源泉"的意思,似不如刘殿爵的 germ 形象、直白。对于"足以保四海"的翻译,无论是理雅各的 protect all within the four seas,还是刘殿爵的 take under his protection the whole realm within the Four Seas,都失之质直,不如意译为 bring about peace to the world 或 pacify the world 更符合儒家治国安邦平天下的理想。

对"原文二"的翻译,在理解方面有一定的困难。如"折枝"一词的解释,历来不一。有的理解为"折草木之枝",有的理解为"幼辈为长者按摩",有的理解为"磬折腰肢,鞠躬作礼"。翻译时无论如何释义,都需要采用文内或文后注解的方法,给读者提供更多的必要信息。

对"原文三"的翻译,刘殿爵充分注意到了原文的语气,使译文与原文的风格较为一致。如孟子连续发问"则如之何",刘殿爵将其译为"then what should he do about it?",即表现出了孟子咄咄逼人的气势。

▶▶ 五、课后练习

(一) 思考题

1.《孟子》的主要内容是什么?
2.《孟子》翻译中的难点是什么?
3.《孟子》在西方的传播如何?

(二) 翻译题

1. 学问之道无他,求其放心而已矣。
2. 君子有三乐,而王天下不与存焉。父母俱存,兄弟无故,一乐也。仰不愧于天,俯不怍于人,二乐也。得天下英才而教育之,三乐也。
3. 恻隐之心,人皆有之;羞恶之心,人皆有之;恭敬之心,人皆有之;是非之心,人皆有之。
4. 恻隐之心,仁也;羞恶之心,义也;恭敬之心,礼也;是非之心,智也。
5. 仁义礼智,非由外铄我也,我固有之也,弗思耳矣。

参考读物

Bloom, Irene. Trans. *Mencius* [M]. New York: Columbia University Press, 2009.

Faber, E. Trans. Arthur B. Hutchinson. Trans. *The Mind Of Mencius: Or, Political Economy Founded Upon Moral Philosophy: A Systematic Digest Of The Doctrines Of The Chinese Philosopher Mencius* [M]. Boston: Houghton, Mifflin & Co., 1882.

Hinton, David. *Mencius* [M]. Washington, D. C.: Counterpoint, 1998.

Lau, D. C. Trans. *Mencius: A Bilingual Edition* [M]. Hong Kong: Chinese University Press, 2003.

Legge, James. Trans. *The Chinese Classics Volume II: The Works of Mencius* [M]. Taipei: SMC Publishing Inc., 1991.

Nivison, David S. On Translating Mencius [J]. *Philosophy East and West*, 1980(1): 93-122.

Van Norden, Bryan W. Trans. *The Essential Mengzi: Selected Passages with Traditional Commentary* [M]. Indianapolis: Hackett Publishing Company, Inc., 2009.

史次耘. 孟子今注今译[M]. 重庆:重庆出版社,2008.

赵甄陶,张文庭,周定之. 孟子:汉英对照[M]. 长沙:湖南人民出版社,1999.

第五课

《荀 子》

▶▶ 一、内容简介

荀子(约前313—前238),名况,字卿,战国末期赵国人,著名思想家、文学家、政治家,儒家代表人物之一,时人尊称"荀卿"。荀子发展了儒家思想,提倡性恶论。荀子是朴素的唯物主义者,反对天命、鬼神迷信之说,主张"天行有常,不为尧存,不为桀亡"。在经济上主张"节用裕民,而善臧其余",提出强本节用、开源节流等主张。在军事上,主张以德兼人,反对争夺。荀子文章长于说理论辩,剖析入微,铺陈排比,善用比喻,风格浑厚。

《荀子》一书,汉代刘向校订为32篇,称《荀卿新书》。唐代杨倞为之作注,改题为《荀子》。清代王先谦撰《荀子集解》,是最精详、最完善的一个注本。现代注译本多以其为底本。《荀子》一书各篇独立成文,又相互关联。性恶篇为荀子学说的基本思想。

《荀子》全书论说方面极广,张觉在他的《荀子译著》说:"纵观荀子全书,凡哲学、伦理、政治、经济、军事、教育,乃至语言学、文学皆有涉猎,且多精论,足以为先秦一大思想宝库。荀子的思想偏向经验以及人事方面,是从社会脉络方面出发,重视社会秩序,反对神秘主义的思想,重视人为的努力。"

荀子和孟子的"性善"说相反,认为人与生俱来就想满足欲望,若欲望得不到满足便会发生争执,因此主张人性生来是"恶"的,须要通过"师化之法,礼义之道"修以为善,所以荀子强调后天的学习。性恶为荀子学说的基础,隆礼为荀子学说的旨趣,强调学习对于化性起伪的重要作用。

▶▶ 二、翻译传播

《荀子》最早在英文世界的介绍可能要追溯到理雅各《中国经典》(*The Chinese*

Classics》第二卷附录中对《性恶篇》(That the Nature is Evil)的翻译,作为《孟子》的对照参考。1924 年,荷兰汉学家戴闻达(J. J. L. Duyvendak)介绍翻译了《正名篇》(Duyvendak, 1924:221 – 254)。1928 年,美国汉学家德效骞(Homer Dubs)翻译出版了《荀子选译》(The Works of Hsüntze)。这是荀子思想早期在英语世界较为全面的译介。

德效骞译本以王先谦《荀子集解》为底本,选译了《荀子》32 篇中的 19 篇,包括《劝学》(An Encouragement to Study)、《修身》(Self-Cultivation)、《荣辱》(On Honour and Shame)、《非相》(Against Physiognomy)、《非十二子》(Against the Ten Philosophers)、《仲尼》(The Confucians)、《儒效》(The Merit of the Confucian)、《王制》(Kingly Government)、《富国》(A Rich Country)、《议兵》(A Debate on Military Affairs)、《天论》(Concerning Heaven)、《正论》(On the Correction of Errors)、《礼论》(On the Rules of Proper Conduct)、《乐论》(On Music)、《解蔽》(The Removal of Prejudices)、《正名》(On the Rectification of Terms)、《性恶》(The Nature of Man Is Evil),以及《王霸》(Kings and Lords Protector)的一个段落和《尧问》末段荀卿弟子对时人谓"孙卿不及孔子"的回应。这些篇章基本上代表了荀子的核心思想。德效骞的译文不仅有脚注,而且还有导读、评论。

德效骞注重译文的准确,因此采用了忠于原文的直译法,这使他的译文在可读性方面有所欠缺。又因为他是第一个较为全面翻译《荀子》的译者,所以错误在所难免。译文一经面世,就遭到了戴闻达的强烈批评(Duyvendak, 1932:1 – 42)。另外,德效骞在《富国篇》中完全省略了荀子对墨家学说的批评,致使此段批评在英语世界长期未受到应有的重视。还有,德效骞还省略了《非十二子篇》中荀子对子思和孟子的批评以及本篇后半部分的翻译。

梅贻宝(Y. P. Mei)自 1951 年起,陆续发表了《正名篇》、《劝学篇》和《王制篇》的译文与介绍。1963 年,美国翻译家及汉学家华兹生(Burton Watson)翻译了《荀子》32 篇中的 11 篇,分别是《劝学》(Encouraging Learning)、《修身》(Improving Yourself)、《王制》(The Regulations of a King)、《议兵》(Debating Military Affairs)、《天论》(A Discussion of Heaven)、《礼论》(A Discussion of Rites)、《乐论》(A Discussion of Music)、《解蔽》(Dispelling Obsession)、《正名》(Rectifying Names)、《性恶》(Man's Nature Is Evil)。华兹生译本也是以清代王先谦的《荀子集解》为底本的,但他同时还参照了《荀子》的日语译本和日本学者的研究成果,以及中国现代刘师培、梁启雄等的注释和研究成果。华兹生的译文注解较少,读来清新流畅,有一定的文学色彩,颇能体现荀子文章的风格,主要以非专业学者为目标读者。

自 1988 年至 1994 年，美国学者约翰·诺布洛克（John Knoblock）先后推出了三卷《荀子》全译本（*Xunzi: A Translation and Study of the Complete Works*）。这是一个学术型译本，注解非常丰富。诺布洛克在《荀子》英译本第一卷用了大约 126 页的篇幅介绍荀子的生平、主要哲学思想以及对《荀子》文本的考证。而且在每篇译文之前，又附有详细的导言，概括全篇的哲学观点及其与其他哲学思想的联系。1999 年，湖南人民出版社推出的《荀子》（《大中华文库（汉英对照）》版），采用的也是诺布洛克的译文，可惜的是这个版本略去了这些极具价值的注解和导言。诺氏的翻译紧扣原文，译文大体准确通顺，但有些地方的表达显得有点生硬或啰唆。诺氏希望能够全面传译荀子的全部哲学思想，因此采用了忠实于原文字面的直译策略，其目标读者是对中国哲学感兴趣的学者，让他们即使在不参照中文原著的情况下仍然能够理解荀子的思想。

三、翻译对比

- 原文一：

吾尝终日而思矣，不如须臾之所学也。吾尝跂而望矣，不如登高之博见也。登高而招，臂非加长也，而见者远；顺风而呼，声非加疾也，而闻者彰。假舆马者，非利足也，而致千里；假舟楫者，非能水也，而绝江河。君子生非异也，善假于物也。（《劝学篇》）

华兹生译文：

I once tried spending the whole day in thought, but I found it of less value than a moment of study. I once tried standing on tiptoe and gazing into the distance, but I found I could see much farther by climbing to a high place. If you climb to a high place and wave to someone, it is not as though your arm were any longer than usual, and yet people can see you from much farther away. If you shout down the wind, it is not as though your voice were any stronger than usual, and yet people can hear you much more clearly. Those who make use of carriages or horses may not be any faster walkers than anyone else, and yet they are able to travel a thousand *li*. Those who make use of boats may not know how to swim, and yet they manage to get across rivers. The gentleman is by birth no different from any other man; it is just that he is good at making use of things.

诺布洛克译文：

I once spent a whole day in thought, but it was not so valuable as a moment in study. I once stood on my tiptoes to look out into the distance, but it was not so effective as climbing up a high place for a broader vista. Climbing to a height and waving your arm does not cause the arm's lenghth to increase, but your wave can be seen farther away. Shouting downwind does not increase the tenseness of the sound, but it is heard more distinctly. A man who borrows a horse and carriage does not improve his feet, but he can extend his travels 1,000 *li*. A man who borrows a boat and paddles does not gain any new ability in water, but he can cut across rivers and seas. The gentleman by birth is not different from other men; he is just good at "borrowing" the use of external things.

- 原文二：

君子之学也，入乎耳，箸乎心，布乎四体，形乎动静。端而言，蠕而动，一可以为法则。小人之学也，入乎耳，出乎口；口耳之间，则四寸耳，曷足以美七尺之躯哉！古之学者为己，今之学者为人。君子之学也，以美其身；小人之学也，以为禽犊。故不问而告，谓之傲，问一而告二，谓之囋。傲，非也，囋，非也；君子如向矣。(《劝学篇》)

华兹生译文：

The learning of the gentleman enters his ear, clings to his mind, spreads through his four limbs, and manifests itself in his actions. His smallest word, his slightest movement can serve as a model. The learning of the petty man enters his ear and comes out his mouth. With only four inches between ear and mouth, how can he have possession of it long enough to ennoble a seven-foot body? In old times men studied for their own sake; nowadays men study with an eye to others. The gentleman uses learning to ennoble himself; the petty man uses learning as a bribe to win attention from others. To volunteer information when you have not been asked is called officiousness; to answer two questions when you have been asked only one is garrulity. Both officiousness and garrulity are to be condemned. The gentleman should be like an echo.

诺布洛克译文：

The learning of the gentleman enters through the ear, is stored in the mind, spreads through the four limbs, and is visible in his activity and repose. In his softest word and slightest movement, in one and all, the gentleman can be taken as a model and pattern. The learning of the petty man enters the ear and comes out the mouth. Since the distance between the mouth and ear is no more than four inches, how could it be sufficient to refine the seven-foot body of a man. In antiquity men undertook learning for the sake of self-improvement; today people undertake learning for the sake of others. The learning of the gentleman is used to refine his character. The learning of the petty man is used like ceremonial offerings of birds and calves. Accordingly, informing where no question has been posed is called "forwardness", and offering information on two points when only one has been raised is called "garrulity". Both forwardness and garrulity are to be condemned! The gentleman is responsive like an echo.

- 原文三：

人之性恶，其善者伪也。今人之性，生而有好利焉，顺是，故争夺生而辞让亡焉；生而有疾恶焉，顺是，故残贼生而忠信亡焉；生而有耳目之欲，有好声色焉，顺是，故淫乱生而礼义文理亡焉。然则从人之性，顺人之情，必出于争夺，合于犯分乱理，而归于暴。故必将有师法之化，礼义之道，然后出于辞让，合于文理，而归于治。(《性恶篇》)

德效骞译文：

The nature of man is evil; his goodness is only acquired training. The original nature of man today is to seek for gain. If this desire is followed, strife and rapacity results, and courtesy dies. Man originally is envious and naturally hates others. If these tendencies are followed, injury and destruction follows; loyalty and faithfulness are destroyed. Man originally possesses the desires of the ear and eye; he likes praise and is lustful. If these are followed, impurity and disorder results, and the rules of proper conduct (Li) and justice (Yi) and etiquette are destroyed. Therefore to give rein to man's original nature, to follow man's feelings, inevitably results in strife and rapacity, together with violations of etiquette and confusion in the proper way of doing things, and reverts to a state of violence. Therefore the civilizing influence of teachers and laws, the guidance of the rules of proper conduct (Li) and justice (Yi) is absolutely necessary. Thereupon courtesy results; public and private etiquette is observed; and good government is the consequence.

诺布洛克译文：

Human nature is evil; any good in humans is acquired by conscious exertion. Now, the nature of man is such that he is born with a love of profit. Following this nature will cause its aggressiveness and greedy tendencies to grow and courtesy and deference to disappear. Humans are born with feelings of envy and hatred. Indulging these feelings causes violence and crime to develop and loyalty and trustworthiness to perish. Man is born possessing the desires of the ears and eyes (which are fond of sounds and colors). Indulging these desires causes dissolute and wanton behavior to result and ritual and moral principles, precepts of good form, and the natural order of reason to perish. This being the case, when each person follows his inborn nature and indulges his natural inclinations, aggressiveness and greed are certain to develop. This is accompanied by violation of social class distinctions and throws the natural order into anarchy, resulting in a cruel tyranny. Thus it is necessary that man's nature undergo the transforming influence of a teacher and the model and that he be guided by ritual and moral principles. Only after this has been accomplished do courtesy and deference develop.

四、翻译赏析

在"原文一"中，荀子言"吾尝终日而思矣，不如须臾之所学也"，与孔子"吾尝终日不食，终夜不寝，以思，无益，不如学也"（《论语·卫灵公》）意颇相似，都强调学的重要。但荀子以性为恶，故其所为学者，乃假之于外，而非发之于内。

总的来说，诺布洛克译本"紧扣原文，照字直译，辅以各种补偿手段，尽量'原汤原汁'地传达原文的含义"（蒋坚松，1999：41）。但是，就本段翻译而言，情况并非如此。相反，这里华兹生的译文更加忠实于原文的句式，尤其是"登高而招，臂非加长也，而见者远；顺风而呼，声非加疾也，而闻者彰"这句话的翻译。但接下来诺布洛克的译文则很符合"照字直译"的原则，尤其是将"假"译为 borrow。但 borrow 一词很难表达"假借，凭借"的意思，因此在最后一句中诺氏就将 borrowing 一词加了引号，这也算是一种补偿手段吧。

在"原文二"中，荀子强调学习要以休养身心为目的，不可为求悦于人、博取名利。入耳箸心是为己之学，入耳出口是为人之学。所谓"古之学者为己，今之学者为人"其实是《论语·宪问》中孔子曾经说过的话。理雅各将其翻译为"In ancient times, men learned with a view to their own improvement. Nowadays, men learn with a view to the approbation of others."比较客观地揭示了原意。诺布洛克的译文"today people undertake learning for the sake of others"意义表达不够准确。另外，诺布洛克在翻译"小人之学也，以为禽犊"时，保留了原文的比喻，但读起来有点让人费解。

"原文三"选自《性恶篇》。荀子开篇即提出"人性恶"的主张，因为人生而好利而有争夺，有欲而易放任，故需"师法之化，礼义之道"，使社会人生"归于治"。

"性"字荀子在《正名篇》中有解释:"生之所以然者谓之性。"在本篇下文他又将"性"与"伪"连起来解释为"不可学,不可事,而在人者,谓之性;可学而能,可事而成之在人者,谓之伪"。由此可见,性乃属于天,而善乃人为;人虽性恶,而人人可以为善。诺布洛克与德效骞都将"性"译为 nature,甚为恰当,译"伪"都用了 acquire 一词,强调了后天学习对于为善的重要,也比较符合原文之意。在《性恶篇》所有的译本中,基本上都把"恶"译为 evil,但这一翻译遭到华盛顿大学东亚语言与文学系鲍则岳(William G. Boltz)教授的强烈反对,其主要根据是 evil 一词带有强烈的基督教"原罪"(original sin)、"至恶"(absolute evil)等宗教暗示。(Boltz, 1991: 414 - 418)事实上,诺布洛克在第一卷的绪论和本篇的引言中已经说明汉语中的"恶"没有英文中 evil 所包含的"罪恶"(sinister, baleful)的含义。(Knoblock, 1988: 99, 1994: 139)这实际上是一种"格义"翻译法。

从行文来说,德效骞的译文句式较能反映荀子文章铿锵的节奏和论辩的逻辑,如对"生而……顺是……亡焉"三个排比句式的处理,诺布洛克译文用 cause ... to 结构,节奏感明显不如德效骞采用分句的译文。

五、课后练习

(一)思考题

1. 《荀子》的基本内容是什么?
2. 荀子的"为学"思想与孔子、孟子的"为学"思想有何异同?
3. 《荀子》英译的难点和要点是什么?

(二)翻译题

1. 学不可以已。青,取之于蓝,而青于蓝;冰,水为之,而寒于水。木直中绳,輮以为轮,其曲中规,虽有槁暴,不复挺者,輮使之然也。故木受绳则直,金就砺则利,君子博学而日参省乎己,则知明而行无过矣。

2. 故不登高山,不知天之高也;不临深溪,不知地之厚也;不闻先王之遗言,不知学问之大也。干、越、夷、貉之子,生而同声,长而异俗,教使之然也。

3. 积土成山,风雨兴焉;积水成渊,蛟龙生焉;积善成德,而神明自得,圣心备焉。故不积跬步,无以至千里;不积小流,无以成江海。骐骥一跃,不能十步;驽马十驾,功在不舍。锲而舍之,朽木不折;锲而不舍,金石可镂。

4. 南方有鸟焉,名曰蒙鸠,以羽为巢,而编之以发,系之苇苕,风至苕折,卵破子死。

巢非不完也，所系者然也。西方有木焉，名曰射干，茎长四寸，生于高山之上，而临百仞之渊，木茎非能长也，所立者然也。蓬生麻中，不扶而直；白沙在涅，与之俱黑。兰槐之根是为芷，其渐之滫，君子不近，庶人不服。其质非不美也，所渐者然也。

5. 君子知夫不全不粹之不足以为美也，故诵数以贯之，思索以通之，为其人以处之，除其害者以持养之。使目非是无欲见也，使口非是无欲言也，使心非是无欲虑也。及至其致好之也，目好之五色，耳好之五声，口好之五味，心利之有天下。是故权利不能倾也，群众不能移也，天下不能荡也。生乎由是，死乎由是，夫是之谓德操。德操然后能定，能定然后能应。能定能应，夫是之谓成人。天见其明，地见其光，君子贵其全也。

参考读物

Boltz, William G. Review on John Knoblock: *Xunzi: A Translation and Study of the Complete Works*. Vol. I. Books 1-6 [J]. *Bulletin of the School of Oriental and African Studies*, 1991(2): 414-418.

Dubs, H. *The Works of Hsüntze: Translation from the Chinese, with Notes* [M]. London: Arthur Probsthain, 1928.

Duyvendak, J. J. L. Hsün-tzǔ on the rectification of names [J]. *T'oung Pao*, 1924(4): 221-254.

Duyvendak, J. J. L. Notes on Dubs' translation of Hsün-tzǔ [J]. *T'oung Pao*, 1932(1/3): 1-42.

Knoblock, John. *Xunzi: A Translation and Study of the Complete Works* [M]. Stanford: Stanford University Press, 1988-1994.

Watson, B. *Hsün-tzu: Basic Writings* [M]. New York: Columbia University Press, 1963.

蒋坚松. 文本与文化——评诺布洛克英译本《荀子》[J]. 外语与外语教学, 1999(1): 40-43.

熊公哲. 荀子今注今译 [M]. 重庆：重庆出版社, 2009.

第六课

《老子》

▶▶ 一、内容简介

老子又称老聃,是春秋末期楚国苦县厉乡曲仁里人,约生于公元前581年,做过东周"守藏室之史",学识精博,智慧不凡,孔子曾向老子问礼。后因周衰,列国乱,国藏史册为人掠走,老子离开东周去秦。过函谷关时,关令尹喜请求老子著书,于是留五千言《道德经》。之后老子在秦隐居,不知所终。

《老子》又称《道德经》,是道家思想的重要著作。《道德经》先秦时只分为上篇《德》、下篇《道》,不分章,也不称经。其分章、定经始于汉代,目前通用的版本基于王弼定本基础之上,5400余字,81章,且改为《道经》在前、《德经》在后。就《道德经》目前的文本特点而言,前后文字之间未呈现密切关联,这也许是分章之后,后人抄写文句的次序错乱所致。

"道"、"德"是《道德经》中的一对重要概念,书中前37章讲"道",后44章言"德",道、德二字有不同的含义。简而言之,道为体,德为用。老子的思想对先秦各家均产生一定的影响,对后世的影响则更为深远。《吕氏春秋》、《淮南子》、《论六家之要指》等西汉前期的作品,多以黄老之学为本。西汉后期和东汉时的《老子河上公章句》、《太平经》、《周易参同契》、《老子指归》等著作,均为老子思想的发挥和传扬。

《老子》书中包括大量朴素辩证法观点,如认为一切事物均具有正反两面,并能由对立而转化。他的哲学思想和由他创立的道家学派,不但对我国古代思想文化的发展作出了重要贡献,而且对我国2000多年来思想文化的发展产生了深远的影响。

《道德经》在流传过程中形成了诸多版本,今天所能见到的最早的《道德经》版本是

1993年在湖北荆门郭店楚墓中出土的战国竹简本;其次则是1973年长沙马王堆汉墓出土的西汉帛书本;历史上流传最广的《道德经》版本是汉代河上公的《河上公章句》和曹魏时期王弼的《老子注》;初唐至五代时期有付奕《道德经古本篇》;两宋至元代时期有王安石《老子注》、苏辙《老子解》、范庆元《老子道德经古本集注》和吴澄《道德真经注》;明代有薛蕙《老子集解》、释德清《老子道德经解》、沈一贯《老子通》、焦竑《老子翼》;清代有王念孙《老子杂志》、俞樾《老子评议》、高延弟《老子证义》、刘师培《老子补》等;民国时期有马叙伦《老子校诂》、劳健《老子古本考》和严灵峰《老子章名新编》。

　　1949年之后有朱谦之《老子校译》、车戴《论老子》、张松如《老子校读》、陈鼓应《老子注译及评价》、任继愈《老子今译》、兰喜并《老子解读》、饶尚宽《老子译注》、刘笑敢《老子古今》等。千百年来,为《道德经》作注疏者不计其数。元代的正一天师张与材曾说:"《道德经》八十一章,注本三千余家。"

▶▶ 二、翻译传播

　　《道德经》不但在中国国学典籍中地位重要,在世界上也影响广泛,普及程度仅次于《圣经》。其译介据记载最早可推至隋朝,被介绍到日本,同在7世纪,又被译为梵文。在西方的传播开始于18世纪中叶,当时《道德经》被译为拉丁文。据说,此间比利时籍耶稣会士卫方济(François Noël)曾将其译为法文。傅圣则(Francois Foucqet)约于1729年将《道德经评注》译为拉丁文和法文。法国汉学家雷慕沙(Abel Remusat)译出《道德经》四章,但后被发现有多处误译。

　　首次的法文全译本《老子道德经》出自汉学家儒莲(Stanislas Julien)之手,1842年在巴黎出版。1870年莱比锡出版了由维克多·施特劳斯(Victor von Straus)翻译的德文本《老子道德经》。最早的俄译本于19世纪上半叶由俄沙皇时期的汉学家丹尼尔·西维洛夫(Д. СивиЛЛов)完成,1915年才发表。最早的英译本出现在19世纪70年代后。1884年,伦敦出版了巴尔弗(Frederic Henry Balfour)的《道书》;1891年,牛津出版了理雅各(James Legge)的《道书》;1898年,美国芝加哥出版了保罗·卡鲁斯(Paul Carus)的《道与德的经典:中英对照本老子〈道德经〉》,一般认为是质量较好的通行本。

　　来华的瑞典传教士艾利克·福尔基(Eric Follee)在1927年用瑞典文译《道德经》,他对老子思想在瑞典的传播起到了重要作用。法国神甫戴遂良(P. Léon Wieger)1913年在巴黎出版的两卷本《道教》,第一卷是《道藏》总目,第二卷是《老子》、《列子》、《庄子》

法汉对照本。此后的法译本还有1967年法籍华裔哲学家刘嘉槐译本(他也是第一个用法文翻译《道德经》的华人)、1974年梅底西斯译本、1978年克娄德·拉尔(Claude Larre)译评本。

老子思想在英国传播较早,二战后的汉学研究则以美国为胜。因此,《道德经》英译本数量颇丰,不乏上乘之作。在英美两国,早期译本有保罗·卡鲁斯的《道与德的经典:中英对照本老子〈道德经〉》(1898年)。20世纪初,海星格(L. W. Heysinger)有《中国之光:〈道德经〉》(1903年),沃尔特·高尔恩(Walter Gorn Old)有《老童纯道》(1904年),沙畹(Édouard Chavannes)有《重大的基石:〈道德经〉》(1905年),麦独斯特(C. Spurgeon Medhurst)有《道德经:比较宗教浅析》(1905年),翟林奈(Lionel Giles)有《老子语录》(1905年),密尔斯(Isabella Mears)有《道德经》(1916年)。东方学家亚瑟·韦利(Arthur David Waley)于1934年在伦敦出版了自己的译本,题为《道与德:〈道德经〉及其在中国思想中的地位研究》,这个译本在英语地区影响较大,至1968年已经再版八次。

20世纪40年代后出版的主要译著有初大告(Chu Ta-kao)的《道德经》(1937年)、吴经熊(John C. H. Wu)的《老子〈道德经〉》(1939—1940年)、宾纳(Witter Bynner)的《老子论生命之道》(1944年)、林语堂的《老子的智慧》(1948年)、布莱克尼(R. B. Blakeney)的《老子:生活之道》(1955年)、霍姆斯·韦尔奇(Holmes H. Welch)的《道之分离:老子和道教运动》(1957年)、阿彻·巴姆(Archie J. Bahm)的《老子〈道德经〉:自然与才智》(1958年)。当时英译本之丰富从陈荣捷(Chan Wing-tsit)1963年《老子之道》中可见一斑:书中说,截至当时,《道德经》已44次被译为英文,其大半在美国出版,在此前的20年,每隔一年就有一个译本产生。

1963年之后,尤其是长沙马王堆汉墓的帛书《老子》甲、乙本出现之后,英译本更加丰富。这些年的主要英译本有:陈荣捷的《老子之道》(1963年)及他与鲁姆堡(Arrienne Rump)合著的《王弼〈老子注〉》(1979年),冯家福(Feng Gia-fu)和英格里希(Jane English)合著的《老子〈道德经〉新译》(1972年),林振述(Paul J. Lin)的《老子〈道德经〉及王弼注》(1977年),陈鼓应著、杨有维(Rhett Y. W. Young)、安乐哲(Roger Thomas Ames)英译并改编的《老子今注今译及评介》(1977年),纽约圣约翰大学哲学系教授陈艾伦(即陈张婉莘 Chen Ellen Marie)的《道德经:新译及评注》(1989年),厄休拉·吉恩(Ursula K. Le Guin)的《老子〈道德经〉:有关道及其力量的一部书》(1990年),陈金梁(Alan Kam-Leung Chan)的《道之二解:王弼与河上公〈老子〉注研究》(1991年),米凯尔·

拉法格(Michael LaFargue)的类编本《〈道德经〉之道:译析》(1992年)及《道与方法:对〈道德经〉的推理探讨》(1994年)。马王堆出土的西汉帛书《老子》译本也有十几种之多,其中较为突出的有:香港中文大学刘殿爵(D. C. Lau)1989年的《老子道德经》,韩禄伯(Robert G. Henricks)1989年的《老子道德经》译本,梅维恒(Victor H. Mair)1990年帛书《老子》译本。

老子的思想影响了东西方的许多著名思想家和作家。德国哲学家海德格尔、戏剧作家莱比锡特思想深受老子影响,也曾译过《道德经》;俄国作家列夫·托尔斯泰、美国戏剧家尤金·奥尼尔、英国汉学博士李约瑟、印度诗人泰戈尔等都曾对《道德经》作过全文或部分翻译;哲学家卡尔·雅斯贝斯在专著中也曾论及老子。

20世纪50年代之后,《道德经》已经在荷兰、匈牙利、罗马尼亚、波兰、西班牙、捷克、希腊、瑞典、丹麦、芬兰、意大利等国都有译本出版。据林振述1977年的《老子〈道德经〉及王弼注》序言所述,各种外文译本有七八十种之多,几乎所有的西方语言都有《道德经》译本,其中瑞典汉学家(如高本汉)的译著尤为值得关注。目前,据可以搜集到的资料显示,《老子》译本有260多种:德文有64种,英文有83种,法文有33种,荷兰文19种,意大利文有11种,日文有10种,西班牙文有10种,丹麦文有6种,俄文、瑞典文、匈牙利文、波兰文各有4种,芬兰文、捷克文各有3种,冰岛文有2种,葡萄牙文、越南文、世界语各有1种(这是统计到20世纪80年代的数字)。其海外发行量居中国传统文化经典之首,在国外翻译出版的版本也很多。截至目前,中国本土学者最新的英译本是北京大学辜正坤教授2007年基于1993年出土的郭店楚简《老子》的译本,西方学者新的译本研究是西尔马·克劳斯(Hilmar Klaus)2009年的汉、英、德译本。

▶▶▶ 三、翻译对比

- 原文一:

道可道,非常道。

名可名,非常名。

无名天地之始。

有名万物之母。

故常无欲以观其妙。

常有欲以观其徼。

此两者同出而异名,同谓之玄。

玄之又玄,众妙之门。

<u>亚瑟·韦利译文:</u>

The Way that can be told of is not an Unvarying Way;

The names that can be named are not unvarying names.

It was from the Nameless that Heaven and Earth sprang;

The named is but the mother that rears the ten thousand creatures, each after its kind.

Truly, "Only he that rids himself forever of desire can see the Secret Essences";

He that has never rid himself of desire can see only the Outcomes.

These two things issued from the same mould, but nevertheless are different in name.

This "same mould" we can but call the Mystery, or rather the "Darker than any Mystery",

The Doorway whence issued all Secret Essences.

<u>道格拉斯·奥尔钦译文:</u>

Who would follow the Way

must go beyond words.

Who would know the world

must go beyond names.

Nameless, all things begin.

Named, all things are born.

Empty of intent, one may be filled with awe.

Full of intent, one may know what's manifest.

One source, different fonts.

Wonders both.

From wonder into wonder,

existence opens.

<u>陈荣捷译文:</u>

The Tao that can be told of is not the eternal Tao;

The name that can be named is not the eternal name.

The Nameless is the origin of Heaven and Earth;

The Named is the mother of all things.

Therefore let there always be non-being, so we may see their subtlety,

And let there always be being, so we may see their outcome.

The two are the same,

But after they are produced, they have different names.

They both may be called deep and profound.

Deeper and more profound,

The door to all subtleties!

辜正坤译文：

The Tao that can be expressed in words

Is not the true and eternal Tao;

The name that can be uttered in words

Is not the true and eternal name.

The word Nothingness may be used to designate the beginning of Heaven and Earth;

The word Existence (Being) may be used to designate the mother of all things.

Hence one should gain an insight into the subtley of Tao by observing Nothingness,

And should gain an insight into the beginning of Tao by observing Existence (Being).

These two things, Nothingness and Existence,

Are of the same origin but different in name.

They are extremely profound in depth

Serving as the door of myriad secret beings.

* The Tao: (Spelled as Dao in Chinese phonetic symbols) a philosophical term first used by Lao Tzu (Lao Zi); traditionally translated as Tao (thus Taoism), logos, path, way, road, etc.

● 原文二：

不尚贤，使民不争。

不贵难得之货，使民不为盗。不见可欲，使民心不乱。

是以圣人之治，虚其心，实其腹，弱其志，强其骨。

常使民无知、无欲，使夫智者不敢为也。

为无为,则无不治。

亚瑟·韦利译文:

If we stop looking for "persons of superior morality" (hsien) to put in power,

There will be no more jealousies among the people.

If we cease to set store by products that are hard to get,

There will be no more thieves.

If the people never see such things as excite desire,

Their hearts will remain placid and undisturbed.

Therefore the Sage rules

By emptying their hearts

And filling their hearts?

Weakening their intelligence

And toughening their sinews

Ever striving to make the people knowledgeless and desireless.

Indeed he sees to it that if there be any who have knowledge,

They dare not interfere.

Yet through his actionless activity all things are duly regulated.

道格拉斯·奥尔钦译文:

Esteem no one especially worthy,

and men are freed from rivalry.

Prize no rarity,

and men are freed from thievery.

Place no treasure where all may see,

and men are freed from envy.

Who governs well

clears minds and fills stomachs,

diffuses ambitions and consolidates bones.

Where hearts and minds are free from want,

no cunning foe can muster discord.

Where no one needs to intervene,

order reigns freely.

陈荣捷译文：

Do not exalt the worthy, so that the people shall not compete.

Do not value rare treasures, so that the people shall not steal.

Do not display objects of desire, so that the people's hearts shall not be disturbed.

Therefore in the government of the sage,

He keeps their hearts vacuous,

Fills their bellies,

Weakens their ambitions,

And strengthens their bones,

He always causes his people to be without knowledge (cunning) or desire,

And the crafty to be afraid to act.

By acting without action, all things will be in order.

辜正坤译文：

Keep the people from contention by disregarding men of abilities;

Keep the people from theft by not valuing rare goods;

Keep the people from the disturbed state of mind by concealing what is desirable.

That is why in governing the people

The sage simplifies their minds

fills up their stomachs,

weakens their wills,

and strengthens their bones.

By keeping the people from knowledge and desires,

He disables wise men from taking any ill desires,

He disables wise men from taking any ill action.

Act in accordance with this principle of inaction

And the world will be kept in order everywhere.

● 原文三：

上善若水。

水善利万物而不争,处众人之所恶,故几于道。

居善地,心善渊,与善仁,言善信,政善治,事善能,动善时。

夫唯不争,故无尤。

<u>亚瑟·韦利译文：</u>

The highest good is like that of water.

The goodness of is that it benefits the ten thousand creatures；

Yet itself does not scramble，

But is content with the places that all men disdain.

It is this makes water so near to the Way.

And if men think the ground the best place for building a house upon，

If among thoughts they value those that are profound，

If in friendship they value gentleness，

In words, truth; in government, good order；

In deeds, effectiveness; in actions, timeliness—

In each case it is because they prefer what does not lead to strife，

And therefore does not go amiss.

<u>道格拉斯·奥尔钦译文：</u>

Utmost virtue, how like water.

Water gives all creatures life

and flows in lowly places，

ever closer to the Way.

Dwell lowly.

Respect deeply.

Trust freely.

Govern justly.

Work authentically.

Act upon opportunity.

Who does not contend

is free of contention.

陈荣捷译文：

The best (man) is like water.

Water is good; it benefits all things and does not compete with them.

It dwells in (lowly) places that all disdain.

This is why it is so near to Tao.

(The best man) in his dwelling loves the earth. In his heart, he loves what is profound.

In his associations, he loves humanity. In his words, he loves faithfulness.

In government, he loves order. In handling affairs, he loves competence.

In his activities, he loves timeliness.

It is because he does not compete that he is without reproach.

辜正坤译文：

The perfect goodness is like water.

Water approaches all things instead of contending with them.

It prefers to dwell where no one would like to say;

Hence it comes close to Tao.

A man of perfect goodness chooses a low place to dwell as water,

He has a heart as deep as water,

He speaks as sincerely as water,

He rules a state as orderly as water,

He does a thing as properly as water,

He takes action as timely as water.

Like water, he never contends with others,

So he never commits a mistake.

- 原文四：

孔德之容，惟道是从。

道之为物，惟恍惟惚。

惚兮恍兮，其中有象。

恍兮惚兮,其中有物。

窈兮冥兮,其中有精。

其精甚真,其中有信。

自古及今,其名不去,以阅众甫。

吾何以知众甫之状哉!

以此。

<u>亚瑟·韦利译文:</u>

Such the scope of the All-pervading Power.

That it alone can act through the Way.

For the Way is a thing impalpable, incommensurable.

Incommensurable, impalpable.

Yet latent in it are forms;

Impalpable, incommensurable

Yet within it are entities.

Shadowy it is and dim;

Yet within it there is a force,

Is none the less efficacious.

From the times of old till now

Its charge has not departed

But cheers onward the many warriors.

How do I know that the many warriors are so?

Through this.

<u>道格拉斯·奥尔钦译文:</u>

Integrity means to follow the Way, fully the Way,

ever so elusive and ineffable.

Elusive and ineffable!

And yet it holds true form.

Ineffable and elusive!

And yet it holds true substance.

How close, how dark, how deep within!

And yet it holds an essence,

a touchstone of one's faith.

Since antiquity, its name has been preserved,

an echoing of how all things began.

How can one know of things remote?

by what is deep within.

陈荣捷译文：

The all-embracing quality of the great virtue follows alone from the Tao.

The thing that is called Tao is eluding and vague.

Vague and eluding, there is in it the form.

Eluding and vague, in it are things.

Deep and obscure, in it is the essence.

The essence is very real; in it are evidences.

From the time of old until now, its name (manifestations) ever remains.

By which we may see the beginning of all things.

How do I know that the beginning of all things are so?

Through this (Tao).

辜正坤译文：

The forms of the great The (virtue)

Exclusive depend on Tao.

Tao as a thing

Is vague an indefinite.

Vague and indefinite,

It presents images;

Indefinite and vague,

It embodied substance.

Distant and dark,

It embraces semen-like essence.

The essence is genuine existence

That can be tested as true.

From ancient tines to now,

Its name has always been accepted,

And with which, the beginning of all things can be surveyed.

How do I know the initial state of all things?

By means of Tao.

- 原文五：

道生一，一生二，二生三，三生万物。万物负阴而抱阳，冲气以为和。人之所恶，唯孤、寡、不谷，而王公以为称。故物或损之而益，或益之而损。人之所教，我亦教之，"强梁者不得其死"。吾将以为教父。

<u>亚瑟·韦利译文：</u>

Tao gave birth to the One;

The One gave birth successively to two things,

Three things, up to ten thousand.

These ten thousand creatures cannot turn their backs to the shade

Without having the sun on their bellies,

And it is on this blending of the breaths that their harmony depends.

To be orphaned, needy, ill-provided is what men most hate;

Yet princes and dukes style themselves so.

Truly, "things are often increased by seeking to diminish them

And diminished by seeking to increase them."

The maxims that others use in their teaching I too will use in mine.

Show me a man of violence that came to a good end,

And I will take him for my teacher.

<u>道格拉斯·奥尔钦译文：</u>

From the Way came one,

from one came two,

from two, a few,

and then a sum,

until a myriad had come.

All these creatures,

with yin on their backs and yang in their breasts,

live by harmonizing their vital breaths.

A commoner is loathe to admit,

while leaders openly submit,

their humble roots or low repute.

One may gain by loss,

and lose by gain.

"Who lives by the sword, dies by the sword."

And "as you live, so shall you die."

What experience confirms,

I will wisely reaffirm.

陈荣捷译文：

Tao produced the One.

The One produced the two.

The two produced the three.

And the three produced the ten thousand things.

The ten thousand things carry the yin and embrace the yang,

and through the blending of the material force they achieve harmony.

People hate to be children without parents, lonely people without spouses,

or men without food to eat,

And yet kings and lords call themselves by these names.

Therefore it is often the case that things gain by losing and lose by gaining.

What others have taught, I teach also: "Violent and fierce people do not die a natural death."

I shall make this the father of my teaching.

辜正坤译文：

Tao begets the One；

The One consists of Two in opposition (the Yin and Yang)；

The Two begets the Three；

The Three begets all things of the world.

All things cannote the Yin and Yang.

The Yin and Yang keep acting upon each other

And thus things keep changing and unifying themselves.

Words like "the solitary",

"the few" and "the unkind"

Are usually detested by people,

Yet lords and kings use them to call themselves.

四、翻译赏析

如何理解和翻译"道"，是《道德经》翻译要解决的首要问题。在"原文一"的翻译中，译文一、二均将其译为 the Way，译文三、四则译为 Tao。据考，"道"字在老子之前的含义均为"道路"，老子将该字用为表万物本体之道，译为 the Way，不免显得表浅。音译为 Tao 当为可取之法。

对于"无名天地之始。有名万物之母"两句开始部分的翻译，前三个译文的处理都十分相似，译为 nameless, the named，但第四个译文则译为了 Nothingness, Existence。这是因为第四个译文在原文的断句上与前三个译文不同，即前三个译文断为"无名，天地之始。有名，万物之母"，而第四个译文断为"无，名天地之始。有，名万物之母"。究竟哪种断句正确，目前仍然见仁见智。

"原文二"的"不尚贤"中"贤"，译文一、二、四分别译为 persons of superior morality, one especially worthy 和 men of abilities，译文三则译为 the worthy。从上下文意来看，"贤"应该指贤德之人。从这个意义上说，译文三的译法似更可取。

"原文三"中"上善若水"的"善"，译文三解作 The best man，其余译文则分别译作 The highest good, utmost virtue 和 The perfect goodness。译文三的理解稍显狭隘，"善"作为老子思想中的重要概念，被视为宇宙的最佳自然状态，隐含于万物之中。

"原文四"中的"象"、"物"、"精"、"信"四个概念的翻译需要慎加推敲。就"象"的翻译而言,译作 image 似乎更符合《周易》所体现的中国古代哲学的特点,译作 form 虽然更显抽象,但却是西方柏拉图哲学中的重要概念 ιδέα(相)。"物"译为 substance 比译为 thing 更能体现本体特征。"精"一般认为译为 essence 比译为 force 更合原文之意。"信"的翻译在四个译本里各不相同,但异曲同工,各有其妙。

"原文五"的"三生万物"中,"万物"乃虚指,故不必逐字译为 ten thousand。在这一点上,译文二、四处理得较为理想。"万物负阴而抱阳"一句的翻译,译文一、三较忠实于原文,译文二、四则对其进行了简化处理,似不足取,因为"负阴而抱阳"是道家"阴、阳"学说的重要理念。

▶▶ 五、翻译练习

（一）思考题

1. 如何理解"上善若水"？
2. 如何理解"道可道,非常道"？
3. 如何理解"道法自然"？

（二）翻译题

1. 是以圣人处无为之事,行不言之教；万物作而弗始,生而弗有,为而弗恃,功成而不居。夫唯弗居,是以不去。

2. 善行无辙迹,善言无瑕谪,善数不用筹策,善闭无关楗而不可开,善结无绳约而不可解。是以圣人常善救人,故无弃人；常善救物,故无弃物。是谓袭明。故善人者,不善人之师；不善人者,善人之资。不贵其师,不爱其资,虽智大迷,是谓要妙。

3. 信言不美,美言不信。善者不辩,辩者不善。知者不博,博者不知。圣人不积,既以为人己愈有,既以与人己愈多。天之道,利而不害；圣人之道,为而不争。

4. 善为士者,不武；善战者,不怒；善胜敌者,不与；善用人者,为之下。是谓不争之德,是谓用人,是谓配天,古之极也。

5. 天下莫柔弱于水,而攻坚强者莫之能胜,以其无以易之。弱之胜强,柔之胜刚,天下莫不知,莫能行。是以圣人云："受国之垢,是谓社稷主；受国不祥,是为天下王。"正言若反。

参考读物

Waley, Arthur. *The Way and Its power, A Study of Tao Te Ching and Its Place in Chinese Thought* [M]. London: George Allen and Uniwin Lit., 1981.

Lau, D. C. *Lao Tzu Tao Te Ching* [M]. Penguin Books, 1963.

Lin, Paul J. *A Translation of Lao Tzu's Tao Te Ching and Wang Bi's Commentary* [M]. Michigan: Michigan Papers in Chinese Studies, 1977.

Takao, Chu. *Tao Te Ching* [M]. London: Hazel Watson and Viney Ltd., 1959.

Wing-tsit, Chan. *The Way of Lao Tzu* [M]. Indianapolis, NewYork: The Bobbs-Merrill Co., Inc., Library of Liberal Arts, 1963.

亚瑟·韦利英译,陈鼓应今译,傅惠生校注. 大中华文库:老子汉英对照[M]. 长沙:湖南人民出版社,1999.

老子著,辜正坤英译. 道德经 汉英对照(附楚简《太一生水》)[M]. 北京:中国对外翻译出版公司,2007.

张园. 郭店楚简《老子》研究述论[D]. 东北师范大学,2006.

张松入. 老子校读[M]. 长春:吉林人民出版社,1981.

陈鼓应. 老子注释及评介[M]. 北京:中华书局,1984.

卢育三. 老子释义[M]. 天津:天津古籍出版社,1987.

第七课

《庄子》

▶▶ 一、内容简介

庄子,姓庄,名周,字子休,约生于公元前369年,卒于公元前286年,宋国蒙人。他做过蒙地的漆园吏,后隐居于陋巷,以织履谋生。庄子是先秦时期继老子之后道家的另外一位重要代表人物。

据《汉书·艺文志》记载,《庄子》一书共计五十二篇,现存的三十三篇为晋人郭象所整理,分为内篇七、外篇十五、杂篇十一,后人对外篇、杂篇的真伪之争较为热烈,认为非庄子本人所作,但总体而言,都可归为庄子学派的思想。庄子散文文字华美,气势磅礴,独具韵味,既可作文学欣赏,也可藉为人生之钥,体现出道家思想的深奥悠远。

庄子的思想精华主要体现在内篇之中,其《逍遥游》展示了道家思想中脱俗不羁、立意高远的精神追求;《齐物论》是庄子认识论的重要表述,认为天下万物皆为"道"所主宰,故皆应以"道"观之,方得万物之妙;《养生主》探讨养生之道,阐述顺应自然、心无旁骛的修心境界;《人间世》讲述以无为处世的高明哲学;《德充符》称颂德行的珍贵,描述了大德之士所追求的修养境界;《大宗师》谈及真人、圣人等道家内在修为的精要之处;《应帝王》从治理天下的角度论述道家治国之方。外篇、杂篇的作者虽然争议颇多,但大致也可作为庄子思想的印证和补充。

总而言之,庄子继承了老子"以道为体"的思想,对道家的思想进行了更为细致、丰富的引申和发挥。

▶▶ 二、翻译传播

巴尔福(Frederic Henry Balfour)1881年所译的《庄子》是最早的英译本。该译本名为

《南华真经——道家哲学家庄子的著作》，但译者本人汉语水平有限，后人评价不高。1889 年翟理斯（Herbert Allen Giles）出版了他的译本，该译本使用维多利亚时期的英语，但翻译上不够严谨，与原本出入较大。1891 年牛津大学出版社出版了理雅各（James Legge）的《道家经典》译本，《庄子》是其中的一部分。该译本为最具好评的英译本之一，影响很大。法文最早的译本 1913 年由河间府（今河北献县）天主教教会发表，译者为戴遂量（Léon Wieger）神父。最早的德文译本是卫礼贤（Richard Wilhelm）1912 年出版的译本。

截至目前，《庄子》的英译本有 20 多种，其中全译本有 10 余种，其余的有简译本、编译本、述译本等。《庄子》的全译本除上文提到的巴尔福、翟理斯和理雅各的译本之外，还有其他一些译本，其中包括 1963 年薪美国图书出版社在纽约出版的威厄（James R. Ware）译本，名为《庄子语录》；1968 年哥伦比亚大学出版社出版的华兹生（Burton Watson）译本，该译本也是一部目前公认的较好译本，译文用词考究，且通俗易懂；1994 年班坦公司出版了梅维恒（Victor H. Mair）译本，书名为《逍遥游——庄子的早期道家故事和寓言》，该译本力求体现《庄子》的文学风格，以英文诗体来翻译书中的汉语诗体，并对书中的术语进行了汇编，颇具特色；1996 年伦敦企鹅丛书出版的帕尔玛（Martin Palmer）译本，该译本从宗教视角解读和翻译《庄子》；2006 年科里亚（Nina Correa）出版了电子译本。

国内的全译本有汪榕培 1997 年出版的译本。摘译本有冯友兰和林语堂分别于 1933 年和 1942 年对《庄子》的选译。随着中西方文化交流的不断深入，《庄子》的译本也在不断增多。其中较为突出的译本为 1981 年葛瑞汉由阿兰公司出版的《庄子》选译本。他认为《庄子》并非出自庄子一人之手，所以"翻译的内容越多，表达的思想越少"，因此采取了节译的方法。另一突出的译本是国内学者冯友兰先生于 1931 年商务印书馆出版的译本，该译本包含了晋人郭象的注疏，并在附录中对注疏予以点评。在该译本的前言和附录中，冯友兰对庄子思想进行了详细论述，是较有价值的译本。

▶▶ 三、翻译对比

- 原文：

庄子·内篇·养生主第三

吾生也有涯，而知也无涯。以有涯随无涯，殆已！已而为知者，殆而已矣！为善无近名，为恶无近刑，缘督以为经，可以保身，可以全生，可以养亲，可以尽年。

庖丁为文惠君解牛，手之所触，肩之所倚，足之所履，膝之所踦，砉然响然，奏刀騞然，莫不中音，合于《桑林》之舞，乃中《经首》之会。

文惠君曰："嘻，善哉！技盖至此乎？"庖丁释刀对曰："臣之所好者道也，进乎技矣。始臣之解牛之时，所见无非全牛者；三年之后，未尝见全牛也；方今之时，臣以神遇而不以目视，官知止而神欲行。依乎天理，批大郤，导大窾，因其固然。技经肯綮之未尝，而况大軱乎！良庖岁更刀，割也；族庖月更刀，折也；今臣之刀十九年矣，所解数千牛矣，而刀刃若新发于硎。彼节者有间而刀刃者无厚，以无厚入有间，恢恢乎其于游刃必有余地矣。是以十九年而刀刃若新发于硎。虽然，每至于族，吾见其难为，怵然为戒，视为止，行为迟，动刀甚微，謋然已解，如土委地。提刀而立，为之而四顾，为之踌躇满志，善刀而藏之。"文惠君曰："善哉！吾闻庖丁之言，得养生焉。"

公文轩见右师而惊曰："是何人也？恶乎介也？天与？其人与？"曰："天也，非人也。天之生是使独也，人之貌有与也。以是知其天也，非人也。"

泽雉十步一啄，百步一饮，不蕲畜乎樊中。神虽王，不善也。

老聃死，秦失吊之，三号而出。弟子曰："非夫子之友邪？"曰："然。""然则吊焉若此可乎？"曰："然。始也吾以为其人也，而今非也。向吾入而吊焉，有老者哭之，如哭其子；少者哭之，如哭其母。彼其所以会之，必有不蕲言而言，不蕲哭而哭者。是遁天倍情，忘其所受，古者谓之遁天之刑。适来，夫子时也；适去，夫子顺也。安时而处顺，哀乐不能入也，古者谓是帝之县解。"

指穷于为薪，火传也，不知其尽也。

理雅各译文：

Nourishing the Lord of Life

There is a limit to our life, but to knowledge there is no limit. With what is limited to pursue after what is unlimited is a perilous thing; and when, knowing this, we still seek the increase of our knowledge, the peril cannot be averted. There should not be the practice of what is good with any thought of the fame (which it will bring), nor of what is evil with any approximation to the punishment (which it will incur): an accordance with the Central Element (of our nature) is the regular way to preserve the body, to maintain the life, to nourish our parents, and to complete our term of years.

His cook was cutting up an ox for the ruler Wen Hui. Whenever he applied his hand, leaned forward with his shoulder, planted his foot, and employed the pressure of his knee, in the audible ripping off of the skin, and slicing operation of the knife, the sounds were all in regular cadence. Movements and sounds proceeded as in the dance of "the Mulberry Forest" and the blended notes of "the King Shou". The ruler said, "Ah! Admirable! That your art should have become so perfect!" (Having finished his operation), the cook laid down his knife, and replied to the remark, "What your servant loves is the method of the Dao, something in advance of any art. When I first began to cut up an ox, I saw nothing but the (entire) carcase. After three years I ceased to see it as a whole. Now I deal with it in a spirit-like manner, and do not look at it with my eyes. The use of my senses is discarded, and my spirit acts as it wills. Observing the natural lines, (my knife) slips through the great crevices and slides through the great cavities, taking advantage of the facilities thus presented. My art avoids the membranous ligatures, and much more the great bones. A good cook changes his knife every year; (it may have been injured) in cutting—an ordinary cook changes his every month—(it may have been) broken. Now my knife has been in use for nineteen years; it has cut up several thousand oxen, and yet its edge is as sharp as if it had newly come from the whetstone. There are the interstices of the joints, and the edge of the knife has no (appreciable) thickness; when that which is so thin enters where the interstice is, how easily it moves along! The blade has more than room enough. Nevertheless, whenever I come to a complicated joint, and see that there will be some difficulty, I proceed anxiously and with caution, not allowing my eyes to wander from the place, and moving my hand slowly. Then by a very slight movement of the knife, the part is quickly separated, and drops like (a clod of) earth to the ground. Then standing up with the knife in my hand, I look all round, and in a leisurely manner, with an air of satisfaction, wipe it clean, and put it in its sheath." The ruler Wen Hui said, "Excellent! I have heard the words of my cook, and learned from them the nourishment of (our) life."

When Gong-wen Xian saw the Master of the Left, he was startled, and said, "What sort of man is this? How is it he has but one foot? Is it from Heaven? or from Man?" Then he added, "It must be from Heaven, and not from Man. Heaven's making of this man caused him to have but one foot. In the person of man, each foot has its marrow. By this I know that his peculiarity is from Heaven, and not from Man."

A pheasant of the marshes has to take ten steps to pick up a mouthful of food, and thirty steps to get a drink, but it does not seek to be nourished in a coop. Though its spirit would (there) enjoy a royal abundance, it does not think (such confinement) good.

When Lao Dan died, Qin Shi went to condole (with his son), but after crying out three times, he came out. The disciples said to him, "Were you not a friend of the Master?" "I was," he replied, and they said, "Is it proper then to offer your condolences merely as you have done?" He said, "It is. At first I thought he was the man of men, and now I do not think so. When I entered a little ago and expressed my condolences, there were the old men wailing as if they had lost a son, and the young men wailing as if they had lost their mother. In his attracting and uniting them to himself in such a way there must have been that which made them involuntarily express their words (of condolence), and involuntarily wail, as they were doing. And this was a hiding from himself of his Heaven (nature), and an excessive indulgence of his (human) feelings; a forgetting of what he had received (in being born); what the ancients called the punishment due to neglecting the Heaven (nature). When the Master came, it was at the proper time; when he went away, it was the simple sequence (of his coming). Quiet acquiescence in what happens at its proper time, and quietly submitting (to its ceasing) afford no occasion for grief or for joy. The ancients described (death) as the loosening of the cord on which God suspended (the life)."

What we can point to are the faggots that have been consumed; but the fire is transmitted (elsewhere), and we know not that it is over and ended.

华兹生译文：

The Secret of Caring for Life

Your life has a limit but knowledge has none. If you use what is limited to pursue what has no limit, you will be in danger. If you understand this and still strive for knowledge, you will be in danger for certain! If you do good, stay away from fame. If you do evil, stay away from punishments. Follow the middle; go by what is constant, and you can stay in one piece, keep yourself alive, look after your parents, and live out your years. Cook Ting was cutting up an ox for Lord Wen Hui. At every touch of his hand, every heave of his shoulder, every move of his feet, every thrust of his knee zip! zoop! He slithered the knife along with a zing, and all was in perfect rhythm, as though he were performing the dance of the Mulberry Grove or keeping time to the Ching Shou music. "Ah, this is marvelous!" said Lord Wen Hui. "Imagine skill reaching such heights!"

Cook Ting laid down his knife and replied, "What I care about is the Way, which goes beyond skill. When I first began cutting up oxen, all I could see was the ox itself. After three years I no longer saw the whole ox. And now I go at it by spirit and don't look with my eyes. Perception and understanding have come to a stop and spirit moves where it wants. I go along with the natural makeup, strike in the big hollows, guide the knife through the big openings, and follow things as they are. So I never touch the smallest ligament or tendon, much less a main joint.

"A good cook changes his knife once a year because he cuts. A mediocre cook changes his knife once a month because he hacks. I've had this knife of mine for nineteen years and I've cut up thousands of oxen with it, and yet the blade is as good as though it had just come from the grindstone. There are spaces between the joints, and the blade of the knife has really no thickness. If you insert what has no thickness into such spaces, then there's plenty of room more than enough for the blade to play about it. That's why after nineteen years the blade of my knife is still as good as when it first came from the grindstone.

"However, whenever I come to a complicated place, I size up the difficulties, tell myself to watch out and be careful, keep my eyes on what I'm doing, work very slowly, and move the knife with the greatest subtlety, until flop! The whole thing comes apart like a clod of earth crumbling to the ground. I stand there holding the knife and look all around me, completely satisfied and reluctant to move on, and then I wipe off the knife and put it away."

"Excellent!" said Lord Wen hui. "I have heard the words of Cook Ting and learned how to care for life!" When Kung wen Hsuan saw the *Commander of the Right*, he was startled and said, "What kind of man is this? How did he come to be footless? Was it Heaven? Or was it man?" "It was Heaven, not man," said the commander. "When Heaven gave me life, it saw to it that I would be one footed. Men's looks are given to them. So I know this was the work of Heaven and not of man. The swamp pheasant has to walk ten paces for one peck and a hundred paces for one drink, but it doesn't want to be kept in a cage. Though you treat it like a king, its spirit won't be content."

When Lao Tan died, Chin Shih went to mourn for him; but after giving three cries, he left the room. "Weren't you a friend of the Master?" asked Lao Tzu's disciples.

"Yes."

"And you think it's all right to mourn him this way?"

"Yes," said Chin Shih. "At first I took him for a real man, but now I know he wasn't. A little while ago, when I went in to mourn, I found old men weeping for him as though they were weeping for a son, and young men weeping for him as though they were weeping for a mother. To have gathered a group like that, he must have done something to make them talk about him, though he didn't ask them to talk, or make them weep for him, though he didn't ask them to weep. This is to hide from Heaven, turn your back on the true state of affairs, and forget what you were born with. In the old days, this was called the crime of hiding from Heaven. Your master happened to come because it was his time, and he happened to leave because things follow along. If you are content with the time and willing to follow along, then grief and joy have no Way to enter in. In the old days, this was called being freed from the bonds of God."

"Though the grease burns out of the torch, the fire passes on, and no one knows where it ends."

林语堂译文：

The Preservation of Life

Human life is limited, but knowledge is limitless. To drive the limited in pursuit of the limitless is fatal; and to presume that one really knows is fatal indeed!

In doing good, avoid fame. In doing bad, avoid disgrace. Pursue a middle course as your principle. Thus you will guard your body from harm, preserve your life, fulfill your duties by your parents, and live your allotted span of life.

Prince Huei's cook was cutting up a bullock. Every blow of his hand, every heave of his shoulders, every tread of his foot, every thrust of his knee, every whshh of rent flesh, every chhk of the chopper, was in perfect rhythm—like the dance of the Mulberry Grove, like the harmonious chords of Ching Shou.

"Well done!" cried the Prince. "Yours is skill indeed!"

"Sire," replied the cook laying down his chopper, "I have always devoted myself to Tao, which is higher than mere skill. When I first began to cut up bullocks, I saw before me whole bullocks. After three years' practice, I saw no more whole animals. And now I work with my mind and not with my eye. My mind works along without the control of the senses. Falling back upon eternal principles, I glide through such great joints or cavities as there may be, according to the natural constitution of the animal. I do not even touch the convolutions of muscle and tendon, still less attempt to cut through large bones."

"A good cook changes his chopper once a year—because he cuts. An ordinary cook, one a month—because he hacks. But I have had this chopper nineteen years, and although I have cut up many thousand bullocks, its edge is as if fresh from the whetstone. For at the joints there are always interstices, and the edge of a chopper being without thickness, it remains only to insert that which is without thickness into such an interstice. Indeed there is plenty of room for the blade to move about. It is thus that I have kept my chopper for nineteen years as though fresh from the whetstone."

"Nevertheless, when I come upon a knotty part which is difficult to tackle, I am all caution. Fixing my eye on it, I stay my hand, and gently apply my blade, until with a hwah the part yields like earth crumbling to the ground. Then I take out my chopper and stand up, and look around, and pause with an air of triumph. Then wiping my chopper, I put it carefully away."

"Bravo!" cried the Prince. "From the words of this cook I have learned how to take care of my life."

When Hsien, of the Kungwen family, beheld a certain official, he was horrified, and said, "Who is that man? How came he to lose a leg? Is this the work of God, or of man?"

"Why, of course, it is the work of God, and not of man," was the reply. "God made this man one-legged. The appearance of men is always balanced. From this it is clear that God and not man made him what he is."

A pheasant of the marshes may have to go ten steps to get a peck, a hundred to get a drink. Yet pheasants do not want to be fed in a cage. For although they might have less worries, they would not like it. When Laotse died, Chin Yi went to the funeral. He uttered three yells and departed. A disciple asked him saying, "Were you not our Master's friend?"

"I was," replied Chin Yi.

"And if so, do you consider that a sufficient expression of grief at his death?" added the disciple.

"I do," said Chin Yi. "I had thought he was a (mortal) man, but now I know that he was not. When I went in to mourn, I found old persons weeping as if for their children, young ones wailing as if for their mothers. When these people meet, they must have said words on the occasion and shed tears without any intention. (To cry thus at one's death) is to evade the natural principles (of life and death) and increase human attachments, forgetting the source from which we receive this life. The ancients called this 'evading the retribution of Heaven'. The Master came, because it was his time to be born. He went, because it was his time to go away. Those who accept the natural course and sequence of things and live in obedience to it are beyond joy and sorrow. The ancients spoke of this as the emancipation from bondage. The fingers may not be able to supply all the fuel, but the fire is transmitted, and we know not when it will come to an end."

汪榕培译文：

Essentials for Keeping a Good Health

Man's life is limited but knowledge is unlimited. To pursue the unlimited with the limited is fatiguing; to know this but still pursue unlimited knowledge with limited life is fatal.

When you do good, don't do it for the sake of fame; when you do bad, don't do it as to incur punishment. If you always keep to the proper way, you will be able to keep a good health, preserve your nature, support your parents and live out your full life-span.

A butcher was carving a bullock for Lord Wenhui. At every touch of his hand, every move of his shoulder, every stamp of his foot and every nudge of knee, there came the sound of slicing the flesh and wielding the knife—a perfect rhythm to the Dance of Mulberry Trees and a perfect tune of the music in King Yao's time.

Lord Wenhui remarked, "Oh, splendid! That you have such a masterful skill!"

The butcher put down his knife and responded, "What I love is Tao, which is much more splendid than my skill. When I first began to carve a bullock, I saw nothing but the whole bullock. Three years later, I no longer saw the bullock as a whole but in parts. Now I work on it by intuition and do not look at it with my eyes. My visual organs stop functioning while my intuition goes its own way. In accordance with natural grain, I cleave along the main seams and thrust the knife into the big cavities. Following the natural structure of the bullock, I never touch veins or tendons, much less the big bones! A good butcher changes his knife once a year because he cuts the flesh; an ordinary butcher changes his knife once a mouth because he hacks the bones. Using this knife for nineteen years, I have carved thousands of bullocks, but the edge of my knife is still as sharp as if it had just come from the whetstone. There are crevices between the joints, but the edge of my knife is very thin. When I insert the thin edge of my knife into these crevices, there is plenty of room for it to pass through. That is why, after nineteen years, the edge of my knife is still as sharp as if it had just come from the whetstone. Nevertheless, whenever I come to a complicated spot and see that there are difficulties here, I proceed with great caution, I keep my eyes on what I am doing and wield the knife slowly. With a very slight movement of the knife, I cut off the flesh—it falls to the ground like a clod of earth. Holding the knife in my hand, I stand there, looking proudly around. Then I clean the knife and put it carefully away."

Lord Wenhui said, "Splendid! From what you just said, I've learned how to keep good health."

When Gongwen Xuan saw Commander of the Right Army, he said in astonishment, "Who are you? How come that you have only one foot? Is this the work of the heaven or of the man?"

Commander of the Right Army replied, "It's the work of Heaven, not of Man. I was born with one foot. Man's appearance is endowed by Heaven. Therefore, I know that it is the work of Heaven, not of Man."

The marsh pheasant has to walk ten steps to find a peck of food and a hundred steps for a peck of drink, but it does not want to be raised in a cage. Even though it might live well in the cage, it would not feel comfortable.

When Laozi died, Qin Shi went to mourn over him and came out after three wails.

A disciple asked him, "Isn't he your friend?"

Qin Shi answered, "Yes, he is."

The disciple said, "Do you think it proper to mourn him like this?"

Qin Shi said, "Of course. I thought that he was a perfect man, but I don't think so now. When I went in to mourn him, old men were weeping as though their son had died and young men were crying as though their mother had died. They have gathered here to say what they should not have said and to cry for what they should not have cried. They have violated the nature of things and have abandoned themselves to sentimentality. In ancient times, this was called 'the crime of violating nature'. Your master's coming to the earth is timely and his departure is natural. A timely coming and a natural departure have nothing to do with joy or sorrow. This was regarded by the ancients as 'emancipation from bondage'."

The resins and the firewood may be consumed, but the fire will burn on. No one knows when the fire will end.

四、翻译赏析

题目"养生主"大意为"生命养护之宗主"。理雅各译文中的 nourishing 一词传递了"养"之意,表达了对人体生命的养护之意;华兹生将其译作 secret of caring for life,似有背离原文之嫌。相比较而言,林语堂的翻译似乎更为可取。

第二句中的"殆已"的翻译,各译本在理解上并无明显差异,但在选词上各有千秋。理雅各将其译为 a perilous thing,华兹生将其译为 danger,林语堂将其译为 fatal,汪榕培将其译为 fatiguing。据王先谦《庄子集解》,"殆"在此处是"窘困"之意;郭象《庄子注》"殆"也为"窘困",但把接下来的"殆而已矣",则解释为"伤害"。几个译文显然都考虑到这个意思,在选词的色彩上各有侧重。

"缘督以为经"的翻译也颇值关注。理雅各将其译作" an accordance with the Central Element (of our nature) is the regular way to …",华兹生将其译作"Follow the middle …",林语堂将其译作"Pursue a middle course as your principle …",汪榕培将其译作"If you always keep to the proper way …"。"督"的意思解为"中"、"正"。理雅各把"督"翻译为与人本性相关的属性,有一定的合理性。在"经"一字的处理上,理雅各和林语堂分别译为 the regular way,principle,另外两个译文则采用意译或略译之法。"督"与"经"后来成为道家学说中的重要概念,翻译时似应慎加处理。

对于"臣之所好者道也,进乎技矣"一句的翻译,四种译本各有千秋。相比之下,林语堂的译文 Tao, which is higher than mere skill 似乎更为可取。华兹生的 the Way, which goes beyond skill,对"道"虽没有采用音译的方法,但整个句子的翻译却与林语堂异曲同工。"神遇而不以目视,官知止而神欲行",即不用客观实体的眼睛去看而是以人的意念去解牛。理雅各和华兹生均将"神"译作 spirit,带有基督教影响的印痕,而林语堂的 mind 一词以及汪榕培的 intuition 则接近原文的实际内涵。

在"遁天倍情,忘其所受"一句中,"遁天"指人不可违背自然。林语堂和汪榕培分别将其译作 evade the natural principle 和 violate the nature,在理解上还是比较到位的。而理雅各以及华兹生的翻译则与原文有较大的差异。

五、课后练习

(一) 思考题

1. 庄子的人生观是怎样的?
2. 《庄子》主要内容是什么?
3. 《庄子》翻译中的难点是什么?

(二) 翻译题

1. 北冥有鱼,其名为鲲。鲲之大,不知其几千里也。化而为鸟,其名为鹏。鹏之背,不知其几千里也;怒而飞,其翼若垂天之云。是鸟也,海运则将徙于南冥。南冥者,天池也。齐谐者,志怪者也。谐之言曰:"鹏之徙于南冥也,水击三千里,抟扶摇而上者九万里,去以六月息者也。"

2. 野马也,尘埃也,生物之以息相吹也。天之苍苍,其正色邪?其远而无所至极邪?其视下也亦若是,则已矣。且夫水之积也不厚,则负大舟也无力。覆杯水于坳堂之上,则芥为之舟,置杯焉则胶,水浅而舟大也。风之积也不厚,则其负大翼也无力。故九万里则风斯在下矣,而后乃今培风;背负青天而莫之夭阏者,而后乃今将图南。蜩与学鸠笑之曰:"我决起而飞,枪榆、枋而止,时则不至而控于地而已矣,奚以之九万里而南为?"

3. 适莽苍者三飡而反,腹犹果然;适百里者宿舂粮;适千里者三月聚粮。之二虫又何知!小知不及大知,小年不及大年。奚以知其然也?朝菌不知晦朔,蟪蛄不知春秋,此小年也。楚之南有冥灵者,以五百岁为春,五百岁为秋;上古有大椿者,以八千岁为春,八千岁为秋。而彭祖乃今以久特闻,众人匹之,不亦悲乎!

参考读物

Legge, James. *The Sacred Books of China: The Texts of Taoism, Part I* [M]. Oxford：Oxford University Press, 1891. Reprint：New York：Dover Publications, 1962.

Giles, Herbert Allen. *Chuang Tzǔ: Mystic, Moralist, and Social Reformer* [M]. Shanghai：Kelly & Walsh, 1926. Reprint：New York：AMS Press, 1974.

Ware, James R. *The Sayings of Chuang Chou* [M]. New York：Mentor Classics, 1963.

Watson, Burton. *The Complete Works of Chuang Tzu* [M]. New York：Columbia University Press, 1968.

Palmer, Martin. *The Book of Chuang Tzu* [M]. London：Penguin Books, 1996.

Mair, Victor H. *Wandering on the Way: Early Taoist Tales and Parables of Chuang Tzu* [M]. New York：Bantam Books, 1994.

Fung, Yu-lan. *Chuang-tzǔ: A New Selected Translation with an Exposition of the Philosophy of Kuo Hsiang* [M]. Shanghai：The Commercial Press, 1933. Reprint：*A Taoist Classic: Chuang-Tzu*. Beijing：Foreign Languages Press, 1964.

Feng, Gia-Fu. *Chuang Tsu: Inner Chapters* [M]. New York：Vintage Books, 1974.

Graham, A. C. *Chuang-tzǔ: The Seven Inner Chapters and Other Writings from the Book Chuang-tzǔ* [M]. London：George Allen & Unwin, 1981. Reprint：*Chuang-tzǔ: The Inner Chapters*. Indianapolis：Hackett Publishing Company, Inc, 2001.

Ziporyn, Brook. *Zhuangzi: The Essential Writings with Selections from Traditional Commentaries* [M]. Indianapolis：Hackett, 2009.

汪榕培. 庄子(英译) 大中华文库[M]. 长沙：湖南人民出版社,北京：外文出版社, 1999. 孙通海译注. 庄子[M]. 北京：中华书局,2007.

班固撰、颜师古注. 汉书[M]. 北京：中华书局,2000.

鲁迅. 汉文学史纲要[M]. 上海：上海古籍出版社,2005.

冯友兰. 英译《庄子》自序. 三松堂全集：第11卷[M]. 郑州：河南人民出版社, 2000.

徐来. 英译《庄子》研究[M]. 上海：复旦大学出版社,2008.

第八课

《孙子兵法》

▶▶ 一、内容简介

孙子,字长卿,春秋末期齐国人。《史记·孙子吴起列传》中记载他到吴国,"以兵法见于吴王阖庐",并以宫中美女"小试勒兵",遂受重用,帮助吴国"西破强楚,入郢,北威齐晋,显名诸侯"。

《孙子兵法》一书"五千言"(今本约6000字),共十三篇。

计篇,开宗明义,指出战争是关系人民生死、国家存亡的大事:"兵者,国之大事,死生之地,存亡之道。"继而提出考察研究战争的"五事"和"七计",以及"兵者,诡道也"的用兵原则,最后总结"未战而庙算胜"的重要。

作战篇,论述战争准备要立足于"速战速决"的军事思想及其客观依据。最后以"兵贵胜,不贵久"总结全篇,并指出贤将的重要:"故知兵之将,民之司命,国家安危之主也。"

谋攻篇,论述谋划攻战策略,犹重以智谋取胜。提出"全敌而胜"、"不战而屈人之兵"、"上兵伐谋"的战略思想。最后的"知彼知己,百战不殆"揭示了战争的一般规律。

形篇,通过对攻守辩证关系的论述,说明要加强和完善、运用和发挥己方的军事实力,使之"若决积水于千仞之溪"。

势篇,论述军队于攻守之中的运动,强调军队通过"奇正之变",达至"激水漂石"、"彍弩"、"转圆石于千仞之山"之势以及"鸷鸟毁折"、"发机"之节。

虚实篇,论述通过对"虚实"的把握,争取在战争中"致人而不致于人",通过"避实击虚"、"因敌变化"而"为敌之司命"。

军争篇,论述争取有利战机,以掌握主动权。首言"军争之难"在于"知迂直之计",

后明"用众"、"治气"、"治心"、"治力"、"治变"之法。

九变篇，论述在特殊条件下机变灵活的作战思想。

行军篇，首先论述"处山"、"处水上"、"处斥泽"、"处平陆"之军的作战原则。总的原则即是"好高而恶下,贵阳而贱阴,养生而处实"。进而说明侦察敌情的方法以及治军原则："合之以文,齐之以武。"

地形篇，论述了"通"、"挂"、"支"、"隘"、"险"、"远"等六种排兵布阵之地形和与之相对应的作战原则，即"地之道"。还论及观察、利用地形的重要性："夫地形者,兵之助也。料敌制胜,计险厄远近,上将之道也。"最后总结"知彼知己,胜乃不殆；知天知地,胜乃可全"的道理。

九地篇，论述了"散地"、"轻地"、"争地"、"交地"、"衢地"、"重地"、"圮地"、"围地"、"死地"九种战略地势和相应的作战与处置方法，其要本于人情："九地之变,屈伸之利,人情之理。"

火攻篇、用间篇，论述较为简单，此不赘述。

《孙子兵法》属兵书，其文章虽"以立意为宗"，但文采也甚为可观，兼有诸子散文之长。结构上，《孙子兵法》大多篇章组织缜密。语言表达上，它多用对句、排比句，使得节律匀称、气势恢宏；通过类比和比喻，展示丰富的内涵。例如："夫兵形象水,水之行避高而趋下,兵之形避实而击虚；水因地而制流,兵因敌而制胜。故兵无常势,水无常形。能因敌变化而取胜者,谓之神。"（《虚实篇》）刘勰于《文心雕龙》称赞"孙武《兵经》,辞如珠玉"。

二、翻译传播

在中国古代典籍中，除《道德经》和《论语》之外，在国外被翻译最多的恐怕就数《孙子兵法》了。

《孙子兵法》的第一个西文译本是法国耶稣会士钱德明（Jean-Joseph-Marie Amiot, 1718–1793）的法语译本。然而英文译本的推出则较晚，第一个英文译本迟至1905年才在东京问世，由卡尔思罗普（E. F. Calthrop）从日文转译，后于1908年在英国由约翰·穆勒出版社（John Murry Ltd.）修订再版。

1910年，时任大英博物馆东方书刊和手稿馆助理馆长的著名汉学家翟林奈（Lionel Giles）翻译了《孙子兵法》，题名为 *The Art of War: The Oldest Military Treatise in the World*，由

Luzac & Co. 出版。此书译文质量较高，富有韵律感，注释详尽，有译者个人的创见，时至今日，仍然不断再版和重印。在献词中，他写到"献给我的弟弟，瓦伦丁·贾尔斯上尉，希望2400年前的这一本书仍有今天的士兵所值得思考的东西。特意奉上此译。"

翟林奈译本是典型的汉学家学术译本。它在体例上仿照理雅各《中国经典》(The Chinese Classics)，有序言和颇为详尽的绪论，介绍孙子其人及其兵法成书的过程和后代注疏的情况。正文包括汉语原文、译文和注释，同页平行排印。还附有参考文献、汉字索引和英文索引。

1963年，美国军事学家、毛泽东军事思想研究专家格里菲斯(Samuel B. Griffith)在牛津大学出版社出版了他翻译的《孙子兵法》(Sun Tzu: The Art of War)。此译本源于其1960年写就的博士论文的一个部分。译本包括英国军事理论家利德尔·哈特(B. H. Liddell Hart)序、前言、致谢、绪论和译文、附录、参考文献，还摘译了部分注家的注解，并且有大量注释。因此，它也是一个严谨的学术译本，但更注重孙子军事思想的传递。

《孙子兵法》更多英语译本的推出是在20世纪90年代和21世纪初，其中较为著名的有哲学家安乐哲(Roger T. Ames)的 The Art of Warfare (1993年Random House出版)，军事理论家苏炀悟(Ralph D. Sawyer)的 Sun Tzu: The Art of War (1994年Westview Press出版)，英国汉学家、文学翻译家闵福德(John Minford)的 The Art of War (2002年Penguin Group出版)。这些译本参照了银雀山汉墓竹简有关《孙子兵法》的最新史料。

闵福德译本无论是在形式还是内容方面都比较独特。他在导言中把《孙子兵法》定位为一部"充满古老智慧的生活之书"(an ancient book of proverbial wisdom, a book of life)。在编排格式上采用自由诗行的形式和中国传统注疏本的印刷风格，除了有中国历代注家的评注，还有翟林奈的注和自我评注，而且其评注常常引用《道德经》、《易经》、《三国演义》的内容，为读者提供语境，使读者了解言外之意。

另外还有一些中国译者的译本，如潘嘉玢、刘瑞祥译本。该译本最初是《孙子校释》(吴九龙主编，军事科学出版社1990年出版)的一个附录，后于1993年单独印行。此外还有林戊荪译本(《孙子兵法 孙膑兵法(大中华文库汉英对照)》，1999年外文出版社出版)，这是一个较为准确、通俗的译本。

三、翻译对比

- 原文一：

兵者，国之大事，死生之地，存亡之道，不可不察也。

翟林奈译文：

The art of war is of vital importance to the State. It is a matter of life and death, a road either to safety or to ruin. Hence it is a subject of inquiry which can on no account be neglected.

格里菲斯译文：

War is a matter of vital importance to the State; the province of life or death; the road to survival or ruin. It is mandatory that it be thoroughly studied.

安乐哲译文：

War is a vital matter of state. It is the field on which life or death is determined and the road that leads to either survival or ruin, and must be examined with the greatest care.

林戊荪译文：

War is a question of vital importance to the state, a matter of life and death, the road to survival or ruin. Hence, it is a subject which calls for careful study.

苏炀悟译文：

Warfare is the greatest affair of state, the basis of life and death, the Way (Tao) to survival or extinction. It must be thoroughly pondered and analyzed.

闵福德译文：

War is

A grave affair of state;

It is a place

Of life and death,

A road

To survival and extinction,

A matter

To be pondered carefully.

● 原文二：

故经之以五事，校之以计，而索其情，一曰道，二曰天，三曰地，四曰将，五曰法。道者，令民与上同意，可与之死，可与之生，而不畏危也。天者，阴阳、寒暑、时制也。地者，远近、险易、广狭、死生也。将者，智、信、仁、勇、严也。法者，曲制、官道、主用也。凡此五者，将莫不闻，知之者胜，不知者不胜。

<u>格里菲斯译文：</u>

Therefore, appraise it in terms of the five fundamental factors and make comparisons of the seven elements later named. So you may assess its essentials. The first of these factors is moral influence; the second, weather; the third, terrain; the fourth, command; and the fifth, doctrine. By moral influence I mean that which causes the people to be in harmony with their leaders, so that they will accompany them in life and unto death without fear of mortal peril. By weather I mean the interaction of natural forces; the effects of winter's cold and summer's heat and the conduct of military operations in accordance with the seasons. By terrain I mean distances, whether the ground is traversed with ease or difficulty, whether it is open or constricted, and the chances of life or death. By command I mean the general's qualities of wisdom, sincerity, humanity, courage, and strictness. By doctrine I mean organization, control, assignment of appropriate ranks to officers, regulation of supply routes, and the provision of principal items used by the army. There is no general who has not heard of these five matters. Those who master them win; those who do not are defeated.

<u>苏炀悟译文：</u>

Therefore, structure it according to [the following] five factors, evaluate it comparatively through estimations, and seek out its true nature. The first is termed the Tao, the second Heaven, the third Earth, the fourth generals, and the fifth the laws [for military organization and discipline]. The Tao causes the people to be fully in accord with the ruler. [Thus] they will die with him; they will live with him and not fear danger. Heaven encompasses yin and yang, cold and heat, and the constraints of the seasons. Earth encompasses far or near, difficult or easy, expansive or confined, fatal or tenable terrain. The general encompasses wisdom, credibility, benevolence, courage, and strictness. The laws [for military organization and discipline] encompass organization and regulations, the Tao of command, and the management of logistics. There are no generals who have not heard of these five. Those who understand them will be victorious; those who do not understand them will not be victorious.

- 原文三：

兵者，诡道也。故能而示之不能，用而示之不用，近而示之远，远而示之近。利而诱之，乱而取之，实而备之，强而避之，怒而挠之，卑而骄之，佚而劳之，亲而离之。攻其无备，出其不意。此兵家之胜，不可先传也。

林戊荪译文：

War is a game of deception. Therefore, feign incapability when in fact capable; feign inactivity when ready to strike; appear to be far away when actually nearby, and vice versa. When the enemy is greedy for gains, hand out a bait to lure him; when he is in disorder, attack and overcome him; when he boasts substantial strength, be doubly prepared against him; and when he is formidable, evade him. If he is given to anger, provoke him. If he is timid and careful, encourage his arrogance. If his forces are rested, wear them down. If he is united as one, divide him. Attack where he is least prepared. Take action when he least expects you. Herein lies a strategist's subtlety of command which is impossible to codify in hard-and-fast rules beforehand.

安乐哲译文：

Warfare is the art (*tao*) of deceit. Therefore, when able, seem to be unable; when ready, seem unready; when nearby, seem far away; and when far away, seem near. If the enemy seeks some advantage, entice him with it. If he is in disorder, attack him and take him. If he is formidable, prepare against him. If he is strong, evade him. If he is incensed, provoke him. If he is humble, encourage his arrogance. If he is rested, wear him down. If he is internally harmonious, sow divisiveness in his ranks. Attack where he is not prepared; go by way of places where it would never occur to him you would go. These are the military strategist's calculations for victory—they cannot be settled in advance.

- 原文四：

凡用兵之法，全国为上，破国次之；全旅为上，破旅次之；全卒为上，破卒次之；全伍为上，破伍次之。是故百战百胜，非善之善者也；不战而屈人之兵，善之善者也。

翟林奈译文：

In the practical art of war, the best thing of all is to take the enemy's country whole and intact; to shatter and destroy it is not so good. So, too, it is better to recapture an army entire than to destroy it, to capture a regiment, a detachment or a company entire than to destroy them. Hence to fight and conquer in all your battles is not supreme excellence; supreme excellence consists in breaking the enemy's resistance without fighting.

苏炀悟译文：

In general, the method for employing the military is this: Preserving the [enemy's] state capital is best, destroying their state capital second-best. Preserving their army is best, destroying their army second-best. Preserving their battalions is best, destroying their battalions second-best. Preserving their companies is best, destroying their companies second-best. Preserving their squads is best, destroying their squads second-best. For this reason attaining one hundred victories in one hundred battles is not the pinnacle of excellence. Subjugating the enemy's army without fighting is the true pinnacle of excellence.

- 原文五：

知彼知己，百战不殆；不知彼而知己，一胜一负；不知彼，不知己，每战必殆。

格里菲斯译文：

Know the enemy and know yourself, in a hundred battles you will never be in peril. When you are ignorant of the enemy but know yourself, your chances of winning or losing are equal. If ignorant both of your enemy and of yourself, you are certain in every battle to be in peril.

安乐哲译文：

He who knows the enemy and himself

Will never in a hundred battles be at risk;

He who does not know the enemy but knows himself

Will sometimes win and sometimes lose;

He who knows neither the enemy nor himself

Will be at risk in every battle.

- 原文六：

故善战者,求之于势,不责于人,故能择人任势；任势者,其战人也,如转木石,木石之性,安则静,危则动,方则止,圆则行。故善战人之势,如转圆石于千仞之山者,势也。

翟林奈译文：

The clever combatant looks to the effect of combined energy, and does not require too much from individuals. Hence his ability to pick out the right men and utilize combined energy. When he utilizes combined energy, his fighting men become as it were like unto rolling logs or stones. For it is the nature of a log or stone to remain motionless on level ground, and to move when on a slope; if four-cornered, to come to a standstill, but if round shaped, to go rolling down. Thus the energy developed by good fighting men is as the momentum of a round stone rolled down a mountain thousands of feet in height. So much on the subject of energy.

安乐哲译文：

The expert at battle seeks his victory from strategic advantage (*shih*) and does not demand it from his men. He is thus able to select the right men and exploit the strategic advantage (*shih*). He who exploits the strategic advantage (*shih*) sends his men into battle like rolling logs and boulders. It is the nature of logs and boulders that on flat ground, they are stationary, but on steep ground, they roll; the square in shape tends to stop but the round tends to roll. Thus, that the strategic advantage (*shih*) of the expert commander in exploiting his men in battle can be likened to rolling round boulders down a steep ravine thousands of feet high says something about his strategic advantage (*shih*).

- 原文七：

故形兵之极,至于无形；无形,则深间不能窥,智者不能谋。

格里菲斯译文：

The ultimate in disposing one's troops is to be without ascertainable shape. Then the most penetrating spies cannot pry in nor can the wise lay plans against you.

苏炀悟译文：

Thus the pinnacle of military deployment approaches the formless. If it is formless, then even the deepest spy cannot discern it or the wise make plans against it.

• 原文八：

夫兵形象水，水之形，避高而趋下；兵之形，避实而击虚；水因地而制流，兵因敌而制胜。故兵无常势，水无常形；能因敌变化而取胜，谓之神。故五行无常胜，四时无常位，日有短长，月有死生。

翟林奈译文：

Military tactics are like unto water; for water in its natural course runs away from high places and hastens downwards. So in war, the way is to avoid what is strong and to strike at what is weak. Water shapes its course according to the nature of the ground over which it flows; the soldier works out his victory in relation to the foe whom he is facing. Therefore, just as water retains no constant shape, so in warfare there are no constant conditions. He who can modify his tactics in relation to his opponent and thereby succeed in winning, may be called a heaven-born captain. The five elements (water, fire, wood, metal, earth) are not always equally predominant; the four seasons make way for each other in turn. There are short days and long; the moon has its periods of waning and waxing.

苏炀悟译文：

Now the army's disposition of force (*hsing*) is like water. Water's configuration (*hsing*) avoids heights and races downward. The army's disposition of force (*hsing*) avoids the substantial and strikes the vacuous. Water configures (*hsing*) its flow in accord with the terrain; the army controls its victory in accord with the enemy. Thus the army does not maintain any constant strategic configuration of power (*shih*), water has no constant shape (*hsing*). One who is able to change and transform in accord with the enemy and wrest victory is termed spiritual. Thus [none of] the five phases constantly dominates; the four seasons do not have constant positions; the sun shines for longer and shorter periods; and the moon wanes and waxes.

▶▶▶ 四、翻译赏析

"原文一"是《孙子兵法》的开篇之言，指出战争关系到人民的生死、国家的存亡，因此需要认真研究。这里的六个译文可谓风格各异。从断句来看，基本上都将其译为两个英文句子，用词还是比较一致的。

"原文二"讲解了考量战争的五种要素。苏炀悟采用直译法，为使译文晓畅而出现的

"衍文",他也一一用方括号标出。对于多义的"道",他也一直采用"不翻"的音译策略。但采取这种翻译策略时,为使读者能够深入理解原著的内涵,往往需要加注说明。格里菲斯主要采用意译法,语言通俗易懂。例如,为使译文晓畅,他添加 I mean 等口语化的词语。对于较难理解的术语,他采用解释翻译法,便于读者接受。例如,他把"阴阳"译为 the interaction of natural forces。

"原文三"讲解了用兵的诡诈之术,这是孙子军事战略战术的一个重要创见,也是历史发展的必然。两个译文都较好地译出了原文的风格。值得一提的是,安乐哲译文句式接近于原文,且前后统一,人称代词也一直用 he,his,符合英文的行文规范。尤其是 entice him with it,代词 it 的使用使句子衔接紧密、逻辑性更强。

"原文四"道出战争的目的是为和平,并非攻城略地。苏炀悟采用直译法,较好地保留了原文双叠排比的句式结构。而翟林奈则打破了原文的句式结构,采用了较为综合的译法。另外,苏炀悟把中国古代军队编制军、旅、卒、伍翻译为 army, battalion, company, squad,体现了其层级结构,相对还是比较准确的。但"国"似乎没有必要翻译为 state capital。还有,"凡用兵之法"在《孙子兵法》中多处出现,是一个固定结构,苏炀悟译文"In general, the method for employing the military is this"更能反映原文的特点。关于"全"字的宾语,原文并未明示是敌人之国、之军、之旅、之卒、之伍,因此在译文中加 enemy 一词,是译者臆断。苏炀悟用方括号将 enemy 标记,是一种不错的处理手法,或者也可加注说明。

"原文五"中的"知彼知己,百战不殆"可说是孙子军事思想的核心。毛泽东在《论持久战》中对它有很高的评价:"战争不是神物,仍是世间的一种必然运动,因此,《孙子》的规律,'知彼知己,百战不殆',仍是科学的真理。""殆"字在这里是"危险"的意思,因此翻译为 be in peril 和 be at risk 都是准确的。安乐哲的译文有诗歌的韵味,这也是符合《孙子兵法》文章风格的。

"原文六"中比喻的使用是《孙子兵法》行文的一大特点。这里把"势"这一范畴用"转圆石于千仞之山"这一通俗易懂的形象的语言表示出来。这与用"决积水于千仞之溪"来比喻"形"这一抽象的范畴有异曲同工之妙。"势"在各个译本中翻译的可谓异彩纷呈。翟林奈和格里菲斯翻将其译作 energy,闵福德将其译作 potential energy,林戊荪将其译作 momentum。苏炀悟和安乐哲则分别将其译作 strategic configuration of power(军事力量的战略部署)和 strategic advantage(战略优势),虽说繁琐了点,但较为贴近孙子的军事思想。

"原文七"在语言表述方面很有老子《道德经》的韵味。然而,要将此种韵味译出,确实非常不易。第一个"形"字是动词,意思是故意表现出假象,有"示形"、"佯动"之义。两个译文 disposing one's troops 和 military deployment 都有"军队部署"之义,符合孙子的战术思想,只不过苏炀悟采用了转换词性的翻译方法。

"原文八"用水作比喻,深入浅出地道出了用兵必须因地制宜的道理。两个译文也都照直译出,保留了这一生动的形象。同时也都采用 wane 和 wax 翻译"月有死生"中的"死生",意义传达非常准确地道。在术语方面,苏炀悟用 spiritual 对应"神",有其实际的用意,而翟林奈将其译作 heaven-born captain,易于为西方读者所接受。

▶▶ 五、课后练习

(一) 思考题

1. 孙子军事思想的核心是什么?
2. 《孙子兵法》在西方的传播如何?
3. 《孙子兵法》翻译的难点是什么?

(二) 翻译题

1. 兵者,诡道也。故能而示之不能,用而示之不用,近而示之远,远而示之近。利而诱之,乱而取之,实而备之,强而避之,怒而挠之,卑而骄之,佚而劳之,亲而离之,攻其无备,出其不意。此兵家之胜,不可先传也。

2. 夫兵形象水,水之形,避高而趋下,兵之形,避实而击虚。水因地而制流,兵因敌而制胜。故兵无常势,水无常形。能因敌变化而取胜者,谓之神。故五行无常胜,四时无常位,日有短长,月有死生。

3. 行千里而不劳者,行于无人之地也;攻而必取者,攻其所不守也。守而必固者,守其所必攻也。故善攻者,敌不知其所守;善守者,敌不知其所攻。微乎微乎,至于无形;神乎神乎,至于无声,故能为敌之司命。

4. 故善用兵者,屈人之兵而非战也,拔人之城而非攻也,毁人之国而非久也,必以全争于天下,故兵不顿而利可全,此谋攻之法也。

参考读物

Ames, R. T. *The Art of Warfare* [M]. New York: Random House, 1993.

Giles, Lionel. *Sun Tzu on the Art of War: The Oldest Military Treatise in the World* [M]. London: Kegan Paul Limited, 2002.

Griffith, S. B. *Sun Tzu: The Art of War* [M]. Oxford: Oxford University Press, 1963.

Minford, John. *The Art of War* [M]. London: Penguin Group, 2002.

Sawyer, R. D. *Sun Tzu: The Art of War* [M]. Boulder: Westview Press, 1994.

李零.《孙子》十三篇综合研究[M]. 北京:中华书局,2006.

孙武撰,曹操注,郭化若今译. 孙子兵法[M]. 上海:上海古籍出版社,2006.

孙子、孙膑著,林戊荪译. 孙子兵法、孙膑兵法:汉英对照(大中华文库)[M]. 北京:外文出版社,1999.

吴九龙. 孙子校释[M]. 北京:军事科学出版社,1990.

吴如嵩. 孙子兵法词典[Z]. 沈阳:白山出版社,1993.

第九课

《易 经》

▶▶ 一、内容简介

《易经》是中国最古老的占筮书。根据《周礼》记载,夏、商、周三代都有《易》。流传至今的只有周代之《易》。《周易》后来被儒家奉为经典,故称《易经》,冠居群经之首。

《易经》最初来自古人的占筮记录,保留了占筮的主要功能,体现了编纂者的哲学思想和生活经验。经过后人的进一步发挥,形成了《易经》的哲学体系,成为中华传统文化的基础,是儒、道、墨、法、兵、名、阴阳等诸子百家思想的重要渊源。

《易经》由一套象征符号系统六十四卦组成。最初用两个最基本的符号阳爻(一)和阴爻(--)来表示宇宙间万事万物的基本分类("爻"音 yáo,含有交错和变化之意),分别象征天和地、男和女、阳和阴、刚和柔、动和静、升和降等,这是古人对宇宙万物矛盾现象直接观察而形成的概念,象征着相互对立的一切事物和现象。阳爻和阴爻这两种符号看来是古人占筮时所用的一节和两节草棒的象形。

传说伏羲画八卦,文王演周易,孔子作易传,《易经》是这"三圣"完成的。伏羲是远古时代的部落首长,据说是他把阳爻、阴爻排列起来,每三爻组成一卦(单卦),得出了八种排列方式,这就是八卦:乾(☰)、坤(☷)、震(☳)、巽(读 xùn,☴)、坎(☵)、离(☲)、艮(读 gěn,☶)、兑(读 duì,☱),分别象征自然界的八种基本事物,即天、地、雷、风、水、火、山、泽。

据说是周文王把八卦两两重叠,演变成了六十四卦(重卦),并且撰写了卦辞和爻辞。将八卦卦符两两重叠、排列组合的结果是六十四种(8×8=64),这就是六十四卦。八卦称为单卦,六十四卦称为重卦。六十四卦分别象征六十四种事物和现象的特定情态,而卦中六爻之间的复杂关系又显示出各种事理的发展规律。这时，便产生了解说六十四卦哲理的卦爻辞。解说某一卦含义的是卦辞。每一卦包含六爻，六十四卦共有三百八十四爻，解说每一爻含义的是爻辞。

由于六十四卦的卦爻辞（即"经文"）写得太简单古奥，相传孔子又对经文加以必要的注释，这就是《易经》的"传文"，易传共有《文言》、《彖传》上下、《象传》上下、《系辞传》上下、《说卦传》、《序卦传》、《杂卦传》七种，计十篇，称为"十翼"。

《易经》关系到哲学思想、天文地理、政治策略、军事计谋、伦理道德、行为科学、思维方式、人际关系、医学养生、信息预测、文艺美学等，甚至还关系到现代的前沿科学如计算机软件、遗传密码、混沌理论、耗散结构等。

《易经》六十四卦可以视为有关社会人生问题的六十四个专题，三百八十四爻可以看做在三百八十四种处境中可能发生的情况和最佳对策。《易经》是古代士大夫必读的高深教科书，今天仍不失为引导人们适应各种复杂环境的宝鉴。

八卦中的每一卦都有其具体的卦名、卦形、象形、意义及象义，具体归纳如下：

卦名	卦形	象形	意义	象义
乾	☰	天	健	父
坤	☷	地	顺	母
震	☳	雷	动	长男
巽	☴	风、木	入	长女
坎	☵	水、雨	陷	中男
离	☲	火、日	附	中女
艮	☶	山	止	少男
兑	☱	泽	悦	少女

要学习八卦，首先得记住八卦的卦形。在熟记八卦卦形的基础上，结合其象形，了解其寓意和象义。这是入门《易经》的第一步。为了帮助初学者牢记八卦的卦形，前人根据其形状和特点，总结了一个24字口诀，即：乾三连（☰），坤六断（☷），震仰盂（☳），艮覆碗（☶），离中虚（☲），坎中满（☵），兑上缺（☱），巽下断（☴）。这个口诀简洁明快、形象生动，非常有助于初学者掌握八卦的卦形。

►► 二、翻译传播

早在16世纪的时候,有关《易经》的信息已经传播到了西方,成为中学西传的重要内容之一。据记载,最早向西方翻译介绍《易经》的是法国传教士金尼阁(Nicola Trigault,1577-1628)。他于1626年在中国杭州用拉丁文翻译出版了《易经》,试图在中国古典思想中寻找与基督教教义之间的结合点。葡萄牙人曾德昭(Alvaro Semedo,1585-1658)1641年在马德里以葡萄牙文出版的《大中国志》一书中,在介绍儒家思想和其经典著作时,也讲到了《易经》。他说《易经》是一部论述自然哲学的著作,根据一些自然原理预知未来和测算祸福。

意大利传教士卫匡国(Martin Martini,1614-1661)1658年在慕尼黑出版的《中国上古史》(Sinicae historiae decas prima)一书中也介绍了《易经》。他认为《易经》是中国最古老的书,也是中国第一部科学数学著作。像许多欧洲汉学家一样,卫匡国也被变幻莫测的《易经》所吸引。他第一次向西方指出了伏羲是《易经》的作者,他第一次向西方初步介绍了《周易》的基本内容,他第一次向欧洲公布了六十四卦图,从而使西方人对《易经》有了直观的理解。这个图要比1687年柏应理(Philippe Couplet)等人在《中国哲学家孔子》一书中所发表的六十四卦图早27年。由于八卦的卦名及其阴爻、阳爻在西方语言中找不到对应语,所以早期向西方介绍《易经》的传教士们虽然煞费苦心,但在概念的介绍和翻译方面还存在着很多需要进一步完善的地方。

在早期的传教士中,对《易经》研究较为深入的当属白晋(Joachin Bouvet,1656-1730)。白晋是法国神父,于康熙年间来华传教并很快得到了康熙帝的信任,在宫中为康熙讲授几何学。白晋在宫中熟读中国典籍,这在当时的传教士中是不多见的。他倾向于从中国古籍之中,尤其是《易经》之中寻找《圣经》的遗迹,从中国传统文化的典籍中寻求基督教的遗迹。他试图从中国文化本身寻求与基督教的共同点,将中国文化说成是基督教文化的派生物。他一方面承认中国文化的合理性,从而使自己能在中国立足,被清政府接受。另一方面,他通过索隐考据的方法,将中国文化归之于基督教文化,从而弥合了自身理论上的冲突,也能取得教廷的支持和欧洲社会对在中国传教的支持。白晋的这一主张得到了来华耶稣会士中部分传教士的赞同和同情,从而形成了一定的力量。

在早期来华传教士中,系统翻译介绍《易经》的是法国传教士雷孝思(Jean-Baptiste Regis,1663-1738),他出版了两卷本的《易经》拉丁文译本,书名为《易经——中国最古之书》(Y-King antiguissimus Sinarum Liber quemexLatina interPretatirn)。在雷孝思之后翻译《易经》的还有传教士宋君荣(Antoine Gauoil,1689-1759)等人。

在英语世界,《易经》的代表译本是英国传教士理雅各(James Legge,1815-1997)1882年翻译出版的译本。理雅各1843年来到中国香港传教,在传教过程中对中国古典文化产生了浓厚的兴趣。在中国学者王韬的帮助下,他开始翻译四书五经等儒家经典。经过15年的艰苦努力,终于完成了28卷本的《中国经典》(The Chinese Classics),由牛津克拉来登公司(Clarendon Press)出版发行。其英译的《易经》题为 The Book of Changes,收录在该书的第二卷,为世界上第一部权威的《易经》英译本。

理雅各的《易经》英译本在西方世界产生了很大的影响,为《易经》在西方的传播和研究奠定了学术基础。自此以后,特别是20世纪以来,《易经》的译本频频问世,使其在西方的传播和影响更加深入。在众多的《易经》译本中,德国汉学家卫礼贤(Richard Wilhelm,1873-1930)的德文译本最为上乘。卫礼贤1923年来华传教,后拜国学大师劳乃宣为师学习《易经》等中国典籍。他翻译的德文版《易经》出版后广受赞誉。20世纪40年代,美国波林根(Bollingen)基金会聘请德译英专家贝恩斯(Cary F. Baynes)将卫礼贤的《易经》德文译本转译为英语,1950年分两卷出版,书名译为 The I Ching or Book of Changes。

21世纪以来,又有一些《易经》译本陆续在西方问世。例如,2008年美国和英国先后出版了科姆·法乃尔(Kin Famell)翻译的《简版易经》(Simply I Ching)。在国内,《易经》的英文译本20世纪末也先后问世,填补了大陆学者翻译《易经》的空白。例如,上海外语教育出版社1993年出版了汪榕培、任秀桦合译的《英译易经》,青岛出版社1995年出版了罗志野的英译本《易经新译》。

▶▶ 三、翻译对比

- 原文一:

☰
☰

乾:元亨利贞

《彖》曰:大哉乾元,万物资始,乃统天。云行雨施,品物流形。大明始终,六位时成,时乘六龙以御天。乾道变化,各正性命,保合太和,乃利贞。首出庶物,万国咸宁。

《象》曰：天行健，君子以自强不息。

初九，潜龙勿用。

九二，见龙在田，利见大人。

九三，君子终日乾乾，夕惕若，厉无咎。

九四，或跃在渊，无咎。

九五，飞龙在天，利见大人。

上九，亢龙有悔。

<u>理雅各译文：</u>

Khien (represents) what is great and originating, penetrating, advantageous, correct and firm. [King Wen's utterances.]

In the first (or lowest) *nine*, undivided, (we see its subject as) the dragon lying hid (in the deep). It is not the time for active doing.

In the second *nine*, undivided, (we see its subject as) the dragon appearing in the field. It will be advantageous to meet with the great man.

In the third *nine*, undivided, (we see its subject as) the superior man active and vigilant all the day, and in the evening still careful and apprehensive. (The position is) dangerous, but there will be no mistake.

In the fourth *nine*, undivided, (we see its subject as the dragon looking) as if he were leaping up, but still in the deep. There will be no mistake.

In the fifth *nine*, undivided, (we see its subject as) the dragon on the wing in the sky. It will be advantageous to meet with the great man.

In the sixth (or topmost) *nine*, undivided, (we see its subject as) the dragon exceeding the proper limits. There will be occasion for repentance.

<u>汪榕培译文：</u>

Qian, the symbol of the heavens, symbolizes supremacy, success, potentiality and perseverance.

Initial Nine: The dragon is lying in wait and avoids taking any action because Yang is in the lower position.

Nine-Second: The dragon appears in the fields. It is time for the great man to emerge from obscurity.

Nine-Third：The gentleman strives hard all day long and is vigilant even at night. By so doing, he will be safe in times of danger.

Nine-Fourth：The dragon will either soar to the sky or remain in the deep. There is nothing to blame in either case.

Nine-Fifth：The dragon is flying in the sky. It is time for the great man to come to the fore.

Terminal Nine：The dragon has soared to the zenith. However, it will regret sooner or later.

- 原文二：

☷
☷

元亨，利牝马之贞。君子有攸往，先迷，后得主，利。西南得朋，东北丧朋。安贞吉。

初六，履霜，坚冰至。

六二，直方大，不习无不利。

六三，含章可贞，或从王事，无成有终。

六四，括囊，无咎无誉。

六五，黄裳，元吉。

上六，龙战于野，其血玄黄。

理雅各译文：

Khwan (represents) what is great and originating, penetrating, advantageous, correct and having the firmness of a mare. When the superior man (here intended) has to make any movement, if he take the initiative, he will go astray; if he follow, he will find his (proper) lord. The advantageousness will be seen in his getting friends in the south-west, and losing friends in the north-east. If he rest in correctness and firmness, there will be good fortune.

In the first *six*, divided, (we see its subject) treading on hoarfrost. The strong ice will come (by and by).

The second *six*, divided, (shows the attribute of) being straight, square, and great. (Its operation), without repeated efforts, will be in every respect advantageous.

The third *six*, divided, (shows its subject) keeping his excellence under restraint, but firmly maintaining it. If he should have occasion to engage in the king's service, though he will not claim the success (for himself), he will bring affairs to a good issue.

The fourth *six*, divided, (shows) the symbol of a sack tied up. There will be no ground for blame or for praise.

The fifth *six*, divided, (shows) the yellow lower garment. There will be great good fortune.

The sixth *six*, divided, (shows) dragons fighting in the wild. Their blood is purple and yellow.

汪榕培译文：

Kun, the symbol of the earth, predicates supremacy and success. There is potentiality in perseverance with submissiveness of a mare. When a gentleman goes anywhere, he will go astray if he takes the lead and he will have guidance if he follows behind. The potentiality lies in finding friends in the southwest and losing friends in the northeast. Peaceful perseverance is a sign of good omen.

Initial Six：When you tread on hoarfrost, solid ice will appear soon.

Six-Second：If you are fair and square, you will reap benefits without exertion.

Six-Third：Keep your brilliance concealed. You'd better persevere in doing this. If you have the chance to serve the king, you should claim no credit but do good service.

Six-Fourth：If you are reticent like a tied-up sack, you will receive neither blame nor praise.

Six-Fifth：You are dressed in yellow like an official. This is a sign of supreme omen.

Terminal Six：When the dragon comes to fight in the wilderness, blood runs black and yellow.

▶▶ 四、翻译赏析

正如卫礼贤所说的那样，对翻译中国古籍的人来说，没有一部比《易经》更难译的了。《易经》的对外翻译和介绍虽然已经有四百多年的历史了，但从目前国内外所出版的各种译本来看,无论是对西方的汉学家而言还是对中国的学者来说,西译《易经》仍然是一个巨大的挑战。尽管在这四百多年的传播和翻译过程中,出现了不少值得肯定的、颇有影响的《易经》译本,但总体来看,基本上仍然是各弹各的调,各吹各的号。

　　翻译中存在的这些看似问题的现象,其实非常自然,毫不奇怪。《易经》是中国最古老的一部"无字天书"。伏羲画八卦的时候,汉字尚未出现,所以伏羲八卦——又称先天八卦——只有卦形而无卦辞,显然是"无字天书"。周文王演八卦——又称后天八卦——之后,卦辞才逐步出现,《易经》也开始由"无字天书"变为"有字天书"。直至孔子作易传,《易经》的思想才得以深刻的揭示和全面的彰显。由于《易经》文字古奥,表述朴直,思想玄秘,结构简约,寓意深远,其解读和诠释自古以来便如孔子所言,"仁者见仁,智者见智"。如今更是"庸者见庸,俗者见俗"。将其翻译成白话文亦颇为不易,更何况翻译成西方语言。

　　从现有的译本来看,中外译者们在翻译《易经》时,风格可谓各有千秋,方法可谓各具色彩,策略可谓各显神通。这是否值得肯定,似乎还有待于"君子终日乾乾"的考察。但对其深加研究,不仅是值得的,而且是必要的。对于任何文本的翻译,从不同的角度和要求进行推究和考察,瑕疵与不足其实都是不可避免的,无论译者多么努力与慎慎。《易经》的翻译尤其如此。因此,要想从现有的《易经》译本找出"使阅者所得之益,与观原文无异"(马建忠之语)的佳作,可谓"难于上青天"。但中西译者数百年来坚持不懈的努力虽然始终是"履霜"而望"坚冰",却是"进无咎也"。不但"无咎",而且"含章可贞"。虽然极少有人能在《易经》的翻译上"黄裳元吉",但"其道"却从未"穷也"。

　　由于语言、文化、思维和审美的差异,现有《易经》译本在诸多方面均有慎加探究之处。这其实也是"自然之道也"。比如坤卦卦辞有"西南得朋,东北丧朋"之说,上面所摘录的两则译文分别将其译作"The advantageousness will be seen in his getting friends in the south-west, and losing friends in the north-east"及"The potentiality lies in finding friends in the southwest and losing friends in the northeast"。译文与原文似乎丝丝相扣,颇为吻合。但从坤卦的基本精神来看,译文似乎还有待于进一步的深化。因为这里的"得朋"和"丧朋",其实是以出行为喻阐述属性之间的关系,故有其特殊的内涵。我们今天看到的《易经》据传是周文王所演。西周起源于陕西岐山,其都城镐京即今日之西安。周朝的本土在秦岭以北,西南方多山而背阴,东北方平坦而向阳,故西南为阴方,东北为阳方。坤卦属阴,西南方亦属阴,所以向西南方走,意味着坤阴趋向阴方,属于同类相聚,所以说"得朋"。东北方属阳,所以向东北走,意味着坤阴走向阳方,即朝属性相反的方向发展,所以说"丧朋"。从客观实际来看,以阴从阳其实是大好之事,只有这样阴阳才能得以合和。从坤卦的发展来说,以阴从阳就是坚持柔顺的坤道,也就是坚持了坤势的正道,当然是吉祥的。因此,对"得朋"与"丧朋"的翻译仅仅从字面解读显然失于表浅。

乾的基本精神是"元亨利贞"。乾代表天,天的本质是沛然刚健、运行不息的阳气,体现出元始(元)、亨通(亨)、和谐有利(利)、正固持久(贞)这四种特征。天之阳气是始生万物的本原,故称为"元";能使万物品类流布成形,无不亨通,故称为"亨";并能使物性和谐,各得其利,故称为"利";又能使万物正固持久地存在,故称为"贞"。总之,天之阳气是万物滋生之本,又制约、主宰着整个自然世界。天有开创万物并使之亨通、富利、正固的"功德",故元、亨、利、贞被称为乾之"四德"。

理雅各将乾的这"四德"译为"Khien (represents) what is great and originating, penetrating, advantageous, correct and firm. [King Wen's utterances.]"汪榕培将其译为"Qian, the symbol of the heavens, symbolizes supremacy, success, potentiality and perseverance."两则译文都在一定程度上揭示了元、亨、利、贞的基本内涵。从跨文化交流的角度来看,似乎还需要别加注解和发挥,方能较为完整地在译文中再现原文概念的精神实质。理雅各将"元"译作 great and originating,将"亨"译作 penetrating,将"利"译作 advantageous,将"贞"译作 correct and firm,其实就含有文内注解之意,只是还略嫌不足。比如将"亨"译作 penetrating 似乎和中文讲的"亨通"(to proceed smoothly, to develop prosperously)就不十分契合,"利"不仅仅指的是 advantageous,还含有 harmonious 之意。

坤的卦辞是"元亨,利牝马之贞。君子有攸往,先迷,后得主,利。西南得朋,东北丧朋。安贞吉"。

理雅各将其译为"Khwan (represents) what is great and originating, penetrating, advantageous, correct and having the firmness of a mare. When the superior man (here intended) has to make any movement, if he take the initiative, he will go astray; if he follow, he will find his (proper) lord. The advantageousness will be seen in his getting friends in the southwest, and losing friends in the north-east. If he rest in correctness and firmness, there will be good fortune."

汪榕培将其译为"Kun, the symbol of the earth, predicates supremacy and success. There is potentiality in perseverance with submissiveness of a mare. When a gentleman goes anywhere, he will go astray if he takes the lead and he will have guidance if he follows behind. The potentiality lies in finding friends in the southwest and losing friends in northeast. Peaceful perseverance is a sign of good omen."。

坤的卦辞中虽然也出现了"元亨"和"利贞",但和乾的卦辞中所说的元、亨、利、贞的寓意却不尽相同。坤阴配合乾阳,才能化生万物,创始万物,并使之生长、发展、亨通。所以坤阴也是元始而亨通的,这是与乾阳的相同之处。不同者,坤卦卦辞在"贞"字之前添上"牝马"二字加以限制,其寓意就有所不同了。雄马的本质是刚健自强,坚持刚健便是雄马的正道,是雄马之"贞";雌马的本质则是柔弱顺从,坚持柔顺便是雌马的正道,是雌马之"贞"。所以"坤"应像雌马那样坚持柔顺之正道。就是说,阳刚而阴柔,乾健而坤顺,所以坤须顺乾。

理雅各将坤卦中的元、亨、利、贞一如乾卦中的元、亨、利、贞译作"Khwan (represents) what is great and originating, penetrating, advantageous, correct and having the firmness of a mare.",而汪榕培的译文则考虑到了乾坤两卦中元、亨、利、贞的不同,所以将"贞"译作 submissiveness,是值得肯定的。

需要说明的是,《易经》言简意赅,寓意深刻。每一卦都有其主旨思想,并以爻位由下而上的顺序呈递进关系,其深奥哲理和思想都隐含在简洁而古奥的卦辞中。译者若只按照字面之意对其加以直译或简单的释译,则无法在译文中再现原文的主旨思想,更无法使读者从中感悟《易经》的精神实质。另外,《易经》中的"象"和"传"是引领读者攀援《易经》高峰的天梯,翻译时若将其加以省略,无疑是自迷其径。

▶▶ 五、课后练习

(一) 思考题

1. 为什么说《易经》是群经之首?
2. 《易经》是怎样形成的?
3. 何为"伏羲八卦"和"文王八卦"?

(二) 翻译题

1. 大哉乾元,万物资始,乃统天。云行雨施,品物流形。大明始终,六位时成,时乘六龙以御天。
2. 乾道变化,各正性命,保合太和,乃利贞。首出庶物,万国咸宁。

3. 至哉坤元,万物滋生,乃顺承天。坤厚载物,德合无疆。含弘光大,品物咸亨。牝马地类,行地无疆,柔顺利贞。

4. 君子攸行,先迷失道,后顺得常。西南得朋,乃与类行;东北丧朋,乃终有庆。安贞之吉,应地无疆。

5. 天行健,君子以自强不息;地势坤,君子以厚德载物。

参考读物

James Legge. *The I Ching or The Book Of Changes* [M]. New York:Dover Publications Inc. ,1963.

Cary F. Baynes. *The I Ching Or Book of Changes* [M]. Princeton:Princeton University Press,1977.

汪榕培,任秀桦. 易经英译[M]. 上海:上海外语教育出版社,1993.

罗志野. 易经新译[M]. 青岛:青岛出版社,1995.

第十课

《诗 经》

▶▶ 一、内容简介

《诗经》是我国最早的一部诗歌总集,原称《诗》或《诗三百》,成书大约在公元前 6 世纪。现今流传的《诗经》是鲁人毛亨、赵人毛苌作注的"毛诗"。

《诗经》全书收诗 305 篇,按音乐的风格和作品的内容分为风、雅、颂三大类。十五国风 160 篇绝大部分是民间乐歌,包括周南、召南、邶风、鄘风、卫风、王风、郑风、齐风、魏风、唐风、秦风、陈风、桧风、曹风、豳风。雅是朝廷正乐,分为大雅和小雅。小雅 74 篇主要为贵族、官吏的作品,多在西周晚期所作,也有东周的作品。大雅 31 篇全部是西周的作品,作者主要是上层贵族。颂是宗庙祭祀之乐,分为周颂、鲁颂和商颂。周颂 31 篇是周王朝宗庙祭祀和典礼仪式所用乐歌,作于西周初年,当出于史官、乐师之手。鲁颂 4 篇为春秋时期鲁国的颂歌和仪式乐歌。商颂 5 篇大约是殷商中后期的作品。

《诗经》中的作品内容非常广泛,深刻反映了殷周时期,尤其是西周初至春秋中叶社会生活的各个方面,当时的政治、经济、军事、文化以及世态人情、风俗习惯在其中都有形象的表现。

赋、比、兴是《诗经》的基本艺术创作手法。赋就是铺陈直叙,既可以叙事描写,也可以议论抒情,是一种基本的表现手法。比就是比方,以彼物比此物。兴是触物兴辞,诗人因客观事物的触发而吟咏歌唱,大多在诗歌的发端。

《诗经》中的作品最初主要用于典礼、讽谏和娱乐,是周代礼乐文化的重要组成部分,也是实行教化的重要工具。诸子百家在著述中常有称诗引诗的现象。孔子就很重视《诗》,他评论《诗》的思想内容说"诗三百,一言以蔽之,思无邪",并且以《诗》教授弟子,说"不学诗,无以言","小子何莫学夫诗?诗可以兴,可以观,可以群,可以怨,迩之事父,远之事君,多识鸟兽草木之名"。

▶▶ 二、翻译传播

最早翻译《诗经》的是法国耶稣会传教士金尼阁(Nicolas Trigult,1577 – 1628),他的拉丁译本《五经》于1626年在杭州印行,但很可能未传至欧洲。第一个在欧洲刊印的是法国传教士孙璋(Alexander de Lacharme,1695 – 1767)的译本,其翻译手稿可以追溯到大约1750年,但迟至1830年才由朱利斯·莫尔(Jules Mohl)编辑,德国斯图加特和蒂宾根(Stuttgartiae et Tubingae)出版社出版,题名为《孔子诗经》(Confucll Chi-King)。

《诗经》的第一个英语译本是理雅各1871年在香港出版的《诗经》全译本(*The She-King, or the Book of Poetry*),这是一个散体本,1876年他用韵体重译了《诗经》。1871年的散体本具有较为显著的学术特点,较准确。1876年的韵体本由于要照顾到诗歌的韵律,准确性有所欠缺。

1891年在英国出版了两个《诗经》韵体全译本。一个是阿连壁(Clement Allen)译本(*Book of Chinese Poetry*)。他的译文相当自由,如他常常将重复出现而缺少变化的诗句压缩在一个诗节内译出,而且还尽量避免直译诗中提及的名物,代之以通俗的名称或不译。从下面他所译的《关雎》一篇,我们即可体会他的这种翻译特点。另一个是詹宁斯(William Jennings)译本(*The Shi King: The Old "Poetry Classic" of the Chinese*)。他翻译之时大量参照了理雅各的散体译本,力求在诗行上与原诗行对应,尽量忠实于原文。他称自己的译文是"切近原作之译"(a close translation)。

King Wen's Epithalamium

Translated by Clement Allen

They sent me to gather the cresses, which lie
And sway on the stream, as it glances by,
That a fitting welcome we might provide
For our prince's modest and virtuous bride.
I heard, as I gathered the cress, from the ait
The mallard's endearing call to its mate;
And I said, as I heard it, "Oh may this prove

An omen of joy to our master's love!"
Long, long for his bride has the prince been yearning,
With such desire has his heart been burning,
That his thoughts by day and his dreams by night
Have had but her as his sole delight.
But a doubt tormented his anxious brain,
And sleep was banished by aching pain,
As tossing in fear and distress he lay
Till the long night watches had passed away.
And how he has won her, this lady fair,
With her modest mind and her gracious air.
Let our lutes and our music and feasting show
The love we to her and our master owe.

  1937年,因翻译中国诗歌而享誉世界的英国汉学家韦利(Arthur Waley)翻译出版《诗经》(*The Book of Songs*)。韦利译本根据诗歌的主题重新编排诗篇顺序,可称是一种文化研究型翻译。其翻译通篇不用韵,讲求忠实和准确。

  1950年,瑞典汉学家高本汉(Bernhard Karlgren)翻译的诗经(*The Book of Odes*)出版。他尽量采取直译法,目的是让学习汉学的学生了解"在中国文学文化历史上占有重要地位的这部宏大的诗集"。

  1954年,庞德(Ezra Pound)的译本(*The Classic Anthology Defined by Confucius*)由哈佛大学出版社出版。庞德对原文进行大量的改写和删节,是创造性翻译的典范。

  《诗经》在国内的翻译主要有:许渊冲的全译本《诗经》(*Book of Poetry*)以汉英对照的形式于1993年在湖南出版社出版;2008年"大中华文库"出版汪榕培翻译的《诗经》(*The Book of Poetry*)。这两个译本都比较注重体现原作的文学性,尤其是音韵美。另外,国内还有杨宪益和戴乃迭的节译本 *Selections from the Book of Songs*,主要选译了《国风》中的诗篇。

三、翻译对比

- 原文一：

关 雎

关关雎鸠,在河之洲。窈窕淑女,君子好逑。
参差荇菜,左右流之。窈窕淑女,寤寐求之。
求之不得,寤寐思服。悠哉悠哉,辗转反侧。
参差荇菜,左右采之。窈窕淑女,琴瑟友之。
参差荇菜,左右芼之。窈窕淑女,钟鼓乐之。

<u>理雅各译文：</u>

Kwan Ts'eu

Kwan-kwan go the ospreys,

On the islet in the river.

The modest, retiring, virtuous, young lady:—

For our prince a good mate she.

Here long, there short, is the duckweed,

To the left, to the right, borne about by the current.

The modest, retiring, virtuous, young lady:—

Waking and sleeping, he sought her.

He sought her and found her not,

And waking and sleeping he thought about her.

Long he thought; oh! long and anxiously;

On his side, on his back, he turned, and back again.

Here long, there short, is the duckweed;

On the left, on the right, we gather it.

The modest, retiring, virtuous, young lady:—

With lutes, small and large, let us give her friendly welcome.

Here long, there short, is the duckweed;

On the left, on the right, we cook and present it.

The modest, retiring, virtuous, young lady:—

With bells and drums let us show our delight in her.

韦利译文：

Fair, Fair, Cry the Ospreys

"Fair, fair," cry the ospreys

On the island in the river.

Lovely is this noble lady,

Fit bride for our lord.

In patches grows the water mallow;

To left and right one must seek it.

Shy was this noble lady;

Day and night he sought her.

Sought her and could not get her;

Day and night he grieved.

Long thoughts, oh, long unhappy thoughts,

Now on his back, now tossing on to his side.

In patches grows the water mallow;

To left and right one must gather it.

Shy is this noble lady;

With great zithern and little we hearten her.

In patches grows the water mallow;

To left and right one must choose it.

Shy is this noble lady;

With gongs and drums we will gladden her.

杨宪益译文：

Crying Ospreys

Merrily the ospreys cry,

On the islet in the stream.

Gentle and graceful is the girl,

A fit wife for the gentleman.

Short and long the floating water plants,

Left and right you may pluck them.

Gentle and graceful is the girl,

Awake he longs for her and in his dreams.

When the courtship has failed,

Awake he thinks of he and in his dreams.

Filled with sorrowful thoughts,

He tosses about unable to sleep.

Short and long the floating water plants,

Left and right you may gather them.

Gentle and graceful is the girl,

He'd like to wed her, the *qin* and *se* playing.

Short and long the floating water plants,

Left and right you may collect them.

Gentle and graceful is the girl,

He'd like to marry her, bells and drums beating.

叶维廉译文：

Kuan-kuan, the Ospreys

Kuan-Kuan, the ospreys.

On the river's isle.

Delicate, a good girl:

A gentleman's fit mate.

Long and short, duckweeds.

Fetch some—left and right.

Delicate, a good girl.

Waking, sleeping: seek her.

To seek her and possess not—

Waking, sleeping: think of her.

So distant, so deep;

Toss and turn in bed.

Long and short, duckweeds.

Pluck some—left and right

Delicate, a good girl:

With music to befriend her.

Long and short, duckweeds.

Pick some—left and right.

Delicate, a good girl:

With bells and drums to meet her.

- 原文二:

桃 夭

桃之夭夭,灼灼其华。之子于归,宜其室家。

桃之夭夭,有蕡其实。之子于归,宜其家室。

桃之夭夭,其叶蓁蓁。之子于归,宜其家人。

詹宁斯译文:

Bridal-Song (General)

Ho, graceful little peach-tree.

Brightly thy blossoms bloom!

Go, maiden, to thy husband;

Adorn his hall, his room.

Ho, graceful little peach-tree,

Thy fruit abundant fall!

Go, maiden, to thy husband;

Adorn his room, his hall.

Ho, graceful little peach-tree.

With foliage far and wide!

Go, maiden, to thy husband;

His household well to guide.

汪榕培译文：

The Beautiful Peach

The peach tree stands wayside,
With blossoms glowing pink.
I wish the pretty bride
Affluence in food and drink

The peach tree stands wayside,
With fruits hanging rife.
I wish the pretty bride
Abundant wealth in life.

The peach tree stands wayside,
With leaves thick and dense.
I wish the pretty bride
A pleasant home e'er hence.

- 原文三：

蒹 葭

蒹葭苍苍，白露为霜。所谓伊人，在水一方。溯洄从之，道阻且长；溯游从之，宛在水中央。

蒹葭萋萋，白露未晞。所谓伊人，在水之湄。溯洄从之，道阻且跻；溯游从之，宛在水中坻。

蒹葭采采，白露未已。所谓伊人，在水之涘。溯洄从之，道阻且右；溯游从之，宛在水中沚。

庞德译文：

Dark, dark be reed and rush,
The white dew turns to frost;
What manner of man is this?
Lost?
Gin I run up,
Gin I go down,

Upstream heavy, there he'd be

In mid water distantly.

Chill, chill be the reeds,

The white dew not yet dry;

What manner of man is he

Under the hanging bank?

Upstream heavily,

Gin I swim down,

On tufted isle

Distantly.

Ever falls dew on bright reeds.

What manner of thing is he

Who seems to be there on the margin

Upstream, to the West, at large?

Hard to go up, to swim, tho' he seem

There on the isle, amid-stream.

许渊冲译文：

Green, green the reed,

Dew and frost gleam.

Where's she I need?

Beyond the stream.

Upstream I go,

The way is long.

Downstream I go,

She's there among.

White, white the reed,

Dew not yet dried.

Where's she I need?

On the other side.

Upstream I go,

Hard is the way.

Downstream I go,

She's far away.

Bright, bright the reed,

Dew and frost blend.

Where's she I need?

At river's end.

Upstream I go,

The way does wind.

Downstream I go,

She's far behind.

四、翻译赏析

关于《关雎》的主旨，传统上将其解说为赞美"后妃之德"，而现代评论家多将其看做是一首恋歌，但也有将其看做是为庆贺新婚而唱的贺婚歌。由于有各种不同的理解，因此不同时代的译者也就见仁见智、各有偏重。就词语理解而言，由于对"淑女"、"君子"、"好逑"等词历来也是解释不一，因此译文也不尽相同。就诗歌语言艺术而言，叶维廉的译文很值得注意。他尽量减少了译者的介入，打破了英语文法的羁绊，采用罗列句式，贴近中国古典诗歌的创作手法，也很有美国现代诗的韵味。

《桃夭》是一首祝贺女子出嫁的诗。此诗首先以桃花喻女子之美，光彩照人，也比喻其芳龄正盛，正值婚嫁。再以桃树的枝繁叶茂和硕果累累祝福女子婚姻生活的幸福美满。詹宁斯的翻译在句式上采用带有命令的祈使句，没有译出祝福的意愿，而且译文也不像他说的那样紧扣原作，如最后一句"宜其家人"在原作中与之前两节的结尾句在句式上是一样的，但译文出现了变换。汪榕培借助 I wish 译出了原诗祝愿之意。就传情达意方面，詹宁斯也确如其所言，是比较忠实于原文的。

《蒹葭》表现对所思慕之人的追求和向往之情。至于所追求的是什么人，后人看法不一，或以为贤人，或以为朋友。今人多从情诗方面理解，与诗的情景较合。诗人渲染出一种凄切惆怅的情调，所追求之人近在身边，却无法靠近。两个译文都将原诗那种朦胧的意境译了出来,也别有一番神韵。庞德的翻译相对比较自由。例如,为了照顾诗的声韵美,他不顾"萋萋"之愿意,而将其译为 chill, chill,"以声象意"。许渊冲译文也可说是形美、声美、意美兼具。

五、课后练习

(一) 思考题

1. 关于《诗经》书名的翻译,众多译家中有的用 poetry 来译其中的"诗",有的用 songs, odes。你认为用哪个词比较好?为什么?
2. 试述你对《诗经》"六义"的理解。
3. 试对比评析《关雎》的四个英译文。

(二) 翻译题

1. 静女其姝,俟我于城隅。爱而不见,搔首踟蹰。
静女其娈,贻我彤管。彤管有炜,说怿女美。
自牧归荑,洵美且异。匪女之为美,美人之贻。
2. 昔我往矣,杨柳依依。今我来思,雨雪霏霏。行道迟迟,载渴载饥。我心伤悲,莫知我哀!
3. 迢迢牵牛星,皎皎河汉女。纤纤擢素手,札札弄机杼。终日不成章,泣涕零如雨。河汉清且浅,相去复几许。盈盈一水间,脉脉不得语。

参考读物

Jennings, William. Trans. *The Shi King: The Old " Poetry Classic" of the Chinese*, *a Close Metrical Translation with Annotations*［M］. London：Routledge, 1891.

Legge, James. Trans. *The Chinese Classics*, Vol. IV, *The She-King, or the Book of Poetry*［M］. Hong Kong：Lane Crawford, 1871.

Minford, John & Joseph S. M. Lau. *Classical Chinese Literature：An Anthology of Translations*, Volume I ［M］. New York：Columbia University Press, Hong Kong：The Chinese University Press.

Waley, Arthur. Trans. *The Book of Songs*［M］. London：Allen & Unwin, 1937.

Yang, Gladys & Yang Xianyi. Trans. *Selections from the " Book of Songs "* [M]. Beijing：Foreign Languages Press, 1983.

海岸. 中西诗歌翻译百年论集[M]. 上海：上海外语教育出版社,2007.

李玉良.《诗经》英译研究[M]. 济南：齐鲁书社, 2007.

吕叔湘. 中诗英译比录[M]. 北京：中华书局,2002.

汪榕培. 诗经(大中华文库汉英对照)[M]. 长沙：湖南人民出版社,2008.

许渊冲. 诗经(汉英对照)[M]. 长沙：湖南出版社,1993.

第十一课

《史 记》

▶▶ 一、内容简介

《史记》是司马迁撰写的中国第一部纪传体通史,记载了上自上古传说中的黄帝时代下至汉武帝初年的三千余年的历史。

司马迁(前145—约前87),字子长,夏阳(今陕西韩城)人,其父司马谈是一位渊博的学者。少年时期的司马迁曾随就任太史令的父亲迁居长安,先后师从董仲舒学习《春秋》,师从孔安国学习《尚书》。青年时代的他又曾几次漫游,行迹几乎遍及全国。这都为后来《史记》的写作奠定了坚实的基础。天汉二年(前99),李陵出击匈奴,兵败投降,汉武帝大怒。司马迁为李陵辩护,触怒武帝,惨遭腐刑。他忍辱含垢"隐忍苟活",秉承先父遗志,在历史著述中实现人生最高价值,完成了"史家之绝唱,无韵之《离骚》"的空前巨著——《史记》。

全书共130卷,52万余字,由本纪、表、书、世家、列传五部分组成。"本纪"是用编年方式叙述历代君主的政绩,为全书之纲;"表"是用表格形式列出每个历史时期的重大事件;"书"是天文、历法、水利等专门事项的记载;"世家"是世袭家族的人物传记;"列传"是本纪、世家以外的各类人物传记。这几种体例互为补充,构成了丰富完整的历史体系。这种以人为本位的纪传体不同于前代的编年体和国别体,对中国史书体例产生了极为深远的影响。

《史记》具有极高的史学和文学成就,并非单纯的历史记录。在《报任安书》中,司马迁指出自己的著述目标是"凡百三十篇,亦欲以究天人之际,通古今之变,成一家之言",这些都淋漓尽致地从书中体现出来。《史记》以"实录"著称,司马迁不虚饰隐讳,同时他又有极高超的叙事艺术,常常营造出高潮迭起、扣人心弦的历史场景和丰满立体的人物形象。日本学者斋藤正谦曾评论道:"读一部《史记》,如直接当事人,亲睹其事,亲闻其语,使人乍喜乍愕,乍惧乍泣,不能自止。"受特殊时代和自身残酷命运的影响,司马迁对历史和人生有深刻的思考,他的《史记》是一部批判性而非歌颂性的史著,书中充满浓郁的悲剧气氛,历史人物有着强烈的传奇色彩。

二、翻译传播

西方对《史记》的翻译研究已有百余年的历史。19世纪中期,奥地利汉学家菲茨迈耶(August Pfizmaier, 1808 – 1887)将《史记》24卷译成德文,陆续发表在《维也纳科学院会议报告》上。法国对《史记》的译介始于19世纪晚期,由著名汉学家沙畹(Edouard Chavannes, 1865 – 1918)译注,共完成52卷。19世纪末,赫伯特·艾伦(H. J. Allen)曾尝试英译《史记》,并在《皇家亚洲文会会刊》上零散发表节选译文。

对《史记》英译本作出重要贡献的当数美国汉学家华兹生,他从20世纪50年代起就开始《史记》的翻译和研究工作。1958年,纽约哥伦比亚大学出版社出版了他的博士论文 *Ssu-ma Ch'ien: Grand Historian of China*(《司马迁:中国伟大的历史学家》);1961年,哥伦比亚大学出版社出版了他译的《史记》(*Records of the Grand Historian of China*),选材集中于汉朝的人物传记。目前,华兹生已翻译《史记》130卷中的80卷,是已经出版的最为完整的英译本。王际真是华兹生在哥大读书时所师从的教授,他出版过不少优秀的中国古典和现代文学的英文译著,主张译文不仅要语义准确,还应行文流畅、赏心悦目。在其影响下,华译《史记》亦注重传递原著的文学内涵,具有很强的可读性。而《史记》的另一位重要的英译者倪豪士(William H. Nienhauser, Jr., 1943 –)正是通过华译本对这部史著产生兴趣的。

倪豪士于1965年进入印第安纳大学东亚语言文学系,专修中国文学,师从旅美作家、学者柳无忌,研究唐代文学。从1989年起,他开始专注于对《史记》的研究,并与郑再发、魏伯特(Robert Reynolds)、吕宗力等组成翻译团体,从1991年起开始翻译《史记》。他们意识到《史记》应该被完整阅读、完整译介,应该译出一种忠实的、具有详细注解并尽可能具有文学性和流畅性的全译本。到目前为止,这一团队已先后出版了《史记·汉以前的本纪》(*The Grand Scribe's Records*; Vol. 1 *The Basic Annals of Pre-Han China*)(1994)等五卷译作。其译本保留了《史记》原有排列顺序,内容包括序言、使用说明、纪年说明、度量衡对照表、缩写表、译文几部分，译文附有详尽的学术考证、文化背景注释、词汇对照表等，文后还列有相关西文和日文译本书目及该卷的中外研究成果。该译本被誉为是西方最完备、最富有学术价值的《史记》译本。

此外，还有杨宪益和戴乃迭的节选本 Selection from Records of the Historian，1979 年 1 月由外文出版社出版。

三、翻译对比

- 原文一：

太子及宾客知其事者，皆白衣冠以送之。至易水之上，既祖，取道，高渐离击筑，荆轲和而歌，为变徵之声，士皆垂泪涕泣。又前而歌曰："风萧萧兮易水寒，壮士一去兮不复还。"复为羽声慷慨，士皆瞋目，发尽上指冠。于是荆轲就车而去，终已不顾。(《史记·刺客列传》)

华兹生译文：

Then he set out. The crown prince and all his associates who knew what was happening put on white robes and caps of mourning to see the party off, accompanying them as far as the Yi River. After they had sacrificed to the god of the road and chosen their route, Gao Jianli struck up his lute and Jing Ke joined in with a song in the mournful *bianzhi* mode. Tears streamed from the eyes of the company. Jing Ke came forward and sang this song:

Winds cry *xiao xiao*,

Yi waters are cold.

Brave men, once gone,

Never come back again.

Shifting to the *yu* mode with its martial air, Jing Ke sang once more; this time the eyes of the men flashed with anger and their hair bristled beneath their caps. Then he mounted his carriage and set off, never once looking back. (*Jing Ke, Assassin*)

杨宪益、戴乃迭译文：

So he set out. The prince and those who knew of the plan, dressed in white mourning clothes, escorted him to the River Yi where they sacrificed to the god of roads before he began his journey. Gao Jianli played the guitar and Jing Ke sang a plaintive air which moved all who heard it into tears. Then he stepped forward and chanted:

The wind is wailing, cold the River Yi,

And a hero sets forth, never to return.

After this he sang a stirring, martial air, which made their eyes bulge with anger and their hair stand on end. Then he mounted his carriage and drove off without further ado. (*The Assassins*)

- 原文二：

秦王谓轲曰："取舞阳所持地图。"轲既取图奏之，秦王发图，图穷而匕首见。因左手把秦王之袖，而右手持匕首揕之。未至身，秦王惊，自引而起，袖绝。拔剑，剑长，操其室。时惶急，剑坚，故不可立拔。荆轲逐秦王，秦王环柱而走。群臣皆愕，卒起不意，尽失其度。……秦王方环柱走，卒惶急不知所为，左右乃曰："王负剑。"负剑，遂拔，以击荆轲，断其左股。荆轲废，乃引其匕首以擿秦王，不中，中铜柱。秦王复击轲，轲被八创。轲自知事不就，倚柱而笑，箕踞以骂曰："事所以不成者，以欲生劫之，必得约契以报太子也。"于是左右既前杀轲，秦王不怡者良久。(《史记·刺客列传》)

华兹生译文：

"Bring the map he is carrying!" said the king to Jing Ke, who took the map container from Qin Wuyang and presented it to the king. The king opened the container, and when he had removed the map, the dagger appeared. At that moment Jing Ke seized the king's sleeve with his left hand, while with his right he snatched up the dagger and held it pointed at the king's breast, but he did not stab him. The king jerked back in alarm and leaped from his seat, tearing the sleeve off his robe. He tried to draw his sword, but it was long and clung to the scabbard and, since it hung vertically at his side, he could not, in his haste, manage to get it out.

Jing Ke ran after the king, who dashed around the pillar of the throne room. All the courtiers, utterly dumbfounded by so unexpected an occurrence, milled about in disorder.

… The king continued to circle the pillar, unable in his confusion to think of anything else to do. "Push the scabbard around behind you!" shouted the king's attendants, and, when he did this, he was at last able to draw his sword and strike at Jing Ke, slashing him across the left thigh. Jing Ke, staggering to the ground, raised the dagger and hurled it at the king, but it missed and struck the bronze pillar. The king attacked Jing Ke again.

Jing Ke, wounded now in eight places, realized that his attempt had failed. Leaning against the pillar, his legs sprawled before him, he began to laugh and curse the king. "I failed because I tried to threaten you without actually killing you and exact the promise that I could take back to the crown prince!" As he spoke, the king's attendants rushed forward to finish him off.

It was a long time before the king regained his composure. (*Jing Ke*, *Assassin*)

杨宪益、戴乃迭译文：

The king bade Jing Ke hand him the map which Qin Wuyang was holding, and he unrolled it to reveal the dagger. Jing Ke seized the king's sleeve with his left hand, snatching up the dagger to stab him with his right. Before he could strike, however, the king leapt up in alarm and his sleeve tore off. He tried to draw his long sword but it stuck in the scabbard, and in his panic he could not pull it out. The king fled behind a pillar with Jing Ke in hot pursuit, while the ministers, taken by surprise, were thrown into confusion.

… Too terrified to know what to do, the king was running round the pillar when some attendants shouted: "Put the sword over your shoulder, Your Majesty!"

He did so and, drawing his sword, struck Jing Ke a blow that shattered his left leg. Unable to move, Jing Ke hurled his dagger at the king, but missed him and hit the bronze pillar instead. The king struck again and again, inflicting eight wounds. Then, knowing that all was up with him, Jing Ke squatted against the pillar with a scornful smile.

"I failed through trying to take you alive," he swore. "And because I was determined to force to agree to our prince's demands!"

At that, attendants ran forward and finished him off. The king brooded in silence for a while …(*The Assassins*)

- 原文三：

政姊荣闻人有刺杀韩相者，贼不得，国不知其名姓，暴其尸而县之千金，乃于邑曰："其是吾弟与？嗟乎，严仲子知吾弟！"立起，如韩，之市，而死者果政也，伏尸哭极哀，曰："是轵深井里所谓聂政者也。"市行者诸众人皆曰："此人暴虐吾国相，王县购其名姓千金，夫人不闻与？何敢来识之也？"荣应之曰："闻之。然政所以蒙污辱自弃于市贩之间者，为老母幸无恙，妾未嫁也。亲既以天年下世，妾已嫁夫，严仲子乃察举吾弟困污之中而交之，泽厚矣，可奈何！士固为知己者死，今乃以妾尚在之故，重自刑以绝从，妾其奈何畏殁身之诛，终灭贤弟之名！"大惊韩市人。乃大呼天者三，卒于邑悲哀而死政之旁。晋、楚、齐、卫闻之，皆曰："非独政能也，乃其姊亦烈女也。"（《史记·刺客列传》）

<u>华兹生译文：</u>

Meanwhile Nie Zheng's elder sister, Rong, heard that someone had stabbed and killed the prime minister of Han, but that the blame could not be fixed since no one knew the culprit's name. His corpse had been exposed in the marketplace with a reward of a thousand pieces of gold hanging above it, she was told. Filled with apprehension, she said, "Could it be my younger brother? Ah—Yan Zhongzi certainly knew what he was capable of!"

Then she set off at once and went to the marketplace of Han, where she found that the dead man was indeed Nie Zheng. Throwing herself down beside the corpse, she wept in profound sorrow, crying, "This man is called Nie Zheng from the village of Deep Well in Zhi!"

The people passing back and forth through the market all said to her, "This man had committed an act of violence and treachery against the prime minister of our state and our king has posted a reward of a thousand gold pieces for anyone who can discover his name—have you not heard? How dare you come here and admit that you were acquainted with him?"

Rong replied, "Yes, I have heard. But Zheng was willing to accept shame and disgrace, throwing away his future and making a living in the market place, because our mother was still in good health and I was not yet married. After our mother had ended her years and departed from the world, and I had found a husband, then Yan Zhongzi, recognizing my brother's worth, lifted him up from hardship and disgrace and became his friend, treating him with kindness and generosity. So there was nothing he could do. A gentleman will always be willing to die for someone who recognizes his true worth. And now, because I am still alive, he has inflicted this terrible mutilation upon himself so as to wipe out all trace of his identity. But how could I, out of fear that I might be put to death, allow so worthy a brother's name to be lost forever?"

Having astounded the people of the marketplace with these words, she cried three times in a loud voice to heaven and then died of grief and anguish by the dead man's side. When the inhabitants of Jin, Chu, Qi, and Wey heard of this, they all said, "Zheng was not the only able one—his sister too proved herself a woman of valor!" (*Nie Zheng*, *Man of Valor*)

杨宪益、戴乃迭译文:

Then Nie Zheng's sister Rong heard of Xia Gui's assassination and the large reward offered for the identification of his unknown assassin, whose corpse had been exposed. "Can this be my brother?" She sobbed. "Ah, how well Yan Sui understood him!"

She went to the market-place in Hann and found that it was indeed he. Falling on corpse she wept bitterly and cried, "This is Nie Zheng from Shenjing Village in Zhi!"

The people in the market warned her, "This man savagely murdered our chief minister and the king has offered a thousand gold pieces for his name. Did you not know this? Why do you come to identify him?"

"I knew this," she replied. "But he humbled himself to live as a tradesman in the market because our mother was living and I had no husband. After our mother died and I was married, Yan Sui raised him from his squalor to be his friend. How else could he repay Yan Sui's great kindness? A man should die for a friend who knows his worth. Because I was still alive, he mutilated himself to hide his identity. But how can I, for fear of death, let my noble brother perish unknown?"

This greatly astounded the people in the market. Having called aloud on heaven three times, she wailed in anguish and died beside his brother.

Word of this reached Jin, Chu, Qi and Wei, and everyone commented, "Not only was Nie Zheng able, his sister was a remarkable woman too." (*The Assassins*)

▶▶ 四、翻译赏析

"原文一"的"易水送别"是《史记》中的名段,也是"荆轲传"中最撼动人心的一幕。两个译本相比较来看,华兹生的译本用词画面感更强,如"击筑"用 struck up、"和而歌"译为 joined in with a song、"垂泪涕泣"用 tears streamed from the eyes,要比杨译本中的 played,sang 和 moved into tears 更具体生动,更有感染力。在句子结构上,杨译本使用长句较多,其中从句出现 7 次,而华译本中从句只出现 3 次。此段译文若长句过多会使原文所渲染的气氛有所削弱。最后一句"终已不顾",华兹生直译为 never once looking back，比杨译本意译为 without further ado（干脆痛快地离开）更能刻画荆轲的复杂心绪。

"原文二"描绘"荆轲刺秦"，二字、三字、四字短句交错出现，将危急惊险的刺杀场景表现得淋漓尽致。华兹生的译文比杨译本长，在于其用词更具体，描绘更细致入微。例如，"群臣皆愕，卒起不意，尽失其度"，华译本为"All the courtiers, utterly dumbfounded by so unexpected an occurrence, milled about in disorder."将群臣先呆若木鸡，继而仓皇失措、乱作一团的景象全部呈现出来。再如"断其左股"，华译本 slashing him across the left thigh 比杨译本 shattered his left leg 更具视觉冲击力。不过，"左右乃曰：'王负剑。'"一句，杨译本中译出了"Your Majesty!"，华译本略去，而这对于体现秦国森严的君臣等级关系是很有必要的。

"原文三"描绘的是"刺客列传"中一位名垂千古的女子聂荣（也有书上称其名为聂嫈），即聂政的姐姐。为报答严仲子的知遇之恩，聂政杀死韩国国相，而后担心连累亲人又自毁面容，暴尸街头。性格刚烈、重义轻生的聂荣不顾自身安危前去认尸，因悲伤过度，死于弟弟聂政身旁。总体说来，这两篇译文都较好地再现了原文的风貌。华译形象生动，注重细节。如原文"立起，如韩，之市"，节奏紧凑，果决利落，体现了聂荣的性格和心境，华译本为"Then she set off at once and went to the marketplace of Han"，再现了原文；华译本还注重对情景的渲染，如"市行者诸众人"被译为 The people passing back and forth through the market，令读者身临其境，而杨译本 The people in the market 较为简略。杨译本的简洁在对话上则显出优势，如"妾其奈何畏殁身之诛，终灭贤弟之名！"一句，华兹生译为"But how could I, out of fear that I might be put to death, allow so worthy a brother's name to be lost forever?"显得过于冗长，杨译本"But how can I, for fear of death, let my noble brother perish unknown?"则简洁有力。

▶▶ 五、课后练习

（一）思考题

1. 《史记》是怎样的一部典籍？
2. 为什么说《史记》是"无韵之《离骚》"？
3. 《史记》的文学性主要体现在哪些方面？在翻译时应该如何传达？

（二）翻译题

1. 黄帝者，少典之子，姓公孙，名曰轩辕。生而神灵，弱而能言，幼而徇齐，长而敦敏，成而聪明。轩辕之时，神农氏世衰。诸侯相侵伐，暴虐百姓，而神农氏弗能征。于是轩辕乃习用干戈，以征不享，诸侯咸来宾从。而蚩尤最为暴，莫能伐。炎帝欲侵陵诸侯，诸侯咸归轩辕。轩辕乃修德振兵，治五气，艺五种，抚万民，度四方，教熊罴貔貅貙虎，以与炎帝战于阪泉之野。三战然后得其志。蚩尤作乱，不用帝命，于是黄帝乃征师诸侯，与蚩尤战于涿鹿之野，遂擒杀蚩尤。而诸侯咸尊轩辕为天子，代神农氏，是为黄帝。（《史记·黄帝本纪》）

2. 太史公曰：诗有之："高山仰止，景行行止。"虽不能至，然心向往之。余读孔氏书，想见其为人。适鲁，观仲尼庙堂车服礼器，诸生以时习礼其家，余祗回留之不能去云。天下君王至于贤人众矣，当时则荣，没则已焉。孔子布衣，传十余世，学者宗之。自天子王侯，中国言六艺者折中于夫子，可谓至圣矣！（《史记·孔子世家》）

3. 陈胜者，阳城人也，字涉。吴广者，阳夏人也，字叔。陈涉少时，尝与人佣耕，辍耕之垄上，怅恨久之，曰："苟富贵，无相忘。"庸者笑而应曰："若为佣耕，何富贵也？"陈涉太息曰："嗟乎，燕雀安知鸿鹄之志哉！"（《史记·陈涉世家》）

4. 高祖为人，隆准而龙颜，美须髯，左股有七十二黑子。仁而爱人，喜施，意豁如也。常有大度，不事家人生产作业。及壮，试为吏，为泗水亭长，廷中吏无所不狎侮，好酒及色。常从王媪、武负贳酒，醉卧，武负、王媪见其上常有龙，怪之。高祖每酤留饮，酒雠数倍。及见怪，岁竟，此两家常折券弃责。高祖常繇咸阳，纵观，观秦皇帝，喟然太息曰："嗟乎，大丈夫当如此也！"（《史记·高祖本纪》）

5. 于是项王乃欲东渡乌江。乌江亭长舣船待，谓项王曰："江东虽小，地方千里，众数十万人，亦足王也。愿大王急渡。今独臣有船，汉军至，无以渡。"项王笑曰："天之亡我，我何渡为！且籍与江东子弟八千人渡江而西，今无一人还，纵江东父兄怜而王我，我何面目见之？纵彼不言，籍独不愧于心乎？"乃谓亭长曰："吾知公长者。吾骑此马五岁，所当无敌，尝一日行千里，不忍杀之，以赐公。"乃令骑皆下马步行，持短兵接战。独籍所杀汉军数百人。项王身亦被十余创，顾见汉骑司马吕马童，曰："若非吾故人乎？"马童面之，指王翳曰："此项王也。"项王乃曰："吾闻汉购我头千金，邑万户，吾为若德。"乃自刎而死。王翳取其头，余骑相蹂践争项王，相杀者数十人。（《史记·项羽本纪》）

参考读物

Nienhauser Jr., William H. & Robert Reynolds. Trans. *The Great Scribe's Records* [M]. Bloomington: Indiana University Press, 1994.

Waston, Burton. Trans. *Courtier and Commoner in Ancient China: Selections from the History of the Former Han* [M]. New York: Columbia University, 1974.

Waston, Burton. Trans. *Records of the Great Historian of China* [M]. New York: Columbia University, 1991.

李秀英.《史记》在西方:译介与研究[J]. 外语教学与研究,2006(4).

司马迁. 史记选[M]. 杨宪益、戴乃迭译. 北京:外文出版社,2000.

第十二课

唐诗宋词

▶▶ 一、内容简介

在中国文学史中,唐诗可谓是一颗璀璨的明珠。"床前明月光,疑是地上霜","慈母手中线,游子身上衣","红豆生南国,春来发几枝",这些令人耳熟能详的诗句皆出自于此。

唐朝是我国历史上国力最为强盛的朝代之一,丰富的物质条件、对自由的崇尚、思想学术的活跃为唐诗的创作提供了丰富的土壤。俗语说"熟读唐诗三百首,不会作诗也会吟",这充分说明了唐诗在中国影响之深远,它作为优质的文化遗产之一,被人们吟诵至今。

唐诗的基本形式主要为:五言古体诗、七言古体诗、五言绝句、七言绝句、五言律诗、七言律诗六种;四个创作阶段为:早唐、盛唐、中唐、晚唐。每个阶段都有其代表的诗人和作品,其中以盛唐时期题材最为广阔,流派最多,是唐诗最为绚烂辉煌的一个时代。各种诗派也是百家齐鸣、百花开放,犹如雨后春笋般令人眼花缭乱。其中既有描写山水田园风光、幽人隐士的山水田园派诗歌,又有描写战争场面、边塞风光,抒发保家卫国情感,向往民族和平的边塞派诗歌。浪漫主义诗人李白与现实主义诗人杜甫是这一时期的杰出代表。

与唐诗相映生辉的,便是宋词。词这一文学载体发端于南北朝,吸取了《诗经》、《楚辞》中的精华,形成于唐,兴盛于两宋。宋朝丰富的文化娱乐生活加快了词的发展,同时随着社会矛盾的激化,词人常用词来表达自己忧国忧民的思想。宋代许多政治家如范仲淹、王安石、司马光、苏轼等都是著名词人。

每首词都有词牌,或调名,如"水调歌头"、"念奴娇"。词按照长短规模可分为小令、中调、长调。创作风格则大致有豪放和婉约派两大派别。婉约派的词多描写儿女风情,情调柔美婉约,其代表人物有李煜、李清照、柳永等;而豪放派则多气势恢宏,创作视野较为广阔,寄托当时士大夫对时代、人生、社会等各方面的感悟和思考,其代表人物有苏轼、辛弃疾等。

▶▶ 二、翻译传播

据考证,西方最早系统进行唐诗英译工作的是18世纪英国汉学家詹尼斯(S. Jenyns),其遗作经后人整理,以《唐诗三百首选读》(Selections from the 300 Poems of the Tang Dynasty)之名于1940年出版,可惜在此之前,詹尼斯的译作并未取得多大反响。

唐诗英译的第一次高潮出现于19世纪末到20世纪初叶,一批西方译介者纷纷投身于此。其中,来华的英国传教士和外交官成为中坚力量。1898年,曾任英国驻华领事的赫本特·翟理斯(Herbert Giles)出版了《中国诗词》(Chinese Poetry in English Verse),开风气之先。其译诗采用韵体或格律体,追求词义和韵律的巧妙结合。

曾任英国驻广州领事馆官员的英国人威廉·弗莱彻(William J. Fletcher)分别于1918年和1919年出版了颇具分量的专著《英译唐诗选》(Gems of Chinese Verse)和《英译唐诗选续集》(More Gems of Chinese Poetry),两书合计译唐诗286首,其特点为英汉对照加注释,译诗通常保持原诗的形式与韵律(Fletcher,1918:i)。在美国,著名意象派诗人埃兹拉·庞德(Ezra Pound)于1915年出版了著名的《神州集》(Cathay),其中包含李白的长干行等多首唐诗。庞德的译作以美学为导向,文字简洁直观,灵活运用直译、意译与创造性翻译,充满着异域风情。继庞德之后,1921年,另一位美国意象派诗人艾米·洛威尔(Amy Lowell)与汉学家Florence Aysough共同推出了"松花笺"(Fir-Flower Tablets: Poems from the Chinese),以诗人的重要性为序,共译中国古代诗歌140余首,其中李白和杜甫的作品居首。其译文采用自由体和拆字法(spilt-up),包含大量注释,以帮助西方读者了解原诗中涉及的典故等。吕叔湘先生评价洛威尔的翻译为"以平实胜"(2002:13)。1923年,日本人小畑薰良(Shigeyoshi Obata)出版了《中国诗人李白》(The Works of Li Po, the Chinese Poet),成为第一部翻译李白个人诗集的作品。这一时期重要的唐诗译介者还包括曾任香港总督的戴维斯(Sir John Francis Davis)、汉学家庄延龄(Edward Harper Parke)、波乃耶(James Dyer Ball)等。他们的译本也许未臻完善,有些甚至褒贬不一,毁誉参半,但无可否认,都对唐诗在海外的传播奠定了坚实基础,起到了不可估量的重要作用。20 世纪 50 年代之后,唐诗英译之风在西方再度盛行,并延续至今。1956 年,英国人格瑞汉(A. C. Graham)出版了《晚唐诗歌》(*Poems of the Late Tang*),在英美等地颇受欢迎,至今仍在重印。新西兰诗人路易·艾黎(Rewi Alley)的作品《杜甫诗选》(*Tu Fu, Selected Poems*)于 1974 年面世,译文采用自由体,汉英对照。美国学者斯蒂芬·欧文(Stephen Owen)分别译有《孟郊、韩愈诗歌》(*The Poetry of Men Chiao and Han Yu*)(1976)、《初唐诗》(*The Poetry of the Early Tang*)(1978)、《盛唐诗》(*The Great Age of Chinese Poetry*)(1981)。1954 年,亚瑟·韦利(Arthur Waley)发表了《寒山诗二十七首》(*27 Poems by Han Shan*),译文采用自由体;伯顿·沃森(Burton Watson)的《唐代诗人寒山诗一百首》(*Cold Mountain: 100 Poems by the Tang Poet Han Shan*)1962 年在纽约出版。

当然,唐诗的翻译推广传播仅有国外译者的作品是远远不够的。早在 1929 年,曾任北洋编译局总办的江亢虎与美国诗人威特·宾纳(Witter Bynner)合作编译了《唐诗三百首:群玉山头》[*The Jade Mountain: A Chinese Anthology (Being 300 Poems of the T'ang Dynasty, 618-906)*],此书的译文采用散体,介于韵体与自由体之间,颇受好评。此后,著名学者林语堂、叶维廉等也从事过唐诗英译工作,并取得不俗成就。

改革开放以后,唐诗翻译作品如雨后春笋般蓬勃涌现。1980 年,吕叔湘的《中诗英译比录》问世,书中收录了许多国外学者英译的中国古典诗词,以供读者比较研究。许渊冲的唐诗英译作品包括《唐诗三百首新译》(1988)、《唐宋诗一百五十首》(1995)、《李白诗选》(2007)等,全部采用韵体。采用韵体翻译的作品还有徐忠杰的《唐诗二百首英译》(1992)和吴均陶的《唐诗三百首》(1997)、《杜甫诗一百七十首》(1985)等。采用自由体的作品则有翁显良的《古诗英译》(1985)和杨宪益、戴乃迭合译的《古诗苑汉英译丛——唐诗》(2001)等。

就宋词英译而言,西方学者较多选取苏轼、李清照的作品集,如美国哥伦比亚大学教授波顿·华兹生(Burton Watson)1965 年出版的《东坡居士轼书》(*Su Tung-p'o: Selections from a Sung Dynasty Poet*),该书收录了苏轼不同创作时期的诗词作品,其中词作品 7 首,并于 1994 年再版。

肯尼斯·雷克斯罗斯(Kenneth Rexroth),中文名王红公,为美国著名诗人兼翻译家。其与钟玲(Ling Chung)合译的《李清照诗词全集》(*Li Ching-chao: Complete Poems*)于 1979 年问世,当即成为李清照作品英译的经典之作,影响极大。1982 年,两人又合作推出了

《兰舟：中国女诗人诗选》(*The Orchid Boat: Women Poets of China*)，其中包含李清照、唐婉等7位女词人的作品。其他翻译李清照作品的译者还有詹姆斯·克莱尔(James Cryer)，其《李清照词选》(*Plum Blossom Poems of Li Ch'ing Chao*)翻译了55首李清照的词作。

此外，白润德(Daniel Bryant)于1982年出版了《南宋词人：冯延巳，李煜》(*Lyric Poets of the Southern T'ang: Feng Yen-ssu（903—960）and Li Yu（937—978）*)。Julie Landau 1994年编译的《春之外：宋词选集》(*Beyond Spring: Tz'u Poems of the Sung Dynasty*)翻译了除苏轼、李清照之外的李煜、欧阳修、辛弃疾等其他13位较为有影响力的词人作品，共158首。

国内学者的宋词译作包括徐忠杰的《词百首英译》(1986)，杨宪益、戴乃迭的《古诗苑汉英译丛——宋词》(2001)，许渊冲的《宋词三百首》(1993)、《唐宋词三百首》(2002)、《许译中国经典诗词：李煜词选》(2005)等。

三、翻译对比

- 原文一：

江　雪

（唐）柳宗元

千山鸟飞绝，

万径人踪灭。

孤舟蓑笠翁，

独钓寒江雪。

宾纳译文：

River-Snow

A hundred mountains and no bird,

A thousand paths without a footprint;

A little boat, a bamboo cloak,

An old man fishing in the cold river-snow.

华兹生译文：

River Snow

From a thousand hills, bird flights have vanished;

on ten thousand paths, human traces wiped out;

lone boat, an old man in straw cape and hat,

fishing alone in the cold river snow.

许渊冲(1984)译文：

Fishing in Snow

From hill to hill no bird in flight;

From path to path no man in sight.

A straw-cloak'd man in a boat, lo!

Fishing on river clad in snow.

- 原文二：

静夜思

(唐)李白

床前明月光，

疑是地上霜。

举头望明月，

低头思故乡。

翟理斯译文：

Night Thoughts

I wake, and moonbeams play around my bed,

Glittering like hoar-frost to my wandering eyes;

Up towards the glorious moon I raise my head,

Then lay me down—and thoughts of home arise.

弗莱彻译文：

The Moon Shines Everywhere

Seeing the Moon before my couch so bright,

I thought hoar frost had fallen from the night.

On her clear face I gaze with lifted eyes：

Then hide them full of Youth's sweet memories.

小畑薰良译文：

On a Quiet Night

I saw the moonlight before my couch,

And wondered if it were not the frost on the ground.

I raise my head and looked out on the mountain moon,

I bowed my head and thought of my far-off home.

许渊冲译文：

A Tranquil Night

Abed, I see a silver light,

I wonder if it's frost aground.

Looking up, I found the moon bright;

Bowing, in homesickness I'm drowned.

洛威尔译文：

Night Thoughts

In front of my bed the moonlight is very bright,

I wonder if that can be frost on the floor?

I lift up my head and look at the full moon, the dazzling moon.

I drop my head, and think of the home of old days.

- 原文三：

声声慢

（宋）李清照

寻寻觅觅，冷冷清清，凄凄惨惨戚戚。

乍暖还寒时候，最难将息。

三杯两盏淡酒，怎敌他，晚来风急？

雁过也，正伤心，却是旧时相识。

满地黄花堆积，憔悴损，而今有谁堪摘？

守着窗儿独自，怎生得黑？

梧桐更兼细雨，到黄昏，点点滴滴。

这次第，怎一个愁字了得！

林语堂译文：

Forlorn

So dim, so dark,

So dense, so dull,

So damp, so dank,

So dead!

The weather, now warm, now cold,

Makes it harder

Than ever to forget!

How can a few cups of thin wine

Bring warmth against

The chilly winds of sunset?

I recognize the geese flying overhead:

My old friends,

Bring not the old memories back!

Let Fallen flowers lie where they fall.

To what purpose

And for whom should I decorate?

By the window shut,

Guarding it along,

To see the sky has turned so black!

And the drizzle on the kola nut

Keeps on droning:

Pit-a-pat, pit-a-pat!

Is this the kind of mood and moment

To be expressed

By one word "sad?"

许渊冲译文：

Autumn Thoughts—To the Tune of Slow, Slow Tune

I look for what I miss;

I know not what it is.

I feel so sad, so drear,

So lonely, without cheer.

How hard is it

To keep me fit

In this lingering cold!

Hardly warmed up

By cup on cup

Of wine so dry,

O how could I

Endure at dust the drift

Of wind so swift?

It breaks my heart, alas!

To see the wild geese pass,

For they are my acquaintances of old.

The ground is covered with yellow flowers,

Faded and fallen in showers.

Who will pick them up now?

Sitting alone at the window, how

Could I but quicken

The pace of darkness that won't thicken?

On plane's broad leaves a fine rain drizzles

As twilight grizzles.

O what can I do with a grief

Beyond belief?

雷克斯罗斯、钟玲译文：

A WEARY SONG TO A SLOW SAD TUNE

Search. Search. Seek. Seek.

Cold. Cold. Clear. Clear.

Sorrow. Sorrow. Pain. Pain.

Hot flashes. Sudden chills.

Stabbing pains. Slow agonies.

I can find no peace.

I drink two cups, then three bowls,

Of clear wine until I can't

Stand up against a gust of wind.

Wild geese fly over head.

They wrench my heart.

They were our friends in the old days.

Gold chrysanthemums litter

The ground, pile up, faded, dead.

This season I could not bear

To pick them. All alone,

Motionless at my window,

I watch the gathering shadows.

Fine rain sifts through the wu-t'ung trees,

And drips, drop by drop, through the dusk.

What can I ever do now?

How can I drive off this word—

Hopelessness?

▶▶▶ 四、翻译赏析

一般文体翻译不易，诗词翻译更难。英国诗人雪莱曾说过，"译诗是徒劳无益的"。

美国诗人弗洛斯特认为,"诗就是在翻译中丧失的东西(Poem is what get lost in translation)"。故有"诗歌不可译"的说法。

从国内外的翻译实践来看,诗词确实不易译,但未必不可译。刘重德教授就曾指出诗可译,但难译。困难当前,如何迎难而上,攻坚克难?许多翻译前辈的宝贵经验可供借鉴。闻一多认为,在诗歌翻译中要注重"气势的翻译、音节的仿佛、保持原作的字数字序"。刘重德教授曾言,"译诗不可满足于达意。力求传神,首先力求保持原诗的意义和意境,其次,使诗具有一定的诗的形式和一定的韵律、节奏"。许渊冲教授在《毛主席诗词四十二首》序言中首次提出了著名的诗歌翻译"三美"原则,即"译诗不但要传达原诗的意美,还要尽可能传达它的音美和形美"。其中,意美指译诗要传达原诗的意境内涵,这也是诗歌翻译的核心要素;音美指译诗的格律及韵式要尽量与原诗相对应;形美指译诗在诗句长短和对仗工整方面要尽量和原诗相似。众所周知,唐诗音韵优美,结构工整,内涵隽永,做到了音、形、义三者的和谐统一。因此,在唐诗翻译中,如能遵循如上原则,通过对遣词、用韵、意境以及内涵的翻译达到形神兼似,即可基本做到"以诗译诗",达到较好的诗词翻译效果。翻译宋词作品也可遵循类似的原则。

《江雪》是柳宗元五言绝句中的代表作,历来为世人所传诵。其言简而意丰,作者用短短 20 字便勾勒出一幅意境开阔、绝美寂静又蕴涵深刻的山水画面,并借此抒发自己政治生涯的失意与苦闷。与此同时,诗压仄韵,使得全诗抑扬顿挫,富于节奏感和音律美。

许译将标题译为 Fishing in Snow,更注重对原诗内容重点的呈现,而宾纳和华兹生的译法在意象传达上与原诗更为贴近。

对前两句"千山鸟飞绝,万径人踪灭"的处理,三译本大不相同,也体现了英汉两种语言的差异。汉语倾向于模糊,而英语倾向于精确,此处"千"和"万"皆为虚指,强调"山"、"径"之多。因此,在翻译时要注意避"实"就"虚"。宾纳和华兹生对此都偏向于采用直译的方法,相对而言,由于英语中 hundred 和 thousand 偶尔也可表示虚指和夸张,宾纳的译法显得更胜一筹,而华兹生的译法就略有生搬硬套之嫌了。许译此处采用意译 From hill to hill 和 From path to path,创造性地兼顾了原诗的诗意和内涵,贴切而传神。而"鸟飞绝,人踪灭"分别译为 no bird in flight 和 no man in sight,准确地传递了原文的意境内涵,且符合英语表达习惯,可谓佳译。

对后两句中"孤舟蓑笠翁,独钓寒江雪"的翻译,许译和华兹生译较为贴切,而宾纳将之译为"A little boat, a bamboo cloak, An old man fishing in the cold river-snow.",人为地

将"蓑笠"和"翁"两个意象割裂开来，可能让读者误以为老翁并未穿着蓑笠，与常识及原意不符。许译中用 river clad in snow 来对应"寒江雪"，将原诗中的苍凉感表现得淋漓尽致，相形之下，宾纳和华兹生的译法 the cold river-snow 和 the cold river snow 则略显平淡无奇。

用韵方面，许译采用 aabb 的韵式，且第三行中 lo 还与行内 cloak 与 boat 押内韵，实属难能可贵，堪称神来之笔，且译诗与原诗每行字数基本相等，音节数基本相同，与原诗对仗工整，译文简练，符合原文风格。唯一稍有遗憾的是，就语义而言，lo 的使用显得有些突兀，与原诗所描述的意境不甚相符。而宾纳更多地采用西方自由诗（free verse）的译法，使用了抑扬格四音步，并未过分追求押韵，而是更关注原诗意义和内容的表达，通过简约地使用几个名词将原诗中的意象逐个鲜明呈现，其所创造的意境效果和原诗更为贴近。华兹生译文也大体如此。

整体来看，尽管译法各有不同，三个译本皆生动展现了原诗描绘的如画景象。相对而言，许译在表达了原诗含义的同时，合理兼顾了原诗的形式和音韵，略胜一筹。

《静夜思》是李白的代表作之一，明胡应麟在《诗薮·内编》中称之为"妙绝古今"，数千年来一直脍炙人口。全诗短短二十言，却意味深长、耐人寻味，引发中外众多学者纷纷进行翻译。

弗莱彻按照自己对原诗含义的理解，采用完全意译的方法，将原标题译为 The Moon Shines Everywhere，月光照耀各处与原意相去甚远，可谓误译。

翟理斯和洛威尔将"静夜思"译为 Night Thoughts，有意无意之间忽视了"静"，而侧重于原诗的核心思想"思"。

许译的 A Tranquil Night 在形式上与原诗的"静夜思"对仗最为贴近，刻画了诗歌的意境，然而与日本学者小烟薰良的翻译类似，皆未译出"思"，似稍有不足。

弗莱彻的译文押 aabb 韵，采用了英文诗歌中用得最多的抑扬格五音步，音律整齐优美，读起来抑扬顿挫。然而其译文虽然做到了形似，在神似上却与原文有点大相径庭，可谓过译（over-translation）。

许译押 abab 韵，采用抑扬格四音步，保持了原诗音韵优美的特点，朗朗上口。第一句中的 a pool of light 翻译颇为精妙传神，又与最后一句的 drowned 相呼应。相对而言，许译与原诗最为形似，简洁精练；内容上也忠实于原文，并尽力传达其言外之意，可谓形神皆似。

翟理斯的翻译也采用abab式的押韵方式。与原诗的简练风格不同，翟译略显冗长，比如在第一句和最后一句增译了 I wake 和 lay me down，而且 lay me down（躺下）也与原诗中"低头"相去甚远。

小畑薰良的译文在几个译本中唯一采用过去时态。其译文第三句没有拘泥于原诗中的"抬头"，而是翻译为 looked out on the mountain moon，有一定创造性及合理性。至于为何会看 mountain moon，据说在日本有《静夜思》另一善本，其中第三句为"举头望山月"。

洛威尔作为中国古典诗歌英译的开拓者之一，其译文侧重于忠于原诗，而欠缺了几分诗意。其独特之处在于，她将第三句中的"明月"译为了 the full moon, the dazzling moon。显然，洛威尔通晓中国文化，了解中国人讲究月圆倍思亲，月圆之刻，正是思乡之情最浓之时。而 the dazzling moon 显然让人晕眩，以至将月光疑为"地上霜"，此等译法虽出人意料，却也颇合情理。

《声声慢》是李清照晚年代表作之一。时值外敌入侵，她被迫流落江南，借此词抒发自己家破人亡、晚年孤苦无依的悲愁。全词不假雕饰，独具匠心，满纸呜咽，动人心弦。

从调名或词牌名"声声慢"的翻译来看，林语堂的译法最有创意。一般而言，词的调名与内容并无多大关联，因此林语堂将其译为 Forlorn（意为"被遗弃的，孤苦伶仃的"），成功地表现出原词伤感凄凉的基调。许渊冲将其译为 Slow, Slow Tune，雷钟版则为 A Slow Sad Tune，两种译文都较为准确地传达了调名的含义，可谓各有千秋、不分伯仲。另外雷钟版增译了 sad 和 a weary song，通过 weary 和 sad 两词的使用，较好地奠定了原词的意境。

李清照此词开端三句叠字"寻寻觅觅，冷冷清清，凄凄惨惨戚戚"历来为人所称道，不仅富于韵律美，而且将女词人晚年孀居之苦、丧夫之痛、亡国之恨展现得淋漓尽致。徐釚在《词苑丛谈》中赞之为"首句连下十四个叠字，真似大珠小珠落玉盘也"。当然，对其的翻译也最见功力。雷钟版将之翻译为"Search. Search. Seek. Seek. Cold. Cold. Clear. Clear. Sorrow. Sorrow. Pain. Pain."，模仿原词的叠字叠韵，工整对仗，然英字如此用法，或许些微失之于汉语叠字独有的美感。许译"I look for what I miss; I know not what it is. I feel so sad, so drear, so lonely, without cheer."乍看似乎过于直白，有失原词叠字叠韵之美，然而细品之下，却发现通过整句和双行押韵的使用，许译既将主人公的空虚寂寞愁惨凄厉的心态描绘得栩栩如生，又对应了原词的叠字叠韵。尤其值得一提的是，译文与原文在 miss 和觅,cheer 和"戚"之间,实现了音似音美。林译则使用了皆以 so 开头的七个双声词,dim, dark, dense, dull, damp, dank, dead 押头韵,与原作的叠字叠韵有异曲同工之妙,且译文所用十四个音节和原文相呼应,形美、意美兼具,惟"寻寻觅觅"之意未直接译出。

再来看"乍暖还寒时候,最难将息"。乍暖还寒,重点在寒,雷钟版对此翻译为"Hot flashes. Sudden chills. Stabbing pains. Slow agonies. I can find no peace.",有一定意义的转化,总体还算四平八稳,无功无过。许译"lingering cold!"可谓切中要害,深合原意。"最难将息"译为"How hard is it to keep me fit",虽有增译,却意韵俱佳。林译将"最难将息"译为"Makes it harder than ever to forget!",较好地展现了主人公萦绕心头、挥之不去的愁思。

"三杯两盏淡酒,怎敌他,晚来风急",此处"三"和"两"皆为虚指,雷钟版 I drink two cups, then three bowls 的译法略显生硬,有生搬硬套之嫌。许译 By cup on cup,将主人公借酒消愁愁更愁的无奈心态展现得淋漓尽致。林译 a few cups of thin wine 也算贴切。

对"雁过也,正伤心,却是旧时相识"的翻译,三个译本都较准确地描绘出原词的意境。相比较而言,许译通过两短句、一长句及韵脚的使用,更好地体现了形美与音美的结合。林译的增译"Bring not the old memories back!",到位传神,颇见功力。

在翻译"满地黄花堆积,憔悴损,而今有谁堪摘?"时,雷钟版通过意义转化,基本符合原诗的意境。许渊冲通过 faded 和 fallen,flowers 和 showers 的使用,既忠于人如黄花、憔悴不堪的原意,又实现了押韵,可谓上选。而林译在保持原意的基础上,通过头韵脚韵的使用,达到音意皆美,与许译旗鼓相当。

最后部分,林译使用的 pit-a-pat 可谓是亮点,不仅生动地描绘出雨打梧桐发出的噼里啪啦声,更暗合主人公无聊苦闷的心情,可谓神来之笔,令人拍案叫绝。许译则通过多义词 grizzle 的使用,既实现了和 drizzle 的押韵,又在表现"天色变灰"的同时,暗含"人悲"之意,可谓巧妙。雷钟译在相对成功表达原意的同时,无韵无调,相形之下,则稍逊一筹。

总的来看,所选的三个译本皆为上乘之作。许译和林译虽在遣词用句、传情达意上各有特点,但都行云流水,意、形、音俱美,不乏传神之笔,可谓各有千秋,不遑多让。雷克斯罗斯倡导在诗词翻译中采用创意英译的方法,基于译者对原诗词作品的理解,在译文中营造相应的诗意境界,即"以表达美感经验,将他们对中国诗的主观感受以优美的英文呈现出来为其目的"(钟铃,2003:34),相比较而言,忠实反映原文的意义信息则并非首要追求。雷克斯罗斯和钟玲合译的《声声慢》典型地体现了这一特点,译文采用自由体的形式,与原文相比有一定的意义转化,未与原文一一对应。但总体而言,还是较为成功营造出了原作空虚忧郁、无可奈何的意境。

▶▶ 五、课后练习

(一) 思考题

1. 唐诗中的常用韵有哪些?平声韵和仄韵的区别何在?
2. 谈谈你对许渊冲诗词翻译"三美"原则的理解和看法。
3. 对诗词翻译中常遇的典故如何处理?比如如何恰当翻译李商隐《锦瑟》中的"庄生晓梦迷蝴蝶,望帝春心托杜鹃"?

(二) 翻译题

1. 春眠不觉晓,处处闻啼鸟。夜来风雨声,花落知多少。(孟浩然,《春晓》)

2. 独怜幽草涧边生,上有黄鹂深树鸣。春潮带雨晚来急,野渡无人舟自横。(韦应物,《滁州西涧》)

3. 岱宗夫如何?齐鲁青未了。造化钟神秀,阴阳割昏晓。荡胸生层云,决眦入归鸟。会当凌绝顶,一览众山小。(杜甫,《望岳》)

4. 春花秋月何时了,往事知多少。小楼昨夜又东风,故国不堪回首月明中。　雕栏玉砌应犹在,只是朱颜改。问君能有几多愁,恰似一江春水向东流。(李煜,《虞美人》)

5. 明月几时有?把酒问青天。不知天上宫阙,今夕是何年。我欲乘风归去,又恐琼楼玉宇,高处不胜寒。起舞弄清影,何似在人间。　转朱阁,低绮户,照无眠。不应有恨,何事长向别时圆?人有悲欢离合,月有阴晴圆缺,此事古难全。但愿人长久,千里共婵娟。(苏轼,《水调歌头》)

参考读物

Graham, A. C. *Poems of the Late T'ang* [M]. Baltimore: Penguin Books, 1965.

Rexroth, Kenneth & Ling Chung. *Li Ching-chao: Complete Poems* [M]. New York: New Directions, 1979.

顾正阳. 古诗词曲英译文化探索[M]. 上海:上海大学出版社,2007.

黄立. 英语世界唐宋词研究[M]. 成都：四川大学出版社，2009.

李照国. 译海心悟——中国古典文化翻译别论[M]. 上海：上海中医药大学出版社，2007.

吕叔湘. 中诗英译比录[M]. 北京：中华书局，2002.

任治稷，余正. 从诗到诗：中国古诗词英译[M]. 北京：外语教学与研究出版社，2006.

王峰，马琰. 唐诗英译集注、比录、鉴评与索引[M]. 西安：陕西人民出版社，2011.

许渊冲. 翻译的艺术[M]. 北京：五洲传播出版社，2006.

许渊冲. 再创作与翻译风格[J]. 解放军外国语学院学报，1999(3).

杨宪益，戴乃迭. 古诗苑汉英译丛——唐诗[M]. 北京：外文出版社，2001.

《中国翻译》编辑部编. 诗词翻译的艺术[M]. 北京：中国对外翻译出版公司，1987.

钟玲. 美国诗与中国梦[M]. 桂林：广西师范大学出版社，2003.

卓振英. 汉诗英译论纲[M]. 杭州：浙江大学出版社，2011.

第十三课

《世说新语》

▶▶ 一、内容简介

《世说新语》是南朝刘宋宗室临川王刘义庆(403—444)编撰的一部笔记小说集,梁刘孝标注,是中国魏晋南北朝时期"志人小说"的代表作。原书为八卷,刘注后分为十卷,现存是宋晏殊删订旧本后成的三卷。全书按类书的形式编排,分为《德行》《言语》《政事》《文学》《方正》《雅量》等36篇,共1130则,主要记载东汉末至魏晋间名士贵族的旧闻轶事和玄言清谈,反映他们的生活情趣、精神风貌和思想状态。

从东汉末到魏晋,天下动乱,军阀混战,儒学式微。士大夫间兴起了精老庄、通周易,摒弃世务、崇尚清谈的玄学之风,此风从魏代何晏、王弼开始,愈演愈烈。清谈由东汉的"清议"发展而来,主要是以人物品鉴为主,一个人的容貌举止、言谈辞气、仪态风度、才情气质无一不是品评的依据,所谓"声名成毁,决于片言",士族名流的品评更是一言九鼎,有时甚至可以左右一个人的前途。《识鉴》《赏誉》《品藻》《容止》等篇都与此有关。例如,形容王羲之"飘如游云,矫若惊龙",形容嵇康"萧萧肃肃,爽朗清举",形容杜弘治"面如凝脂,眼如点漆,此神仙中人"。任情放旷是魏晋风度的另一面,《任诞》《伤逝》《栖逸》等篇就对蔑视礼法、自由放达、纵酒吟啸的名士作了描写。"圣人忘情,最下不及于情,然则情之所钟,正在我辈。"和"礼岂为我辈设也?"都是魏晋名士的自白或宣言。此书也被鲁迅先生称为"一部名士的教科书"。此外,书中还记录了士族骄奢残暴、吝啬刻薄或忿狷轻躁的一面,如《汰侈》《俭啬》《忿狷》等篇。

在玄学清谈中,士人常聚集论辩,由此培养了语言表达的机敏智慧和简洁隽永。《世说新语》语言简约传神,人物风貌活脱欲出。明代文艺评论家胡应麟曾赞曰:"读其语言,晋人面目气韵,恍惚生动,而简约玄澹,真致不穷。"鲁迅将其艺术特色概括为:"记言则玄远冷峻,记行则高简瑰奇。"现在许多广泛应用的成语如"卿卿我我"、"拾人牙慧"、"咄咄怪事"、"一往情深"等皆出自此书。

▶▶ 二、翻译传播

《世说新语》在西方世界的第一个译本是由贝莱佩尔(Bruno Belpaire)1974年翻译的法文译本。1976年,美国汉学家、明尼苏达大学东亚系教授马瑞志(Richard B. Mather,1913—)的英译本 *A New Account of Tales of the World* 问世。这是第一部也是迄今为止唯一一部完整的《世说新语》英译本。

马瑞志1913年生于中国河北保定,其父是清朝末年来华传教士。40年代他在加州大学攻读东方语言专业博士学位时,曾受业于著名白俄学者卜弼德(Peter A. Boodberg)教授和我国语言学家赵元任教授。50年代末期开始,马瑞志的学术重点由中国中古时代佛学转向《世说新语》,1976年明尼苏达大学出版了他历时近二十年潜心翻译的《世说新语》英译本。译本吸收了大量前人和同时代中、日学者的研究成果,对原文的理解与注释、史料的收集和筛选都做了细致的工作,受到学术界高度评价。全书由三大部分组成:前言、正文和附录。前言部分又分自序、引论和译者注,其中主要部分是长达十八页的引论《〈世说新语〉的世界》(The World of the Shi-shuo Hsin-yü);附录则包括人物传略、术语和官衔表、缩写、参考书目和索引五种。2002年密歇根大学出版社再版此书,2007年又被引进收录"大中华文库",由中华书局出版。

事实上,早在20世纪40年代,著名翻译家梁实秋就曾尝试英译《世说新语》。他在《读马译〈世说新语〉》一文中回忆自己曾于英文版《自由中国评论》杂志上试译《世说新语》,但"译了二三十段之后即知难而退,以为《世说》全部英译殆不可能"。总结起来,这本著作的翻译难点主要表现在:"文字简奥",史实典故多,人名异称,别号官衔容易混淆,"谈玄论道之语固常不易解,文字游戏之作更难移译"(梁实秋,2005:473)。遗憾的是,梁实秋先生的这些零散译稿后来也没有被收录他的文集。以下我们赏析马瑞志的译本中的部分精彩片段。

▶▶▶ 三、翻译对比

• 原文一：

嵇康身长七尺八寸，风姿特秀。见者叹曰："萧萧肃肃，爽朗清举。"或云："肃肃如松下风，高而徐引。"山公曰："嵇叔夜之为人也，岩岩若孤松之独立；其醉也，傀俄若玉山之将崩。"（《容止》）

译文：

Chi K'ang's body was seven feet, eight inches tall, and his manner and appearance conspicuously outstanding. Some who saw him sighed, saying, "Serene and sedate, fresh and transparent, pure and exalted!" Others would say, "Soughing like the wind beneath the pines, high and gently blowing."

Shao T'ao said, "As a person Chi K'ang is majestically towering, like a solitary pine tree standing alone. But when he is drunk he leans crazily like a jade mountain about to collapse."

• 原文二：

有人诣王太尉，遇安丰、大将军、丞相在坐。往别屋，见季胤、平子。还，语人曰："今日之行，触目见琳琅珠玉。"（《容止》）

译文：

Someone went to visit Grand Marshal Wang Yen. He happened to arrive when Wang Tun, Wang Jung, and Wang Tao were also present. Passing into another room, he saw Wang Yen's younger brothers, Wang Yu and Wang Ch'eng. Returning, he said to others, "On today's trip wherever I cast my eyes I saw tinkling and dazzling pearls and jade."

• 原文三：

王孝伯问王大："阮籍何如司马相如？"王大曰："阮籍胸中垒块，故须酒浇之。"（《任诞》）

译文：

Wang Kung once asked Wang Ch'en, "How could Juan Chi compare with Ssu-ma Hsing-ju?" Wang replied, "In Juan Chi's breast it was a rough and rugged terrain; that's why he needed wine to irrigate it." (The Free and Unrestrained)

第十三课 《世说新语》

- 原文四：

王蓝田性急。尝食鸡子，以箸刺之，不得，便大怒，举以掷地。鸡子于地圆转未止，仍下地以屐齿碾之，又不得。瞋甚，复于地取内口中，啮破即吐之。（《忿狷》）

译文：

Wang Shu was by nature extremely short-tempered. Once while he was attempting to eat a hard-boiled egg, he speared it with his chop-sticks, but failed to get hold of it. Immediately flying into a great rage, he picked it up and hurled it to the ground. The egg rolled around on the ground and had not yet come to rest when he got down on the ground and stamped on it with the cleats of his clogs, but again failed to get hold of it. Thoroughly infuriated, he once more picked it up from the ground and put it in his mouth. After biting it to pieces, he immediately spewed it out. (Anger and Irascibility)

- 原文五：

周处年少时，凶强侠气，为乡里所患。又义兴水中有蛟，山中有遭迹虎，并皆暴犯百姓。义兴人谓为"三横"，而处尤剧。或说处杀虎斩蛟，实冀三横唯余其一。处即刺杀虎，又入水击蛟。蛟或浮或没，行数十里，处与之俱。经三日三夜，乡里皆谓已死，更相庆。竟杀蛟而出，闻里人相庆，始知为人情所患，有自改意。乃入吴寻二陆。平原不在，正见清河，具以情告，并云"欲自修改，而年已蹉跎，终无所成。"清河曰："古人贵朝闻夕死，况君前途尚可。且人患志之不立，亦忧令名不彰邪？"处遂改励，终为忠臣孝子。（《自新》）

译文：

When Zhou Chu was young his cruel and violent knight-errantry was a source of distress to his fellow villagers. Furthermore, in the stream which flowed his native Yixing (in modern Jiangsu) there was a scaly dragon, and in the hills a roving tiger, both of which were terrorizing the local population. The people of Yixing called the three of them the "Three Scourges", but Zhou Chu was the most dreaded of them all. Someone suggested to Chu that he kill the tiger and behead the dragon, in reality hoping that the "Three Scourges" only one would be left.

Chu promptly stabbed the tiger to death and proceeded to enter the stream to attack the dragon. But the dragon, now afloat, now submerged, swam on for several tens of li, with Chu swimming beside it all the way. After a full three days and three nights, the villagers all assumed he was dead and were congratulating each other more than ever.

Finally, however, Chu killed the dragon and emerged from the water. It was only after he heard that the villagers were congratulating each other that he realized what a source of distress he had been to the feelings of others, and he made up his mind to reform himself.

Accordingly, from Wu Commandery (modern Suzhou) he sought out the two Lu brothers, Lu Ji and Lu Yun. Since Lu Ji was not at home at the time, he saw only Lu Yun. After reporting the situation to him in detail, Chu added, "I've wanted to reform my ways, but the years have already slipped by and until now I haven't accomplished it."

Yun said, "The man of antiquity honored the principle of 'Hearing the Way in the morning and dying content in the evening.' How much more promising is your future course! What's more, even though people are distressed that your ambition has not yet been established, why, indeed, should you worry that your good name will not someday become well known?"

Chu thereupon exerted all his energies in a new direction, and in the end he became a loyal minister and a filial son. (Self-Renewal)

▶▶ 四、翻译赏析

《世说新语》中有大量的双声叠韵词、拟声拟态词以及重叠词,如"温润恬和","温润"是叠韵词;"洛中铮铮冯惠卿","铮铮"是拟声拟态词;重叠词如"亭亭"、"察察"、"黯黯"、"谡谡"、"濯濯"、"萧萧肃肃"、"落落穆穆"等。这类词的运用使得文辞音节铿锵,有音乐之美,诗意盎然。马瑞志的译文在处理这些语词时也颇费苦心。有时用英语押头韵(alliteration)的方法来译,如"原文一"中的"萧萧肃肃"译为 Serene and sedate,《赏誉》一篇中"世目李元礼'谡谡如劲松下风'"译为 brisk and bracing like the wind beneath sturdy pines;有时甚至用中英相似的拟声词,如本段中的"肃肃如松下风"译为 Soughing like the wind beneath the pines,"肃肃"与 sough [sʌf] 同为风的拟声词,读来相近,可谓妙译。

"原文二"中的"琳琅"一词既指精美的玉石,又指玉石相击声。《楚辞》中有"抚长剑兮玉珥,璆锵鸣兮琳琅"之句,琳琅也泛指清脆美妙的声音。此段中"琳琅"译为 tinkling and dazzling 可谓声色俱佳、达意传神。

"原文三"中的"垒块",亦作"块垒",泛指郁积之物,比喻胸中郁结的愁闷或气愤。

此段中译文将"垒块"化译为 a rough and rugged terrain（崎岖不平之地），"浇"没有用 drown one's sorrows（借酒浇愁），而是自然而然地用 irrigate（灌溉），可谓合情合理，水到渠成。梁实秋曾评论马瑞志的译文"偶有神来之笔，达出会心之处，则尤难能可贵"（梁实秋，2005：476）。此段译文应可算作是"神来之笔"的例证之一。

鲁迅先生在《中国小说史略》中指出，志人小说"记人间事者已甚古，列御寇、韩非皆有录载，惟其所以录载者，列在用以喻道，韩在储以论政。若为赏心所作，则实萌芽于魏而盛大于晋。虽不免追随俗尚，或供揣摩，然要为远实用而近娱乐矣"。这里点出志人小说的目的，虽然有记录史实供人揣摩的考虑，但也有了很强的欣赏和娱乐的特点。"原文四"这段文字用吃鸡蛋来呈现王蓝田急性轻躁的性格特点，写得惟妙惟肖，令人忍俊不禁。英语译文也很好地表达出了这种幽默，所选的动词都体现出性急之人怒气冲冲，动作幅度大、速度快的特点：从 spear 开始就显得来势汹汹，flying into a great rage 之后的一系列动作 hurl, stamp, spew 无一不是如此，译文中 rolled around on the ground, with the cleats of his clogs 分别用了押尾韵和头韵手法，读来朗朗上口。

"原文五"写周处年少时纵情肆欲，为祸乡里，为了改过自新去找名人陆机、陆云，后浪子回头、洗心革面。译文简洁生动地将"凶强侠气"的少年周处呈现在读者面前，如"处即刺杀虎，又入水击蛟"译为"Chu promptly stabbed the tiger to death and proceeded to enter the stream to attack the dragon."利落明快，显出周处强悍好斗的性格；"蛟或浮或没，行数十里，处与之俱"译为"But the dragon, now afloat, now submerged, swam on for several tens of li, with Chu swimming beside it all the way"，将汉语的节奏一并译出，周处与蛟龙在水中周旋酣战的画面如在眼前。

五、课后练习

（一）思考题

1. 结合鲁迅《魏晋风度及文章与药及酒之关系》一文，思考魏晋风度的特点及成因。

2. 冯友兰先生把魏晋名士风度概括成八个字"玄心、洞见、妙赏、深情"，阅读《世说新语》，谈谈你对这八个字的理解。

3.《世说新语》的翻译难点主要体现在哪些方面？为什么？

（二）翻译题

1. 时人目王右军"飘如游云，矫若惊龙"。（《容止》）

2. 卫玠从豫章至下都，人闻其名，观者如堵墙。玠先有羸疾，体不堪劳，遂成病而死，时人谓看杀卫玠。(《容止》)

3. 王子猷尝暂寄人空宅住，便令种竹。或问："暂住何烦尔？"王啸咏良久，直指竹曰："何可一日无此君？"(《任诞》)

4. 王孝伯言："名士不必须奇才，但使常得无事，痛饮酒，熟读离骚，便可称名士。"(《任诞》)

5. 王子猷居山阴，夜大雪，眠觉，开室命酌酒，四望皎然。因起彷徨，咏左思招隐诗。忽忆戴安道。时戴在剡，即便夜乘小舟就之。经宿方至，造门不前而返。人问其故，王曰："吾本乘兴而行，兴尽而返，何必见戴？"(《任诞》)

参考读物

Mather, Richard B. Trans. *A New Account of Tales of the World* [M]. Minneapolis, MN: University of Minnesota Press, 1976.

Kao, Karl S. Y. Ed. *Classical Chinese Tales of the Supernatural and the Fantastic: Selections from the Third to the Tenth Century* [M]. Bloomington: Indiana University Press, 1985.

范子烨. 马瑞志博士的汉学研究[J]. 世界汉学, 2003(1).

梁实秋. 雅舍谈书[M]. 济南:山东画报出版社, 2006.

鲁迅. 中国小说史略[M]. 桂林:广西师范大学出版社, 2010.

马瑞志.《世说新语》法译本审查报告[J]. 读书, 2002(4).

杨勇. 世说新语校笺[M]. 北京:中华书局, 2006.

第十四课 《聊斋志异》

➤➤ 一、内容简介

　　志怪小说是中国古典小说形式之一,以记叙神异鬼怪传说为主,产生和流行于魏晋南北朝,相沿不衰,至唐人传奇发扬光大,清代蒲松龄的《聊斋志异》则达到顶峰。蒲松龄(1640—1715)字留仙,别号柳泉居士,山东淄川(今淄博)人,出身于没落世家,19岁应童子试,接连考取县、府、道试第一,补博士弟子员,名震一时。然其此后的科场经历却异常坎坷,直至71岁才成岁贡生。为生活所迫,在科场跋涉的数十年,蒲松龄主要靠做私塾教师糊口。大概从中年开始,他一边教书一边撰写《聊斋志异》。

　　《聊斋志异》,简称《聊斋》,俗名《鬼狐传》,全书共有短篇小说491篇(一说431篇)。书中的故事主要分为两类:一类是篇幅短小的奇闻异谈的记录;一类是真正意义上的小说,关于狐妖、鬼神、花精的故事。民间相传蒲松龄在路边摆设茶摊供路人享用,同时与之闲谈,搜罗各种异闻。而据作者在《聊斋自志》中所言,"喜人谈鬼,闻则命笔,遂以成编。久之,四方同人又以邮筒相寄,因而物以好聚,所积益夥"。《聊斋志异》尚未脱稿就在亲朋中传阅,竞相传抄,尤获同乡好友王士祯的激赏,他为全书题诗:"姑妄言之姑听之,豆棚瓜架雨如丝。料应厌作人间语,爱听秋坟鬼唱诗。"

　　蒲松龄自述其书:"集腋为裘,妄续幽冥之录;浮白载笔,仅成孤愤之书。""孤愤"二字可以看做这部著作的灵魂,承载了作者对现实和人生的悲愤抑郁之情,全书占主导地位的亦多为现实批判性作品,如《三生》、《司文郎》、《王子安》等篇写尽科考之路的苦楚辛酸,《席方平》、《促织》等篇淋漓尽致地揭露官场腐化、政治黑暗。然而,《聊斋》长久以来受读者青睐最主要的原因是其关于狐鬼花怪与人恋爱的故事,如《婴宁》、《聂小倩》、

《莲香》、《小谢》、《晚霞》、《青凤》、《葛巾》等名篇。书中女性超脱于现实社会的礼教束缚,能自由抒发内心情感,敢于追求自己所爱所想,她们或憨直顽皮,或温柔娇弱,或慧黠灵巧,或果敢侠义,形象极富生气,令人过目难忘。

《聊斋》结合了志怪和传奇两类文言小说的传统,既能建构奇幻迷离的情节,同时又能塑造写实生动的人物形象,语言简洁优雅。郭沫若先生曾赞其曰:"写鬼写妖高人一等,刺贪刺虐入骨三分。"

▶▶ 二、翻译传播

《聊斋志异》在英语世界的传播始于1842年,早期译介以在华传教士及外交官为主。目前发现的英文《聊斋》研究资料的最早记载是德籍传教士郭实腊(Karl Gützlaff)在《中国丛报》刊登的"Extraordinary Legends from Liao Chai",其中讲述了九个《聊斋》故事。美国汉学家、传教士卫三畏(Samuel Williams)1848年编著的 The Middle Kingdom 第一卷收录了《种梨》和《骂鸭》两篇英译文。

1880年,翟理斯(Herbert A. Giles)英译的两卷本 Strange Stories from a Chinese Studio 出版,共164篇,这是《聊斋》首个英译本,在英语世界影响甚大,被多次再版。1946年,纽约潘西恩图书公司(Pantheon Books Inc.)出版了由邝如丝(Rose Quong)翻译的 Chinese Ghost and Love Stories,共选译40篇。此后,Strange Stories from a Chinese Studio、Chinese Tales of the Supernatural 等小说集陆续选译《聊斋》。1981年,中国文学杂志社出版了由杨宪益和戴乃迭翻译的 Selected Tales of Liaozhai,共17篇。1989年,外文出版社出版了美国汉学家梅丹理(Denis C. Mair)和梅维恒(Victor H. Mair)翻译的 Strange Tales from Make-do Studio,其中选译51篇。2006年,著名汉学家闵福德(John Minford)历时14年,翻译出版了 Strange Tales from a Chinese Studio,该译本由英国企鹅出版社出版,选译了104个故事。

2007年,外文出版社出版了大中华文库之 Selections from Strange Tales from the Liaozhai Studio,共四卷,含216篇,是迄今为止选译《聊斋》篇目最多的版本。该书中文版采用张友鹤的点校本,英译主要采用黄友义、张庆年、张慈云、杨毅、梅丹理、梅维恒等人的译文。2008年,美国 Jain Publishing Company 出版了由宋贤德(Sidney L. Sondergard)博士翻译的 Strange Tales from Liaozhai 前两卷,含166篇。

《聊斋》虽尚未出现全译本,但从其被选译和节译的情况来看,在英语世界是颇受欢迎的,考虑到中国志怪小说与西方奇幻文学(fantasy literature)的共通之处,这亦是情理之中的事情。

三、翻译对比

- 原文一：

蹑足而窗窥之,见一狞鬼,面翠色,齿巉巉如锯。铺人皮于榻上,执彩笔而绘之;已而掷笔,举皮,如振衣状,披于身,遂化为女子。(《画皮》)

梅丹理、梅维恒译文：

He tiptoed to a window and peeped in to see a frightful demon with green face and jagged, saw-like teeth. It spread a human skin on the bed, and painted the skin with color-dipped brushes. That done, the demon threw the brushes aside, lifted the skin and shook wrinkles out as if it were a piece of clothing. The demon pulled the skin over its body and changed instantly into a young woman. (*Painted Skin*)

闵福德译文：

Creeping stealthily up to a window, he peeped through and saw the most hideous sight, a green-faced monster, a ghoul with great jagged teeth like a saw, leaning over a human pelt, the skin of an entire human body, spread on the bed—on *his* bed. The monster had a paintbrush on its hand and was in the process of touching up the skin in lifelike color. When the painting was done, it threw down the brush, lifted up the skin, shook it out like a cloak and wrapped itself in it— whereupon it was instantly transformed into his pretty young 'fugitive' friend. (*The Painted Skin*)

- 原文二：

母见其绰约可爱,始敢与言,曰:"小娘子惠顾吾儿,老身喜不可已。但生平止此儿,用承祧绪,不敢令有鬼偶。"女曰:"儿实无二心。泉下人既不见信于老母,请以兄事,依高堂,奉晨昏,如何？"母怜其诚,允之……女即入厨下,代母尸饔。入房穿榻,似熟居者。日暮母畏惧之,辞使归寝,不为设床褥。女窥知母意,即竟去。(《聂小倩》)

梅丹理、梅维恒译文：

Seeing how ethereal and lovely she was, the mother found the courage to speak to her: "I am delighted by the gracious favor you have shown my son, young lady, but I have only this one son to carry on the offering of ancestral sacrifices, and I dare not let him have ghost mate."

"Rest assured, there is no other aim in my heart. Since you, venerable mother, cannot give your trust to a person from the nether world, I beg leave to treat him as an elder brother. I will place myself in your hands and serve you day and night. May I?"

The mother, moved to pity by her earnestness, gave approval … Then the girl entered the kitchen and presided over preparation of meals in the mother's stead. She threaded her way in and out of the rooms and around the furniture like a long-time resident. At sundown, the mother, frightened by her presence, bid her goodnight without setting out a bed and covers. Seeing what the mother had in mind, the girl finally left the house. (*Nie Xiaoqian*)

<u>闵福德译文</u>：

Ning's mother had to admit to herself that she was very charming. "I am indeed delighted," she replied at last, "that you should be so attached to Ning. But he is my only son, the sole hope of our family. The continuation of our ancestral sacrifices depends on him. I cannot possibly have him marrying a ghost!"

"Truly I wish him no harm," replied the girl. "If you do not trust me, because I am a spirit from the Nether World, then let me serve him as a sister. That would allow me to wait upon you, morning and evening, as a daughter."

Ning's mother was moved by her obvious sincerity, and agreed to this unusual arrangement … Little Beauty took herself off to the kitchen and supervised the cooking in the old lady's stead, seeming to know her way around every room of the house as if it were her own home. At nightfall, Ning's mother began to feel afraid and sent Little Beauty off to sleep "somewhere else", pointedly not preparing a bed for her. Little Beauty understood her meaning and went outside …(*The Magic Sword and the Magic Bag*)

● 原文三：

逾岁，媪果亡。灵舆至殡宫，有女子缞绖临穴。众惊顾，忽而风激雷轰，继以急雨，转瞬已失所在。松柏新植多枯，至是皆活。福海稍长，辄思其母，忽自投入海，数日始还。龙宫以女子不得往，时掩户泣。一日昼暝，龙女急入，止之曰："儿自成家，哭泣何为？"乃赐八尺珊瑚一株，龙脑香一帖，明珠百粒，八宝嵌金合一双，为嫁资。生闻之突入，执手啜泣。俄顷，迅雷破屋，女已无矣。(《罗刹海市》)

第十四课 《聊斋志异》

梅丹理、梅维恒译文：

Sure enough, after a year passed, the old woman died. When the hearse reached the final resting place, a woman in hempen morning clothes stood before the tomb. Suddenly, as the mourners stared in surprise, a fierce wind began to blow and thunder rumbled. This was followed by heavy rain. In the blink of an eye she was gone. Many of the pines and catalpas had died from being transplanted, but after this they all came to life.

As Blessing-Sea grew a little older he thought often of his mother. One day he was seen threw himself into the sea, and he did not return until several days later. Dragon Palace, being a girl, could not go, and so she cried in her room day after day. One day the light of the sun dimmed; in an instant the dragon lord's daughter appeared and calmed her: "Someday you will have a family of your own. What good will crying do?" She gave her daughter a dowry consisting of an eight-foot tree of coral, a packet of borneol camphor, one hundred gleaming pearls and a pair of small gold boxes set with eight sorts of gems. Hearing her voice, the scholar burst into the room and took her by the hand, sobbing. In a moment a sharp clap of thunder shook the room, and she was gone. (*The Raksasas and the Ocean Bazaar*)

翟理斯译文：

The following year the old lady did die, and her coffin was borne to its last resting-place, when lo! There was the princess standing by the side of the grave. The lookers-on were much alarmed, but in a moment there was a flash of lightning followed by a clap of thunder and a squall of rain, and she was gone. It was then noticed that many of the young pine-trees which had died were one and all brought to life.

Subsequently, Fu-hai went in search of the mother for whom he pined so much, and after some days' absence returned. Lung-kung, being a girl, could not accompany him, but she mourned much in secret. One dark day her mother entered and bade her dry her eyes, saying, "My child, you must get married. Why these tears?" She then gave her a tree of coral eight feet in height, some Baroos camphor, one hundred valuable pearls, and two boxes inlaid with gold and precious stones, as her dowry. Ma having found out she was there, rushed in, and, seizing her hand, began to weep for joy, when suddenly a violent peal of thunder rent the building and the princess had vanished. (*The Lo-Ch'a Country and the Sea-market*)

▶▶ 四、翻译赏析

鲁迅先生在《中国小说史略》中评《聊斋志异》云："而以志怪，变幻之状，如在目前；又或易调改弦，别叙畸人异行，出于幻域，顿入人间；偶述琐闻，亦多简洁，故读者耳目，为之一新。"（鲁迅，2010:136）此评论用来形容"原文一"的文字可谓贴切之至，寥寥数语，王生"窗窥"所见骇人景象如现眼前。两个译本都忠实再现了此番情景，各有优势。梅译本在用词和句式上更简洁利落，节奏紧凑，更能体现出王生临窗偷窥的紧张感；闵福德更注重细节以及与前文的呼应，如"遂化为女子"译为 it was instantly transformed into his pretty young "fugitive" friend，呼应小说开头与王生初次见面时，女鬼自道"在亡之人，乌有定所"（I am a fugitive. I have no place to go.），读来颇显讽刺意味。

"原文二"描写女鬼聂小倩随书生宁采臣回家拜见母亲的情形，生动地刻画了她灵秀乖巧、善解人意的特征。梅译本在用词上更为考究，着力传递女鬼行动姿态轻盈翩然，将"绰约"译为 ethereal，体现其飘逸优雅、不食人间烟火的气质，比译文二的 charming 更为形象；又将"入房穿榻"译为 threaded her way in and out of the rooms and around the furniture，将小倩殷勤侍奉宁母忙而不乱的画面逼真地呈现出来，而译文二将这个动作略去不译，甚为可惜。"明末志怪群书，大抵简略，又多荒怪，诞而不情，《聊斋志异》独于详尽之外，示以平常，使花妖狐媚，多具人情，和易可亲，忘为异类……"（鲁迅，2010:136）诚哉斯言。此段聂小倩面对宁母的言辞与行为无不体现出"多具人情，和易可亲"的特点。一番诚恳自白释去宁母疑虑，结尾一句"如何？"更显其乖巧，译文一译为 May I? 恰到好处，译文二则未能译出。不过，"奉晨昏"闵福德译为 to wait upon you, morning and evening，比译文一 serve you day and night 更能体现小倩心细如发，也在一定程度上预示了下文宁母婉拒小倩夜晚留宿的情节。

《聊斋》中人与狐鬼神怪的爱情故事虽然脱离世俗礼教的桎梏，有其浪漫奔放的一面，但他们的结合往往是短暂的，缺乏世俗生活的明朗欢悦，总是带着幽凄悲怆的色彩，如《罗刹海市》中的马骥和龙女。《罗刹海市》写主人公马骥出海的一系列奇遇，他先至罗刹国，后入龙宫，成为龙王的驸马，因系念故土，只身返回人间。临别时，与龙女约定，三年之后他将泛舟南岛，领回儿子福海和女儿龙宫。"原文三"描写马骥带儿女回到人间生活，龙女不能相伴，但时时牵念，在关键时刻两次现身，却又不得不立刻分离。她先身着丧服为婆婆送行，以尽孝道；又不忍女儿思念母亲，伤心垂泪，现身抚慰。亲人殊途，每次相见未及叙旧话别就生生分离,令人叹惋。

　　译文一生动简洁,且用动词多,画面感强。如"忽而风激雷轰,继以急雨,转瞬已失所在"这句,译文一为"A fierce wind began to blow and thunder rumbled. This was followed by heavy rain. In the blink of an eye she was gone."将龙女现身时天空出现的异相从色到声都传递出来,而译文二为"there was a flash of lightning followed by a clap of thunder and a squall of rain, and she was gone.",用there be句式加三个名词短语,将动态刻画转为静态描述。再如龙女在家中现身劝慰女儿时,"生闻之突入,执手啜泣",译文一为"Hearing her voice, the scholar burst into the room and took her by the hand, sobbing."译文二为"Ma having found out she was there, rushed in, and, seizing her hand, began to weep for joy"。马骥与龙女分离数年却时时牵挂,此时的相见应是百感交集,"相顾无言,唯有泪千行",并不只是weep for joy,所以译文一的直译反而更能表达男主人公的心绪。

五、课后练习

（一）思考题

1. 谈谈中国志怪小说产生、流行的时代并思考其历史成因。
2. 读《聊斋志异》,思考中国的志怪小说与英国的哥特小说有哪些异同之处。
3. 蒲松龄称《聊斋志异》为"幽冥之录"和"孤愤之书",在翻译过程中如何着力呈现这两点?尤其需要注意哪些层面?

（二）翻译题

1. 东壁画散花天女,内一垂髫者,拈花微笑,樱唇欲动,眼波将流。朱注目久,不觉神摇意夺,恍然凝思;身忽飘飘如驾云雾,已到壁上。见殿阁重重,非复人世。(《画壁》)

2. 一夕归,见二人与师共酌。日已暮,尚无灯烛。师乃剪纸如镜黏壁间,俄顷,月明辉室,光鉴毫芒。(《崂山道士》)

3. 忽大风起,尘气莽莽然,城市依稀而已。既而风定天清,一切乌有;惟危楼一座,直接霄汉。楼五架窗扉皆洞开,一行有五点明处,楼外天也。(《山市》)

4. 曾烂醉如泥,沉睡座间。陶起归寝,出门践菊畦,玉山倾倒,委衣于侧,即地化为菊,高如人;花十余朵,皆大如拳。马骇绝,告黄英。英急往,拔置地上,曰:"胡醉至此!"覆以衣,要马俱去,戒勿视。既明而往,则陶卧畦边。马乃悟姊弟皆菊精也,益敬爱之。(《黄英》)

5. 宁采臣,浙人,性慷爽,廉隅自重。每对人言:"生平无二色。"适赴金华,至北郭,解装兰若。寺中殿塔壮丽,然蓬蒿没人,似绝行踪。东西僧舍,双扉虚掩,惟南一小舍,扃键如新。又顾殿东隅,修竹拱把,阶下有巨池,野藕已花。意甚乐其幽杳。会学使案临,城舍价昂,思便留止,遂散步以待僧归。(《聂小倩》)

参考读物

Giles, Herbert. Trans. *Strange Stories from a Chinese Studio* [M]. Honolulu: University Press of the Pacific, 2003.

Mair, Denis C. & Victor H. Mair. Trans. *Strange Tales from Make-do Studio* [M]. Beijing: Foreign Language Press, 2001.

Minford, John. Trans. *Strange Tales from a Chinese Studio* [M]. London: Penguin Group, 2006.

何敏.英语世界《聊斋志异》译介述评[J].外语教学与研究,2009(2).

李伟昉. 英国哥特小说与中国六朝志怪小说比较研究[M].北京:中国社会科学出版社,2004.

鲁迅.中国小说史略[M].桂林:广西师范大学出版社,2010.

第十五课

晚明小品

▶▶ 一、内容简介

"小品"原是佛家用语,指大部佛经的略本。这一名称较早见于《世说新语·文学》,文中有言:"殷中军读小品,下二百签,皆是精微,世之幽滞,尝欲与支道林辩之,竟不得。今小品犹存。""殷中军被废东阳,始看佛经。初见维摩诘,疑'般若波罗蜜'太多;后见小品,恨此语少。"以后经唐、宋、元数代,到晚明时小品大盛。

明中叶后,宦官擅权,奸臣当道,内忧外患。思想界涌现出以王艮、李贽为代表的反理学思潮,主张童心本真,率性而行。在这种思潮的推动下,文人士子对社会黑暗绝望之余,将精神转托于山水风光与日常生活情趣。明人所谓"小品"是指轻灵隽永、活泼新鲜而有情韵的"小文小说"、"小札戏墨",尺牍、游记、传记、日记、序跋等生活化、个人化的文体均包含在内,有别于庄重古板的"高文大册"。晚明小品强调"真"、"诚"、表现率真自然之情,不虚伪矫饰,反对"伪理学、伪经济",真情至性,任性而发。

"公安派"是晚明小品的开端,代表人物袁宗道、袁宏道和袁中道,他们深受李贽和徐渭等人的影响,反对复古派,主张"独抒性灵,不拘格套",认为文学是时代生活的反映,应随时代变化,不必模拟古人,具有鲜明的反道学色彩。"三袁"之中,袁宏道成就最大,著有《满井游记》、《徐文长传》等名篇。继"公安派"而起的还有以钟惺、谭元春等人为代表的"竟陵派",追求"幽深孤峭,奇理别趣"的艺术风格。

晚明散文的一位集大成者是张岱(1597—1679),字宗子,号陶庵,山阴(今浙江绍兴)人,出身于官宦世家,早年生活繁华靡丽,自称"少为纨绔子弟,极爱繁华。好精舍,好美婢,好娈童,好鲜衣,好美食,好骏马,好华灯,好烟火,好梨园,好鼓吹,好古董,好花鸟,兼以茶淫橘虐，书蠹诗魔"(《自为墓志铭》)。他的小品文既有公安派的清新，又有竟陵派的冷峭，且不乏诙谐之趣，所涉题材广泛，风景名胜、戏曲杂技、世情风俗无所不记。有《陶庵梦忆》、《琅嬛文集》、《西湖梦寻》等文集。

▶▶ 二、翻译传播

晚明小品在英语世界的传播与 20 世纪 30 年代以林语堂为首的"论语派"所掀起的小品文热是分不开的。"论语派"推崇明末清初的小品，其主要刊物有《论语》、《人间世》、《宇宙风》，以刊登小品文为主，提倡幽默、闲适、性灵，主张"以自我为中心，以闲适为笔调"，采取与政治保持距离的自由主义立场，以审美的态度谛视日常生活，追求生活的艺术化。

林语堂钟爱的明清小品作家有徐渭、陈继儒、张岱、金圣叹、公安三袁、屠隆、袁枚、李笠翁、郑板桥、沈复等。早在 20 世纪 30 年代，他就英译了沈复的《浮生六记》，后来又选译了屠隆的《冥寥子游》。金圣叹的《论游》、《西厢记序·留赠后人》、《〈水浒传〉序》，陈继儒的《闲居书付儿辈》，张岱的《扬州瘦马》、《西湖七月半》，李笠翁的《闲情偶寄》，郑板桥的《养鸟》、《家书》，张潮的《幽梦影》，蒋坦的《秋灯琐忆》等名篇。这些小品文也直接影响了林语堂的英文著作 The Importance of Living (《生活的艺术》)，此书 1937 年在美国出版后反响甚大，连续再版四十余次。

1972 年，美国汉学家白芝(Cyril Birch)在《中国文学选集》第二卷(Anthology of Chinese Literature. Volume 2: From the Fourteenth Century to the Present Day)中收录部分小品文；1978 年，师从夏志清先生的美国汉学家齐皎瀚(Jonathan Chaves)翻译出版了《白云的朝圣者：袁宏道及其兄弟诗文集》(Pilgrim of the Clouds: Poems and Essays by Yüan Hung-tao and His Brothers)。1988 年，华裔学者周质平(Chou, Chih-p'ing)出版著作《袁宏道与公安派》(Yüan Hung-tao and the Kung-an School)。1999 年，美国加州大学教授叶扬翻译出版了《晚明小品文》(Vignettes From the Late Ming: A Hsiao-pin Anthology)，其中包括李贽、张岱、屠隆、"公安三袁"等 14 位作家共 70 篇作品，这是小品文在英语世界的一次系统的译介。"大中华文库"于 2011 年出版了王宏和张顺生英译的《明清小品文》，收录 87 位作家的 127 篇作品，是目前小品文英译篇目最多的作品集。

下面就来赏析林语堂和叶扬所译的张岱名作《西湖七月半》。

三、翻译对比

- **原文一：**

西湖七月半，一无可看，止可看看七月半之人。看七月半之人，以五类看之。其一，楼船箫鼓，峨冠盛筵，灯火优傒，声光相乱，名为看月而实不见月者，看之；其一，亦船亦楼，名娃闺秀，携及童娈，笑啼杂之，环坐露台，左右盼望，身在月下而实不看月者，看之；其一，亦船亦声歌，名妓闲僧，浅斟低唱，弱管轻丝，竹肉相发，亦在月下，亦看月而欲人看其看月者，看之；其一，不舟不车，不衫不帻，酒醉饭饱，呼群三五，跻入人丛，昭庆、断桥，嚣呼嘈杂，装假醉，唱无腔曲，月亦看，看月者亦看，不看月者亦看，而实无一看者，看之；其一，小船轻幌，净几暖炉，茶铛旋煮，素瓷静递，好友佳人，邀月同坐，或匿影树下，或逃嚣里湖，看月而人不见其看月之态，亦不作意看月者，看之。

林语堂译文：

There is nothing to see during the harvest moon on West Lake [Hangchow]. All you can see are people who come out to see the moon. Briefly there are five categories of these holidaymakers. First, there are those who come out in the name of looking at the harvest moon, but never even take a look at it: the people who, expensively dressed, sit down at gorgeous dinners with music in brightly illuminated boats or villas, in a confusion of light and noise. Secondly, those who do sit in the moonlight, but never look at it: ladies, daughters of high families, in boats and towers, also handsome boys [homosexuals] who sit in open spaces and giggle and chatter and look at other people. Thirdly, boat parties of famous courtesans and monks with time on their hands who enjoy a little sip and indulge in song and flute and string instruments. They are in the moonlight, too, and indeed look at the moon, but want people to see them looking at the moon. Fourthly, there are the young men, who neither ride nor go into boats, but after a drink and a good dinner, rush about in their slovenly dress and seek the crowd at Chaoching and Tuanchiao where it is thickest, shouting, singing songs of no known melody, and pretending to be drunk. They look at the moon, look at the people looking at the moon, and also look at those not looking at the moon, but actually see nothing. Lastly, there are those who hire a small boat, provided with a clay stove and a clean table and choice porcelain cups and pots for serving newly brewed tea, and who get into the boat with a few friends and their sweethearts; they hide under a tree or row out into the Inner Lake in order to escape from the crowd, and look at the moon without letting people see that they are looking at the moon and even without consciously looking at it. (*Harvest Moon on West Lake*)

叶扬译文:

On the fifteenth night of the seventh month, there was nothing worth seeing at West Lake except the people milling around. If you looked at people who came out on that night, you could classify them into five types.

First, there were those who came in a storied galley, bringing with them musicians playing flutes and drums. They were fully dressed up, and they ordered sumptuous meals. At a brightly lit place they enjoyed themselves in a tumult of light and sound. They were supposed to be "viewing the moon", but actually they could not see it. We could look at them.

There were also those who came in a boat or sat in a storied mansion. They were accompanied either by celebrated beauties or gentlewomen, and sometimes they also brought with them handsome boys. Laughs and sobs burst out in turn. They sat in a circle on the balcony and glanced right and left. Although they were right there under the moon, they really did not bother to give it a look. We could look at them.

There were those who came in a boat, with musicians waiting upon their pleasure, in the company of famous courtesans and Buddhist monks who had time to spare. They sipped their wine slowly and sang in a low voice, accompanied by the soft music of pipes and strings. Human voice and the sound of musical instruments set each other off. They were indeed beneath the moon, and they did view the moon, but they also wanted people to see them viewing the moon. We could look at them.

There were those who came neither in a boat nor in a carriage. They were casually dressed. After having eaten and drunk their fill, they met in groups of three to five and joined the crowd, making a lot of noise shouting and yelling at the Celebration Temple or on the Broken Bridge. They pretended to be drunk and sang tuneless songs. They looked at the moon, at those who were looking at the moon, and also at those who were not looking at the moon, but actually did not look at anything in particular. We could look at them.

There were those who came in a small boat with gauzy curtains. They sat by a clean table and a clay stove, and had water boiled in the pot to make tea; then they passed it to one another in white porcelain teacups. They came with good friends and beautiful women, and invited the moon to be their company. They either hid themselves in the shade of the trees or stayed away from the clamor on the Inner Lake. They came to view the moon, but people couldn't see how they conducted themselves while viewing the moon. Nor did they ever look at the moon with full intent. We could look at them. (*West Lake on the Fifteenth Night of the Seventh Month*)

- 原文二:

杭人游湖,巳出酉归,避月如仇。是夕好名,逐队争出,多犒门军酒钱,轿夫擎燎,列俟岸上。一入舟,速舟子急放断桥,赶入胜会。以故二鼓以前,人声鼓吹,如沸如撼,如魇如呓,如聋如哑。大船小船,一齐凑岸,一无所见,止见篙击篙,舟触舟,肩摩肩,面看面而已。少刻兴尽,官府席散,皂隶喝道去。轿夫叫船上人,怖以关门,灯笼火把如列星,一一簇拥而去。岸上人亦逐队赶门,渐稀渐薄,顷刻散尽矣。

林语堂译文:

The local Hangchow people come out on the lake, if they do at all, between eleven in the morning and eight in the evening, as if they had morbid fear of the moon. But on this night, they all come out in groups, wanting to be seen. They overtip the guards at the citygate and their sedan chair carriers, holding torches, wait along the bank for their return. The moment they get into a boat, they tell the boatman to hurry and row across to the Tuanchiao area, and get lost in the crowd, therefore in that area before the second watch [ten o'clock], the place is filled with noise and music bands in a weird, boiling confusion, like a roaring sea or a landside, or a nightmare, or like Bedlam let loose, with all the people in it rendered deaf and dumb for the moment. Large and small boats are tied up along the bank, and one can see nothing except boats creaking against boats, punting poles knocking punting poles, shoulders rubbing shoulders, and faces looking at faces. Soon the fervor cools, the officials leave their feasts, the yamen runners shout to clear the way, the sedan chair carriers scream for fare, the boatmen give warning that the city gates will soon be closed. A grand procession of torches and lanterns, with swarms of retainers, passes on. Those on land also hurry to get into the city before the closing of the gate, and very soon almost the entire crowd is gone.

叶扬译文：

When the local people in Hangchow made their trip around the lake, they usually came out around ten o'clock in the morning and returned before six in the evening. They stayed away from the moon as if from a personal enemy. On that night, however, they all came out of the city in groups, merely for the purpose of having something to brag about. They paid heavy tips to the gatekeepers. Their sedan-chair carriers held torches in hand and stood in a row on the bank. As soon as they got into their boats, they instructed the boatmen to hurry for the Broken Bridge to join in the big party there. Therefore, before the second beat of the night watches, the boiling hullabaloo of human voices and music there was like that during an earthquake or in a nightmare, loud enough to make everyone deaf and mute. Boats big and small were all moored along the bank. There was nothing there to watch except the boats and the punt-poles hitting one another, and people rubbing shoulders and looking into the faces of one another. After a while their frenzy was exhausted. Government officials left after their banquets were over, yamen runners shouted to clear the way, and sedan-chair carriers yelled and scared people in the boats by saying that the city gates were closing. Lanterns and torches moved like a trail of stars, and people hurried away surrounded by their retainers. Those on the shore also hurried to go back in groups before the city gates closed. The crowd got sparser and thinner, and in a short while they were all gone.

- 原文三：

吾辈始舣舟近岸，断桥石磴始凉，席其上，呼客纵饮。此时月如镜新磨，山复整妆，湖复颒面，向之浅斟低唱者出，匿影树下者亦出，吾辈往通声气，拉与同坐。韵友来，名妓至，杯箸安，竹肉发。月色苍凉，东方将白，客方散去。吾辈纵舟，酣睡于十里荷花之中，香气拍人，清梦甚惬。

林语堂译文：

Only then do we move the boat to Tuanchiao. The rocks have become cool by this time, and we spread a mat on the ground and invite ourselves to a great drink. At this time, the moon looks like a newly polished mirror, the hills appear draped in a new dress, and the face of lake is like a lady after a fresh make-up. Those who have been hiding themselves under a tree come out and those who have been enjoying a quiet sip and a little song come out now also. We exchange names and invite them to join us. There we have charming friends and famous courtesans; cups and chopsticks are in place, and songs and music begin, in the chilly dream world of moonlight. The party breaks up at dawn, and we get into the boat again and move it into the miles of lotus-covered surface, where we catch a nap in an air filled with its fragrance, and have a perfect sleep.

叶扬译文：

Only then would people like us move our boats to the shore. The stone steps of the Broken Bridge had just cooled down. We placed mats on them and sat down, and invited our friends to drink to their hearts' content. Now the moon was like a newly polished mirror. The hills and the lake seemed to have just washed their faces and put on new makeup. Those who had been sipping their wine slowly and singing in a low voice came out. Those who had been hiding themselves in the shade of the trees also emerged. We greeted them and pulled them over to sit among us. Poetic friends and famous courtesans arrived on the scene. Wine cups and chopsticks were brought out. Human voices and musical instruments blended in unison. Only when the moon was fading fast and the east was gradually turning white would our guests take their leave. We set our boats adrift to find ourselves among miles of lotus flowers and to sleep soundly. There, with the fragrance assailing our nostrils, we would have sweet, sweet dreams.

▶▶▶ 四、翻译赏析

这篇小品文描述的是农历七月十五中元节的情景。晚明时，杭州西湖的各大寺院这天晚上都会举行盂兰盆佛会，故夜间游人甚众。这便是此篇小品的缘起。"原文一"，即首段写各色人等汇聚西湖内外，有炫耀富贵的，有卖弄风情的，有粗俗招摇的，有故作矜持的，也有闲静清雅的，可笑中透着可爱，语气诙谐，褒贬暗寓。林译本语言流畅自然，有英文随笔之意趣，对先描述后总结的原文顺序做了调整，每小节都先译某类人看月的特点，再译其行迹，符合英语行文习惯。相比之下，叶译本更为忠实地呈现原文的全貌，每小节后面的"We could look at them."一方面似乎在提醒读者，"你站在桥上看风景，看风景的人在楼上看你"，同时也传达出原文寓谐于庄的调侃意味。

"原文二"写"二鼓以前"看月人嘈杂喧哗的场景，讽其看月只为"好名"，只是来凑热闹，并不解其中雅趣。寥寥几笔，喧嚣纷扰尽在眼前。"人声鼓吹，如沸如撼，如魇如呓，如聋如哑"一句，叶译本略去部分细节，林译本为"like a roaring sea or a landside, or a nightmare, or like Bedlam let loose, with all the people in it rendered deaf and dumb for the moment"，将原文中的"沸"、"撼"、"魇"、"呓"全都具象化，活泼生动，读来令人忍俊不禁。"篙击篙，舟触舟，肩磨肩，面看面"一句，林译本按原文的节奏传递此番景象："boats creaking against boats, punting poles knocking punting poles, shoulders rubbing shoulders, and faces looking at faces."熙熙攘攘，好不热闹。本段结尾林译本中 A grand procession of, swarms of 和叶译本中 like a trail of stars 这些量词的使用都简洁形象地表现出喧嚣将散的场景。

"原文三"由动入静，写人潮散去，真正看月者方与韵友同道共坐月下，伴着明月清风浅斟低唱，就着十里荷香沉入梦乡。此时的高雅清寂映衬出彼时的庸俗粗陋，高下立见。两个译本各有千秋，林译简洁明快，叶译细致入微。"月色苍凉，东方将白，客方散去。吾辈纵舟，酣睡于十里荷花之中，香气拍人，清梦甚惬"一句，叶译本甚佳："Only when the moon was fading fast and the east was gradually turning white would our guests take their leave. We set our boats adrift to find ourselves among miles of lotus flowers and to sleep soundly. There, with the fragrance assailing our nostrils, we would have sweet, sweet dreams."其中，"Only when … was"的句式道出雅士尽兴方散；"set our boats adrift to find ourselves …"一句巧妙地译出"纵舟"的随性任情，无所拘碍；"we would have sweet, sweet dreams"中两个 sweet 连用，好似香梦沉酣中的呓语，让人再不敢多言，恐扰其清梦。

五、课后练习

(一) 思考题

1. 谈谈小品文兴盛于晚明的历史原因。
2. 小品文与英国的随笔(familiar essay)有何异同？
3. 考察林语堂小品文翻译与散文创作之间的互动关系。

(二) 翻译题

1. 崇祯五年十二月，余住西湖。大雪三日，湖中人鸟声俱绝。是日，更定矣，余挐一小舟，拥毳衣炉火，独往湖心亭看雪。雾凇沆砀，天与云、与山、与水，上下一白。湖上影子，惟长堤一痕、湖心亭一点、与余舟一芥，舟中人两三粒而已。到亭上，有两人铺毡对坐，一童子烧酒，炉正沸。见余大喜，曰："湖中焉得更有此人？"拉余同饮。余强饮三大白而别，问其姓氏，是金陵人，客此。及下船，舟子喃喃曰："莫说相公痴，更有痴似相公者。"（张岱，《湖心亭看雪》）

2. 文长既已不得志于有司，遂乃放浪曲蘖，恣情山水，走齐、鲁、燕、赵之地，穷览朔漠。其所见山奔海立、沙起云行、雨鸣树偃、幽谷大都、人物鱼鸟，一切可惊可愕之状，一一皆达之于诗。其胸中又有勃然不可磨灭之气，英雄失路、托足无门之悲；故其为诗，如嗔如笑，如水鸣峡，如种出土，如寡妇之夜哭、羁人之寒起。虽其体格时有卑者，然匠心独出，有王者气，非彼巾帼而事人者所敢望也。文有卓识，气沉而法严，不以摸拟损才，不以议论伤格，韩、曾之流亚也。文长既雅不与时调合，当时所谓骚坛主盟者，文长皆叱而怒之，故其名不出于越，悲夫！（袁宏道，《徐文长传》）

3. 十年别友，抵暮忽至。开门一揖毕，不及问其船来陆来，并不及命其坐床坐榻，便自疾趋入内，卑辞叩内子："君岂有斗酒如东坡妇乎？"内子欣然拔金簪相付。计之可作三日供也。不亦快哉！（金圣叹，《三十三不亦快哉》）

参考读物

Chaves, Jonathan. *Pilgrim of the Clouds: Poems and Essays by Yüan Hung-tao and His Brothers* [M]. New York: Weatherhill, 1978.

Chou, Chih-p'ing. *Yüan Hung-tao and the Kung-an School* [M]. Cambridge: Cambridge University Press, 1988.

Ye, Yang. *Vignettes From the Late Ming: A Hsiao-pin Anthology* [M]. University of Washington Press, 1999.

林语堂. 林语堂英文作品集：古文小品译英 [M]. 北京：外语教学与研究出版社，2009.

林语堂. 生活的艺术 [M]. 北京：外语教学与研究出版社，2009.

第十六课

《水浒传》

▶▶ 一、内容简介

《水浒传》是我国古典文学史上一部著名的长篇章回体白话小说，是元末明初施耐庵在宋元民间传说和话本的基础上整理、加工而成的。它以北宋末年以宋江为首的一支"全忠仗义"、"替天行道"的武装队伍在梁山聚义为题材，艺术地再现了中国古代农民起义的发生、发展和失败的全过程。

《水浒传》的创作手法极为精湛。金圣叹说："《水浒传》方法，都从《史记》出来，却有许多胜似《史记》处。若《史记》妙处，《水浒》已是件件有。"

《水浒传》前七十一回以聚义梁山为线索，将一个个、一批批人物串联起来。先集中写一个或一组人物，将其上梁山前的故事记述完毕，再引出另一个或另一组人物。作者以酣畅淋漓的笔墨集中描写了史进、鲁智深、林冲、杨志、宋江、武松、李逵等108位英雄，个个人物都写得活灵活现。第一位将《水浒传》翻译为英文的美国文学家、诺贝尔文学奖得主赛珍珠曾在演讲中说："《水浒传》被认为是最伟大的三部小说之一，并不是因为它充满了刀光剑影的情节，而是因为它生动地描绘了108个人物，这些人物各不相同，每个都有其独特的地方。"

七十一回之后，以时间为顺序，写两赢童贯、三败高俅、寻求招安、北破大辽、平贼灭寇等，以报效朝廷为主干，将故事贯穿始终。但情节显得有些松散、拖沓，多有雷同、失真之处，正如明代批评家叶昼所说："文字至此，都是强弩之末了，妙处还在前半截。"金圣叹将《水浒传》腰斩为七十一回，缘由也正在于此。

《水浒传》的语言也有极高的成就。它是在民间口语的基础上加以提炼、净化了的文学语言。特别是在人物语言个性化方面,《水浒传》能"一样人,便还他一样说话"(金圣叹《读第五才子书法》)。作者通过人物对话、动作、心理等多方位、多层次地刻画人物性格,在浓墨重彩描绘惊心动魄的故事时,也注意在细节上精雕细琢。

二、翻译传播

在中国古典小说中,《水浒传》因其以通俗的口语写成,在国外流传相当广泛。早在鸦片战争之前,国外就开始了对《水浒传》的译介活动。迄今为止已分别被译成了英语、法语、德语、俄语、拉丁语、意大利语、匈牙利语、捷克语、波兰语、日语、朝鲜语、越南语、泰语、印尼语等。其中较为流行的英文译本有1933年赛珍珠(Pearl S. Buck)译本(*All Men Are Brothers*)、1963年杰克逊(J. H. Jackson)译本(*The Water Margin*)、1980年沙博理(Sidney Shapiro)译本(*Outlaws of the Marsh*)和1994—2002年登特-杨父子(John and Alex Dent-Young)译本(*The Marshes of Mount Liang*)。

赛珍珠译《水浒传》书名为 *All Men Are Brothers*,启发自《论语·颜渊》"四海之内,皆兄弟也",其译本依据的是金圣叹评点的七十回本。赛珍珠主要采取直译法,有时甚至是亦步亦趋的字字翻译(word-for-word translation)。例如:

赵员外说:"要是留提辖在此,恐怕会有些山高水低,他日教提辖怨恨。"

Chao said, "If I let the captain stay here, it will be as dangerous as mountains too high and waters too deep. Then if trouble comes, you will hate me."

杰克逊译本依据的仍是金圣叹评点的七十回本,主要采取了意译法,有时甚至有删减,显得过于自由。例如:

话说宋江因躲一杯酒,去净手了,转出廊下来,趾了火锨柄,引得那汉焦躁,跳将起来就欲要打宋江,柴进赶将出来,偶叫起宋押司,因此露出姓名来。那大汉听得是宋江,跪在地下哪里肯起,说道:"小人'有眼不识泰山'!一时冒渎兄长,望乞恕罪!"宋江扶起那汉,问道:"足下是谁?高姓大名?"

We have already related how Sung Chiang, in order to avoid drinking more wine, went outside to the toilet and while on the veranda he upset the charcoal brazier, and burnt a man, and how this resulted in Sung Chiang's name being disclosed to the man. When the man heard Sung Chiang's name how could he get up after kowtowing! He said, "I failed to recognize your eminence and I hope that you will forgive me for that blunder."

Sung Chiang raised him up and asked who he was.

沙博理译本 1980 年由北京外文出版社以精装 3 卷本的形式出版,依据的是《水浒传》一百回本,1981 年又由美国印第安纳大学出版社与北京外文出版社联合再版,1993 年外文出版社又出版了修订本。其译本通俗易懂,可读性很高。例如:

两个公人看那和尚时,穿一领皂布直裰,跨一口戒刀,提着禅杖,轮起来打两个公人。林冲方才闪开眼看时,认得是鲁智深。林冲连忙叫道:"师兄!不可下手!我有话说!"智深听得,收住禅杖。两个公人呆了半晌,动弹不得。

Dressed in a black cassock, he was wearing a knife and carried a Buddhist staff which he brandished at the two guards. Lin Chong, who had just opened his eyes, recognized Sagacious Lu, and he hastily cried: "Brother! Stay your hand. I have something to say!" Sagacious lowered his iron staff. The guards gaped at him, too frightened to move.

《水浒传》的最新译本是登特-杨翻译的五卷本 The Marshes of Mount Liang,于 1994 至 2002 年由香港中文大学出版社出版。2011 年又由上海外语教育出版社出版了中英对照本。这是一个一百二十回的全译本,依据的原文底本是香港商务印书馆出版的《水浒》(1969 年,1987 年),偶尔也参阅了香港中华书局出版的《水浒全传》(1958 年)。英译本的总标题为 The Marshes of Mount Liang,各分卷标题为 The Broken Seals(1—22 回),The Tiger Killers(23—43 回),The Gathering Company(44—62 回),Iron Ox(63—90 回)和 The Scattered Flock(91—120 回),分卷方式本身就体现了译者的匠心。关于文本的翻译,译者在前言中写道:"本译文的对象是不通中文的普通读者。《水浒》是中国文学里最畅销的作品之一,会讲中文的人几乎尽人皆知。因此,这个英译本必须尽量具有可读性,同时对原文又不作任何删改。所以,我们既要保留中国古代的情趣,又要把注释减少到最低程度,用流畅的英语表达中国的方言和成语。"从语言风格方面讲,这是一个非常地道的译本。

▶▶ 三、翻译对比

- 原文:

这武松提了哨棒,大着步,自过景阳冈来。约行了四五里路,来到冈子下,见一大树,刮去了皮,一片白,上写两行字。武松也颇识几字,抬头看时,上面写道:

近因景阳冈大虫伤人,但有过往客商可于巳午未三个时辰结伙成队过冈。勿请自误。

武松看了笑道:"这是酒家诡诈,惊吓那等客人,便去那厮家里歇宿。我却怕甚么鸟!"横拖着哨棒,便上冈子来。

那时已有申牌时分,这轮红日厌厌地相傍下山。武松乘着酒兴,只管走上冈子来。走不到半里多路,见一个败落的山神庙。行到庙前,见这庙门上贴着一张印信榜文。武松住了脚读时,上面写道:

阳谷县示:为景阳冈上新有一只大虫伤害人命,见今杖限各乡里正并猎户人等行捕未获。如有过往客商人等,可于巳午未三个时辰结伴过冈;其余时分,及单身客人,不许过冈,恐被伤害性命。各宜知悉。政和……年……月……日。

武松读了印信榜文,方知端的有虎,欲待转身再回酒店里来,寻思道:"我回去时须吃他耻笑不是好汉,难以转去。"存想了一回,说道:"怕甚么鸟!且只顾上去看怎地!"

武松正走,看看酒涌上来,便把毡笠儿掀在脊梁上,将哨棒绾在肋下,一步步上那冈子来;回头看这日色时,渐渐地坠下去了。此时正是十月间天气,日短夜长,容易得晚。武松自言自说道:"那得甚么大虫!人自怕了,不敢上山。"

武松走了一直,酒力发作,焦热起来,一只手提哨棒,一只手把胸膛前袒开,踉踉跄跄,直奔过乱树林来。见一块光挞挞大青石,把那哨棒倚在一边,放翻身体,却待要睡,只见发起一阵狂风。那一阵风过了,只听得乱树背后扑地一声响,跳出一只吊睛白额大虫来。武松见了,叫声"阿呀",从青石上翻将下来,便拿那条哨棒在手里,闪在青石边。那大虫又饥又渴,把两只爪在地上略按一按,和身望上一扑,从半空里撺将下来。武松被那一惊,酒都作冷汗出了。

说时迟,那时快,武松见大虫扑来,只一闪,闪在大虫背后。那大虫背后看人最难,便把前爪搭在地下,把腰胯一掀,掀将起来。武松只一闪,闪在一边。大虫见掀他不着,吼一声,却似半天里起个霹雳,振得那山冈也动,把这铁棒也似虎尾倒竖起来只一剪。武松却又闪在一边。原来那大虫拿人只是一扑,一掀,一剪;三般捉不着时,气性先自没了一半。那大虫又剪不着,再吼了一声,一兜兜将回来。

武松见那大虫复翻身回来,双手轮起哨棒,尽平生气力,只一棒,从半空劈将下来。只听得一声响,簌簌地将那树连枝带叶劈脸打将下来。定睛看时,一棒劈不着大虫,原来打急了,正打在枯树上,把那条哨棒折做两截,只拿得一半在手里。那大虫咆哮,性发起来，翻身又只一扑扑将来。武松又只一跳，却退了十步远。那大虫恰好把两只前爪搭在武松面前。武松将半截棒丢在一边，两只手就势把大虫顶花皮胳嗒地揪住，一按按将下来。那只大虫急要挣扎，被武松尽力气捺定，那里肯放半点儿松宽。

武松把只脚望大虫面门上、眼睛里只顾乱踢。那大虫咆哮起来，把身底下爬起两堆黄泥做了一个土坑。武松把大虫嘴直按下黄泥坑里去。那大虫吃武松奈何得没了些气力。武松把左手紧紧地揪住顶花皮，偷出右手来，提起铁锤般大小拳头，尽平生之力只顾打。打到五七十拳，那大虫眼里、口里、鼻子里、耳朵里，都迸出鲜血来，更动弹不得，只剩口里兀自气喘。（第二十三回　横海郡柴进留宾　景阳冈武松打虎）

登特-杨译文：

Wu Song picked up his cudgel and strode off towards the Jingyang Pass. After little more than a mile, he arrived at the foot of the pass. Here he saw a big tree, with a white patch where the bark had been stripped off to make room for two lines of writing. Wu Song was a passable reader. He raised his eyes and read：

In view of the recent attacks by a tiger in the Jingyang Pass, travellers are advised to make the crossing only in the morning, at noon, or in the afternoon, and furthermore to organize themselves into groups for the said crossing. Ignore this advice at your peril！

Wu Song did not take it seriously. "It must be a trick by that scoundrel of an innkeeper to frighten travellers into staying at his inn. That sort of bullshit won't scare me！" he said, and with his cudgel at the slope he began to climb the pass.

By now the afternoon was drawing on and the sun's red disk was starting to sink behind the mountains. But Wu Song, spurred on by the wine he had drunk, was determined to conquer that pass. He had not gone more than a few hundred yards, however, when he came upon a tumbledown little temple dedicated to the spirits of the mountain. Approaching, he saw that there was a notice bearing an official seal fixed to the door. He paused to read it. It said：

Yanggu district office announces that due to the recent appearance of a fierce man-eating tiger and the fact that the local hunters commissioned to trap it have not yet succeeded in their objective, all merchants and travellers are accordingly advised not to attempt the crossing of the pass except between the hours of nine and three, and furthermore single travellers are not to attempt the journey alone, lest they perish in the process.

Traveller take heed!

After reading this, Wu Song realized that there was indeed a tiger. At first he thought of turning back and going to the inn, but then he said to himself: "If I go back there, I'll have to endure his mockery. It'll look as if I'm scared. So I can't very well turn back." He turned it over in his mind for a while and then concluded: "What the hell am I afraid of? I'll just go on and see what happens."

So on he went. And as the wine began to mount to his head, he took off his hat and strung it on his back, and tucked the cudgel under his arm. Step by step, he trudged on up the pass. Turning to look at the sun, he saw that it was slowly setting. This was real November weather, when the days are short and the nights long, and it's easy for nightfall to catch you unawares. "What's all this nonsense about a big tiger," Wu Song was muttering to himself. "People are scared of the mountain that's all, they don't have the guts to climb it."

He walked on a bit further and the wine began to make itself felt still more. He was feeling hot, so holding his cudgel in one hand he used the other to loosen his clothing and bare his chest. He was swaying and stumbling as he advanced towards a dense thicket. There happened to be a smooth black boulder here, so he laid his cudgel aside and sank down to rest upon the boulder. He was just drifting off to sleep when there came a fierce gust of wind.

When the gust had passed, he heard something crashing through the trees and out sprang an enormous tiger, with bulging eyes and a white forehead. When Wu Song saw this a horrified "Aiya!" broke from his lips. He rolled off the boulder and grabbing his cudgel dodged behind it.

Now the tiger was ravenous. It struck the ground with two paws and sprang upwards, intending to land on its prey like a thunderbolt. Wu Song had such a shock that he felt all the wine start out of him in an icy sweat!

It's slow in the telling, but happens in a flash. When he saw the tiger spring, Wu Song leapt out of the way, ending up behind it. That's exactly what the tiger didn't like, to have a man at its back. Thrusting upward off its front paws, it flexed its back and twisted round to pounce again. But again Wu Song dodged to one side. Failing to grasp its prey, the tiger gave a roar like half the heavens exploding, a roar that seemed to shake the very mountains, and lashed out at Wu Song with its tail, rigid as a steel bar. Once more Wu Song leapt aside.

Now when the tiger attacks a man, it generally has these three strategies: the spring, the pounce and the tail-swipe. When all these three methods failed, this tiger's spirit was half broken. After failing to catch Wu Song with its tail it gave a loud roar and turned away. Seeing the tiger had turned its back on him, Wu Song grasped his cudgel in both hands and brought it down with all the strength of his body. There was a resounding crash.

But what he had done was demolish a whole tree, branches and all. He looked for the tiger. His staff had not even touched it. He'd rushed his stroke and all he'd achieved was to bring down a dead tree. Now his cudgel was broken in two and he was left with only the broken half in his hand.

The tiger roared, it was enraged, it turned and sprang at him again. Wu Song leapt back, covering ten paces in a single bound. The tiger reared up on its hind legs and came at him with all its claws out. Wu Song threw away his broken stick and suddenly grabbing the tiger's striped neck with his bare hands began forcing it down to the ground. The beast tried to struggle, but all Wu Song's strength was employed against it, not for a moment did he relax his grip. With his legs he delivered fearful kicks to its nose and eyes. The tiger roared furiously, and as it thrashed about under this onslaught its paws churned up two mounds of mud. Wu Song thrust the beast's head down into the mud and irresistibly its power began to ebb. Still gripping the striped coat tightly with his left hand, Wu Song managed to work his right hand free and began raining down blows with an iron fist, hammering the beast with all his might. He got in fifty or sixty blows, till from the tiger's eyes, mouth, nose and ears the red blood began to gush. For a moment it lay helpless, faintly panting. (*Chapter 23 Chai Jin entertains his guests with class; Wu Song kills the tiger of Jingyang Pass*!)

沙博理译文:

Staff in hand, Wu Song strode off towards Jingyang Ridge. After walking four or five li he came to the foot of it. A piece of bark had been peeled from a large tree, and on the white patch words were written. Wu Song could read quite well, and he saw that it was a notice with this inscription: *Of late a tiger on Jingyang Ridge has been killing people. Travellers must form bands and cross only between late morning and early afternoon. Do not take risks.*

Wu Song grinned. "That host is a crafty one. Scares his customers into staying the night. Well, he can't scare me!"

He proceeded up the slope, holding his staff level. It was late afternoon by then, and the red sun was pressing on the mountains in the west. Still primed by all the wine he had consumed, Wu Song continued climbing the ridge. Before he had gone another half li he came upon a dilapidated Mountain Spirit Temple. A notice was posted on the door. It read:

Yanggu County Notice: Lately, a big tiger has been killing people on Jingyang Ridge. Although all township leaders, village chiefs and hunters have been ordered to capture the beast or be beaten, they have so far failed. Travellers are permitted to cross the ridge only between late morning and early afternoon, and only in bands. At other times, and to single travellers at any time, the ridge is closed, lest the tiger take their lives. Let this be known to all.

So there really was a tiger! The notice with its official seal confirmed that. Wu Song considered returning to the tavern. But then he said to himself: "If I do that, the host will laugh at me for a coward. I can't go back." He thought a moment. "What's there to be afraid of," he exclaimed. "Just keep climbing and see what happens."

He walked on. The warmth of the wine rose in him, and he pushed back the felt hat till it was hanging by the string on his shoulders. Clapping the staff under one arm, he plodded up the slope. When he looked back at the sun, it was almost gone. The days are short in late autumn, and the nights are long. It gets dark early.

"There isn't any tiger," he said to himself. "People just scare themselves and don't dare come up the mountain."

The wine was burning inside him as he walked. With his staff in one hand, he unbuttoned his tunic with the other. His gait was unsteady now, and he staggered into a thicket. Before him was a large smooth rock. He rested his staff against it, clambered onto its flat surface, and prepared to sleep.

Suddenly a wild gale blew, and when it passed a roar come from behind the thicket and out bounded a huge tiger. Its malevolent upward-slanting eyes gleamed beneath a broad white forehead.

"Aiya!" cried Wu Song. He jumped down, seized his staff, and slipped behind the rock.

Both hungry and thirsty, the big animal clawed the ground with its front paws a couple of times, sprang high and came hurtling forward. The wine poured out of Wu Song in a cold sweat. Quicker than it takes to say, he dodged, and the huge beast landed beyond him. Tigers can't see behind them, so as its front paws touched the ground it tried to side-swipe Wu Song with its body. Again he dodged, and the tiger missed. With a thunderous roar that shook the ridge, the animal slashed at Wu Song with its iron tail. Once more he swivelled out of the way.

Now this tiger had three methods for getting its victim—spring, swipe and slash. But none of them had worked, and the beast's spirit diminished by half. Again it roared, and whirled around.

Wu Song raised his staff high in a two-handed grip and swung with all his might. There was a loud crackling, and a large branch, leaves and all, tumbled past his face. In his haste, he had struck an old tree instead of the tiger, snapping the staff in two and leaving him holding only the remaining half.

Lashing itself into a roaring fury, the beast charged. Wu Song leaped back ten paces, and the tiger landed in front of him. He threw away the stump of his staff, seized the animal by the ruff and bore down. The tiger struggled frantically, but Wu Song was exerting all his strength, and wouldn't give an inch. He kicked the beast in the face and eyes, again and again. The tiger roared, its wildly scrabbling claws pushing back two piles of yellow earth and digging a pit before it. Wu Song pressed the animal's muzzle into the pit, weakening it further. Still relentlessly clutching the beast by the ruff with his left hand, Wu Song freed his right, big as an iron mallet, and with all his might began to pound.

After sixty or seventy blows the tiger, blood streaming from eyes, mouth, nose and ears, lay motionless, panting weakly. (Chapter 23 *Lord Chai Accommodates Guests in Henghai County*; *Wu Song Kills a Tiger on Jingyang Ridge*)

▶▶ 四、翻译赏析

"武松打虎"是《水浒传》中的著名片段,也是家喻户晓、妇孺皆知的故事。本回的高潮是"打虎",但在开打之前的层层渲染体现了《水浒传》高超的文学技巧。《水浒传》第四十三回也写"李逵杀虎",两回情节相近,但并非简单重复。这种"特犯不犯"的文学技巧,正是《水浒传》的艺术成就之一。两个译者也都极尽英文之能事,运用不同的手法,从遣词、造句、篇章和修辞方面努力传递了原文的文学风格。

《水浒传》是章回体小说,每回都有回目。登特-杨在翻译这些回目时采用意译法,以英雄双行体诗歌的形式,较好地对应了原著对仗的特点。沙博理采用直译法,也较好地保留了原文对仗的形式,而且意义的传达也很到位。采用诗歌体翻译每个回目是登特-杨译文的一个特点,但也有意思传达不当之处,如第九回"柴进门招天下客;林冲棒打洪教头"的译文"Chai Jin comes home and finds a guest; Lin Chong's mastery is put to the test!"。相较之下,沙博理的译文"Chai Jin keeps open house for all bold men; Lin Chong defeats instructor Hong in a bout with staves"则较好地表达了原文的意思。

《水浒传》是从宋元话本的基础上发展而来的,因此在语言上保留了大量说书人的口气。例如每回开篇会有"话说",结尾会有"且听下回分解",描写人物或场景之前会有"但见",以及"当下"、"只说"、"正是"、"原来"等。这些语词在登特-杨的译文中几乎都保留了下来,且做了巧妙的处理,没有影响英语的行文。而在沙博理的译文中,几乎全部去除了这些语词。例如,登特-杨在本回开篇就是"Let me remind you",而沙博理的译文则是紧承上回,没有像原著那样,对上回之事作一总结重复。但是,登特-杨在碰到这些说书人的语词时,也并非采用同样的英文翻译,常常是有变化的。例如,第一回开头"话说大宋仁宗天子在位"的译文是"The story in the days when the Great Emperor Ren Zong reigned",而第二回开头"话说当时主持真人对洪太尉说道"的译文是"Then the superior said to Marshal Hong"。即使是每回结尾的"且听下回分解",登特-杨的译文也会有所变化:"turn to the next chapter","read the next chapter","you must read the next chapter","you have to read the next chapter"。他的遣词造句避免重复的译文特征也体现在其他地方,如本回中提及"哨棒"的几处。这就使得他的译文富于变化,有浓重的文学色彩,非常耐读。这也可说是体现了《水浒传》"特犯不犯"的文学技巧。

《水浒传》对人物生动逼真的描绘主要是通过人物自身的行为和语言来实现的,而不是靠作者进行解释,因此才能"一个人还他一个样"。登特-杨在翻译人物语言时,大量地使用英语口语和习语,非常生动。例如,"Well, I thought I'd killed him, so I cleared off and came here to Mr. Chai's, waiting for it to blow over."(小弟只道他死了,因此一径地逃来,投奔大官人处,躲灾避难。)中的 well, blow over。再比如武松在酒店与店家的对话,登特-杨的译文充满口语体甚至俗语,使得人物形象非常鲜明。例如,"This wine's got a real kick","how about something to line the stomach","Balls","Enough of your bullshit","I will turn your bloody house upside down"。当然,沙博理的译文在人物语言的处理方面也不逊色,只是有点直白。没有了 well, see, you know 等这样的插入语,使得人物对话显得有些呆板。这也体现在江湖套语及俗语的翻译上。例如"有眼不识泰山",登特-杨的译文是"(I) couldn't see what was staring me in the face","(you) can't see the nose on the end of your face",而沙博理的译文是"(I) have eyes but didn't recognize Mount Taishan"。

本选段对老虎和武松的动作描写可说是惟妙惟肖,尤其表现在动词的连用上。两个译文也发挥了英语动词连用的长处,较好地传达了原文的风格。例如,老虎欲吃武松时"按"、"扑"、"掀"、"掀"、"剪",虎威尽显,在登特-杨译文中是 struck, sprang, land, thrusting upward, lashed out,在沙博理译文中是 clawed, sprang, came hurtling, side-swipe, slashed;武松打虎时是"双手轮起哨棒"、"劈将下来"、"两只手就势把大虫顶花皮胳嗒地揪住"、"按将下来",真乃神人,在登特-杨译文中是"(Wu Song) grasped his cudgel in both hands and brought it down","suddenly grabbing the tiger's striped neck with his bare hands","forcing it down to the ground",沙博理译文中是"(Wu Song) raised his staff high in a two-handed grip and swung with all his might","seized the animal by the ruff and bore down"。

另外,本选段描写老虎出场,很有声势。若对比第一回和四十三回老虎出场情景,则真正见的作者笔下之真功夫。虽都先写"风",再是"吼",再是"跳出",然用语变化多端,绘声绘色。译文也不逊色。先看第一回:"只见山凹里起一阵风,风过处,向那松树背后奔雷也似吼一声,扑地跳出一个吊睛白额锦毛大虫来。"登特-杨的译文是"He felt a sudden gust of wind rush out from a hollow in the mountainside. When this gust passed, a thunderous roar burst from behind a pine tree, and out sprang a savage-eyed, white-browed tiger with a brilliantly-patterned coat."沙博理的译文是"A strong wind blew through the hollow. When it had passed, a roar thundered from behind the pines and out leaped a huge tiger, with bulging eyes, a white forehead and striped fur."再看第四十三回:"只见就树边卷起一阵狂风,吹得败叶树木如雨一般打将下来。自古道:'云生从龙,风生从虎。'那一阵风起处,星月光辉之下,大吼了一声,忽地跳出一只吊睛白额虎来。"登特-杨的译文是

"when from behind the trees a sudden gale arose. It blew so furiously the leaves were shaken from the trees like rain. According to the old saying: 'Clouds originate from dragons, and wind is produced by tigers.' At that moment, amid a storm of wind and by the light of the stars and the moon, a great roar burst out and a huge tiger with sad eyes and a white forehead appeared."沙博理的译文是"when a sudden gale arising among the trees brought down a shower of leaves and branches, 'Clouds herald dragons, gales foretell tigers,' as the old saying goes. From the place where the wind blew, a roaring tiger leaped out. It had upward-slanting eyes and a white forehead"。

另外,对公文的翻译也很值得玩味。公文语言与文学语言差别很大,两位译者自然明白这一点。因此,在翻译"阳谷县示"时,遣词造句与其他地方有很大的不同。登特-杨的译文中使用了一些很正式的表达法,如 be advised to 和 be to 短语。

五、课后练习

(一) 思考题

1. 比较《水浒传》四个译本的书名,谈谈你对《水浒传》书名翻译的看法。
2. 两则译文的各自特点是什么?
3. 与原文比较,译文在句子长短和段落方面有哪些变化?试述这些变化的原因。

(二) 翻译题

1. 再说林冲踏着那瑞雪,迎着北风,飞也似奔到草场门口,开了锁入内看时,只叫得苦。原来天理昭然,佑护善人义士。因这场大雪,救了林冲的性命。那两间草厅,已被雪压倒了。林冲寻思:"怎地好?"放下花枪、葫芦在雪里,恐怕火盆内有火炭延烧起来。搬开破壁子,探半身入去摸时,火盆内火种,都被雪水浸灭了。林冲把手床上摸时,只拽的一条絮被。林冲钻将出来,见天色黑了。寻思:"又没打火处,怎生安排?"想起:"离了这半里路上,有个古庙,可以安身。我且去那里宿一夜。等到天明,却做理会。"把被卷了,花枪挑着酒葫芦,依旧把门拽上锁了,望那庙里来。

2. 林冲投东去了两个更次,身上单寒,当不过那冷。在雪地里看时,离的草场远了。只见前面疏林深处,树木交杂,远远地数间草屋,被雪压着。破壁缝里透出火光来。林冲径投那草屋来。推开门,只见那中间坐着一个老庄家,周围坐着四五个小庄家向火。地炉里面焰焰寺烧着柴火。林冲走到面前,叫道:"众位拜揖。小人是牢城营差使人,被雪打湿了衣裳,借此火烘一烘,望乞方便。"庄客道:"你自烘便了,何妨得。"林冲烘着身上湿衣服,略有些干,只见火炭边煨着一个瓮儿,里面透出酒香。林冲便道:"小人身边有些碎银子,望烦回些酒吃。"老庄客道:"我们每夜轮流看米囤,如今四更天气正冷,我们这几个吃,尚且不勾,那得回与你。休要指望。"

3. 当晚武行者辞了张青夫妻二人,离了大树十字坡,便落路走。此时是十月间天气,日正短,转眼便晚了。约行不到五十里,早望见一座高岭。武行者趁着月明,一步步上岭来。料道只是初更天色。武行者立在岭头止看时,见月从东边上来,照得岭上草木光辉。看那岭时,果然好座高岭。但见:高山峻岭,峭壁悬崖。石角棱层侵斗柄,树梢仿佛接云霄。烟岚堆里,时闻幽鸟闲啼;翡翠阴中,每听哀猿孤啸。弄风山鬼,向溪边侮弄樵夫;挥尾野狐,立岩下惊张猎户。好似峨眉山顶过,浑如大庾岭头行。

4. 今日山寨幸得众多豪杰到此相扶相助,似锦上添花,如旱苗得雨。此人只怀妒贤能之心,但恐众豪杰势力相压。夜来因见兄长所说众位杀死官兵一节,他便有些不然,就怀不肯相留的模样;以此请众豪杰来关下安歇。

5. 众豪杰休生见外之心。林冲自有分晓。小可只恐众豪杰生退去之意;特来早早说知。今日看他如何相待。若这厮语言有理,不似昨日,万事罢论;倘若这厮今朝有半句话参差时,尽在林冲身上!

参考读物

Shapiro, S. *Outlaws of the Marsh* [M]. Beijing:Foreign Languages Press,1993.
金圣叹. 金圣叹批评本水浒传[M]. 南京:凤凰出版社,2010.
罗贯中著,罗慕士(Moss Roberts)译. 三国演义(大中华文库汉英对照)[M]. 北京:外文出版社,1999.
施耐庵、罗贯中著,登特-杨(John and Alex Dent-Young)译. 水浒传(汉英对照)[M]. 上海:上海外语教育出版社,2011.

第十七课

《红楼梦》

▶▶ 一、内容简介

  《红楼梦》,中国四大古典名著之一,章回体长篇小说,成书于1784年(清乾隆四十九年)。作者曹雪芹(约1715—1763),名霑,字梦阮,号雪芹,又号芹溪、芹圃。他出身于"百年望族",曾祖曹玺任江宁织造,曾祖母孙氏做过康熙的保姆,祖父曹寅做过康熙的伴读,后任江宁织造,兼任两淮巡盐监察御使,极受康熙信任。康熙六下江南,其中四次由曹寅负责接驾,并住在曹家。曹寅病故后,其子曹颙、曹頫先后继任江宁织造。曹雪芹就在这种"花柳繁华地,富贵温柔乡"中度过了少年时代。

  康熙死后,政治剧变,曹頫下狱,家产没收,曹家从此一蹶不振,子弟最终沦落至社会底层。曹雪芹后随全家迁往北京,生活困顿,其晚年生活更加艰难到"举家食粥酒常赊"的地步。在经历了此番人生剧变之后,曹雪芹对社会世情有了不同寻常的体悟,他将自己的心血都投入到《红楼梦》的创作中,"披阅十载,增删五次","字字看来皆是血,十年辛苦不寻常"。

  《红楼梦》原名《石头记》,乾隆四十九年梦觉主人序本正式题为《红楼梦》,后来这一名字取代《石头记》成为更通行的书名。《红楼梦》的版本有两大系统。一为"脂本",是流行于乾隆十九年到五十六年间,附有"脂砚斋"评语的版本,共八十回;一为"程本",由程伟元于乾隆五十六年首次以活字排印,全书一百二十回,后四十回一般认为由高鹗所续。

  小说以宝、黛、钗三人的感情和婚姻纠葛为线索,在揭示贾府由繁盛到衰败的过程中,折射出不同人物,尤其是"闺阁女子"的悲剧命运。从烈火烹油似的繁华景象到"好一似食尽鸟投林,落了片白茫茫大地真干净",可谓是"彻头彻尾之悲剧"(王国维语)。全书宏大而精致,上至皇宫贵族,下至市井乡野,每个阶层的特殊风貌都有呈现,具有很强的写实性。书中出现的人物,从小姐太太到丫鬟书僮,都刻画得惟妙惟肖、气韵生动,绝无概念化、脸谱化的涂抹。

《红楼梦》中还有大量诗、词、曲及骈文,妥帖紧密地与故事情节结合在一起,其中不少堪称佳作。这部著作历来被看做是中国古典小说的巅峰之作,问世不久,其抄本很快在全国流传,到嘉庆初年,已出现"遍于海内,家家喜闻,处处争购"的盛况,甚至有"开谈不说《红楼梦》,读尽诗书也枉然"的说法。

▶▶ 二、翻译传播

《红楼梦》在英语世界的流传已有一百多年的历史,大致可以分为三个时期。早期的译者主要是在华任职的官员,以节译为主,翻译的目的多为汉语学习。1830 年(道光十年),英国驻华公使德庇时(John Francis Davis)在《英国皇家亚洲学会学刊》(*The Royal Asiatic Transaction*)上发表《汉文诗解》(*On the Chinese Poetry*),其中讲解并翻译了《红楼梦》第三回中的两首"西江月";1846 年(道光二十六年),英国驻宁波首任领事罗伯聃(Robert Thom)将《红楼梦》第六回的片段译为英语,登载于《正音撮要》(*The Chinese Speaker*),供外国人学习中文参考。1868 年(同治七年),清政府海关税务司英国人鲍拉(Edward Charles Bowra)译出第一至八回,连载于《中国杂志》(*China Magazine*)。1892—1893 年(光绪十八年—十九年),英国驻澳门副领事乔利(H. Bencraft Joly)译出第一至五十六回,*Hung Lou Meng, or The Dream of the Red Chamber*,采用逐行直译的方法,未能呈现原著的文学性。

第二个时期《红楼梦》的英语译者由官员转向文学研究者,翻译目的开始从语言学习转向文学译介。1929 年,美国哥伦比亚大学教授王际真(Wang Chi-chen)翻译出版了 *Dream of the Red Chamber*,将原著压缩为 39 章,分为三册。1958 年,美国人麦克休姐妹(Florence Mchugh 和 Isabel Mchugh)将库恩(Franz Walter Kuhn)的德文版《红楼梦》进行转译,出版了 *The Dream of the Red Chamber*。这两个译本都面向普通读者,使用现代语汇,虽然在内容增删与意义呈现上有所缺失,但对《红楼梦》作为文学作品的译介功不可没。

第三个时期是全译本时期。1973—1980 年,英国汉学家霍克斯(David Hawkes)将《红楼梦》前八十回译出,书名译为 *The Story of the Stone*,将全书分为三卷(Vol. I *The*

Golden Days, Vol. II The Crab-Flower Club, Vol. III The Warning Voice)。霍克斯在序中说,"如果能够将这部中国小说带给我的欢乐表达出一小部分,我也就不枉此生了",他的译本很好地呈现了原文的双关、典故、俗语等修辞手法,很大程度上使英美读者感受到原作的文学魅力。1982—1986 年,霍克斯的女婿、汉学家闵福德(John Minford)译出高鹗后续的四十回,分为两卷(Vol. IV The Debt of Tears, Vol. V The Dreamer Wakes)。1978 年至 1980 年,杨宪益、戴乃迭夫妇的译本 A Dream of Red Mansions 问世,由外文出版社出版。他们的译本严谨忠实,最大限度地保留了中国文化意象,与霍克斯的译本各有千秋,可谓《红楼梦》英译版的"双璧"。

▶▶ 三、翻译对比

- 原文一:

这熙凤携着黛玉的手,上下细细打量了一回,仍送至贾母身边坐下,因笑道:"天下真有这样标致的人物,我今儿才算见了!况且这通身的气派,竟不像老祖宗的外孙女儿,竟是个嫡亲的孙女,怨不得老祖宗天天口头心头一时不忘。只可怜我这妹妹这样命苦,怎么姑妈偏就去世了!"说着,便用帕拭泪。贾母笑道:"我才好了,你倒来招我。你妹妹远路才来,身子又弱,也才劝住了,快再休提前话。"这熙凤听了,忙转悲为喜道:"正是呢!我一见了妹妹,一心都在他身上了,又是喜欢,又是伤心,竟忘记了老祖宗。该打,该打!"又忙携黛玉之手,问:"妹妹几岁了?可也上过学?现吃什么药?在这里不要想家,想要什么吃的,什么玩的,只管告诉我,丫头老婆们不好了,也只管告诉我。"一面又问婆子们:"林姑娘的行李东西可搬进来了?带了几个人来?你们赶早打扫两间下房,让他们去歇歇。"说话时,已摆了茶果上来。熙凤亲为捧茶捧果。(第三回 贾雨村夤缘复旧职 林黛玉抛父进京都)

霍克斯译文:

Xi-feng took Dai-yu by the hand and for a few moments scrutinized her carefully from top to toe before conducting her back to her seat beside Grandmother Jia.

'She's a beauty, Grannie dear! If I hadn't set eyes on her today, I shouldn't have believed that such a beautiful creature could exist! And everything about her so *distingué*! She doesn't take after your side of the family, Grannie. She's more like a Jia. I don't blame you for having gone on so about her during the past few days—but poor little thing! What a cruel fate to have lost Auntie like that!' and she dabbed at her eyes with a handkerchief.

'I've only just recovered,' laughed Grandmother Jia. 'Don't you go trying to start me off again! Besides, your little cousin is not very strong, and we've only just managed to get her cheered up. So let's have no more of this!'

In obedience to the command Xi-feng at once exchanged her grief for merriment.

'Yes, of course. It was just that seeing my little cousin here put everything else out of my mind. It made me want to laugh and cry all at the same time. I'm afraid I quite forgot about you, Grannie dear. I deserve to be spanked, don't I?'

She grabbed Dai-yu by the hand.

'How old are you dear? Have you begun school yet? You mustn't feel homesick here. If there's anything you want to eat or anything you want to play with, just come and tell me. And you must tell me if any of the maids or the old nannies are nasty to you.'

Dai-yu made appropriate responses to all these questions and injunctions.

Xi-feng turned to the servants.

'Have Miss Lin's things been brought in yet? How many people did she bring with her? You'd better hurry up and get a couple of rooms swept out for them to rest in.'

While Xi-feng was speaking, the servants brought in tea and various plates of food, the distribution of which she proceeded to supervise in person.

杨宪益、戴乃迭译文：

Hsi-feng took her hand and carefully inspected her from head to foot, and led her back to her seat by the Lady Dowager.

"Well," she cried with a laugh, "this is the first time I've set eyes on such a ravishing beauty. Her whole air is so distinguished! She doesn't take after her father, son-in-law of our Old Ancestress, but looks more like a Chia. No wonder our Old Ancestress couldn't put you out of her mind and was for ever talking or thinking about you. But poor ill-fated little cousin, losing your mother so young!" With that she dabbed her eyes with a handkerchief.

"I've only just dried my tears. Do you want to start me off again?" said the old lady playfully. "Your young cousin's had a long journey and she's delicate. We've just got her to stop crying. So don't reopen that subject."

Hsi-feng switched at once from grief to merriment. "Of course," She cried. "I was so carried away by joy and sorrow at sight of my little cousin, I forgot our old Ancestress. I deserve to be caned." Taking Tai-yu's hand again, she asked, "How old are you, cousin? Have you started your schooling yet? What medicine are you taking? You mustn't be homesick here. If you fancy anything special to eat or play with, don't hesitate to tell me. If the maids or old nurses aren't good to you, just let me know."

She turned then to the servants. "Have Miss Lin's luggage and things been brought in? How many attendants did she bring? Hurry up and clear out a couple of rooms where they can rest."

Meanwhile refreshments had been served. And as Hsi-feng handed round the tea and sweetmeats …

- 原文二：

"他说一是一，说二是二，没人敢拦他。又恨不得把银子钱省下来堆成山，好叫老太太，太太说他会过日子，殊不知苦了下人，他讨好儿。估着有好事，他就不等别人去说，他先抓尖儿；或有了不好事或他自己错了，他便一缩头推到别人身上来，他还在旁边拨火儿。如今连他正经婆婆，大太太都嫌了他，说他'雀儿拣着旺处飞，黑母鸡一窝儿，自家的事不管，倒替人家去瞎张罗'"……

"我告诉奶奶，一辈子别见他才好。嘴甜心苦，两面三刀，上头一脸笑，脚下使绊子，明是一盆火，暗是一把刀：都占全了。只怕三姨的这张嘴还说他不过。好，奶奶这样斯文良善人，那里是他的对手！"（第六十五回 贾二舍偷娶尤二姨 尤三姐思嫁柳二郎）

霍克斯译文：

"… whatever she says goes, nobody else dares stand up to her. She's a great one for saving. She must have saved a mountain of money by now. That's why Their Ladyships are always saying what a good manager she is. They don't realize how much we servants have to suffer so that she can take the credit. Whenever anything good happens, you can be sure that she'll get in with the news first, before anyone else does, so that she can reap the benefit. But when things go wrong or she's made a slip herself, she'll very quickly step aside and fasten the blame for it on someone else. She'll even fan the flames up and make it hotter for that other person once she's safely out of it herself. Even her mother-in-law can't stand her. 'The magpie looking for a bigger nest who set up house with the crow' she calls her."...

"It would be much better if you never set eyes on her as long as you live. She's 'soft of tongue and hard of heart', 'two faces and three knives', she'll 'give you a smile and trip you up the while', she's 'a welcoming fire when you see her, but a stab in the back when it's dark'—all those things and more. I don't think even Miss You here could get the better of her in an argument, so I'm sure a quiet, gentle lady like you would be no match for her."

杨宪益、戴乃迭译文：

"Whatever she says goes, and no one dares stop her. She tries to save up piles of silver so that Their Ladyships will praise her for being a good manager; but of course we servants are the ones to suffer while she takes all the credit.

If anything good happens, she rushes to take the credit before anyone else can report it. If anything bad happens, or if she herself makes some mistake, she ducks and shifts the blames on to other people, stirring up more trouble too on the side. Now even her own mother-in-law, the Elder Mistress, can't stand her, calling her a fair-weather sparrow, or a black hen that neglects her own nest but keeps butting in everywhere else…

"Take my word for it, it will be best for you never to meet her all you life. She'll give you sweet talk when there's hatred in her heart, she's so double-faced and tricky. All the time she's smiling she tries to trip you up, making a show of great warmth while she stabs you in the back. That's the way she is. I'm afraid not even Third Aunt could outtalk her, so how could a gentle, kindly lady like you be a match for her?"

- 原文三：

好了歌

世人都晓神仙好，唯有功名忘不了！
古今将相在何方？荒冢一堆草没了！
世人都晓神仙好，只有金银忘不了！
终朝只恨聚无多，及到多时眼闭了！
世人都晓神仙好，只有娇妻忘不了！
君生日日说恩情，君死又随人去了。
世人都晓神仙好，只有儿孙忘不了！

痴心父母古来多,孝顺儿孙谁见了?

(第一回 甄士隐梦幻识通灵 贾雨村风尘怀闺秀)

霍克斯译文:

Won-Done Song

Men all know that salvation should be won,
But with ambition won't have done, have done.
Where are the famous ones of days gone by?
In grassy graves they lie now, every one.

Men all know that salvation should be won,
But with their riches won't have done, have done.
Each day they grumble they've not made enough.
When they've enough, it's goodnight everyone!

Men all know that salvation should be won,
But with their loving wives they won't have done.
The darlings every day protest their love:
But once you're dead, they're off with another one.

Men all know that salvation should be won,
But with their children won't have done, have done.
Yet though of parents fond there is no lack,
Of grateful children saw I ne'er a one.

杨宪益、戴乃迭译文:

All good things must end

All men long to be immortals,
Yet to riches and rank each aspires;
The great ones of old, where are they now?
Their graves are a mass of briars.

All men long to be immortals,

Yet silver and gold they prize;
And grub for money all their lives
Till death seals up their eyes.

All men long to be immortals,
Yet dote on the wives they've wed,
Who swear to love their husband evermore,
But remarry as soon as he's dead.

All men long to be immortals,
Yet with getting sons won't have done.
Although fond parents are legion,
Who ever saw a really filial son?

▶▶ 四、翻译赏析

"原文一"描述的是林黛玉初见王熙凤的情形，将王熙凤的八面玲珑写得有声有色，令人绝倒。其目光、嘴巴处处在黛玉身上，而心思却时时念着贾母，既讨好黛玉，又向贾母承欢邀宠，看贾母的眼色，忽悲忽喜，"转悲为喜"，同时还不忘彰显当家少奶奶的身份，一面安顿黛玉，一面吩咐婆子丫鬟。霍译本中的人物对话更加生动活泼，如"竟忘记了老祖宗。该打，该打！"译为"I'm afraid I quite forget you, Grannie dear. I deserve to be spanked, don't I?"一个反义疑问，更显"泼皮破落户儿"的调皮；贾母说"快再休提前话"译为"So let's have no more of this!"比"don't reopen that subject"更自然亲切。"况且这通身的气派，竟不像老祖宗的外孙女儿，竟是个嫡亲的孙女"一句，杨译本为了使读者更好理解，换一个角度叙述为"She doesn't take after her father, son-in-law of our Old Ancestress, but looks more like a Chia.", 将王熙凤的谄媚奉承之术更鲜明地表现出来。

"原文二"描写的是贾琏的小厮兴儿对尤二姐介绍王熙凤之为人，写得甚为热闹。"抓尖儿"、"拨火儿"、"雀儿拣着旺处飞，黑母鸡一窝儿，自家的事不管，倒替人家去瞎张罗"、"嘴甜心苦"、"上头一脸笑，脚下使绊子"、"明是一盆火，暗是一把刀"，将王熙凤的阴险狠毒刻画得惟妙惟肖、淋漓尽致。霍译本中的"get in with the news first"，"fan the flames up"，"soft of tongue and hard of heart"，"a welcoming fire when you see her, but a stab in the back when it's dark","The magpie looking for a bigger nest who set up house with the crow",杨译本中的"ducks and shifts the blames","double-faced and tricky"都很口语化,生动活泼,符合兴儿的人物身份和形象。

"原文三"《好了歌》出现在《红楼梦》的第一回,可以视为这部小说的总纲。甄士隐听见道人唱此歌,"便迎上来道:'你满口说些什么?只听见些"好"、"了"、"好"、"了"。'那道人笑道:"你若果听到'好'、'了'二字还算你明白。可知世上万般,好便是了,了便是好。若不了,便不好;若要好,须是了。我这歌儿,便名《好了歌》。"杨译本简洁流畅,韵脚活泼多变,比较忠实地传达了原歌意味。霍克斯的译本充分考虑到这首歌中的意蕴,采用 won 和 done 来翻译"好"和"了",不但让译文与原文一样音形俱美,而且还与小说后文中甄士隐和跛脚道人之间的对话有机地结合在一起,实为佳作。

五、课后练习

(一) 思考题

1. 《红楼梦》在英语世界的流传大致可分为几个时期?每个时期有何译介特色?
2. 比较霍克斯和杨宪益、戴乃迭的译本,指出其在处理文化语词上所采用的不同策略。
3. 《红楼梦》包罗万象、博大精深,在翻译《红楼梦》的过程中,译者会遇到哪些文化信息需要特别处理?

(二) 翻译题

1. 今风尘碌碌,一事无成,忽念及当日所有之女子,一一细考较去,觉其行止见识皆出于我之上。何我堂堂须眉,诚不若彼裙钗哉?实愧则有馀,悔又无益之大无可如何之日也!当此,则自欲将已往所赖天恩祖德,锦衣纨袴之时,饫甘餍肥之日,背父兄教育之恩,负师友规训之德,以至今日一技无成,半生潦倒之罪,编述一集,以告天下人:我之罪固不免,然闺阁中本自历历有人,万不可因我之不肖,自护己短,一并使其泯灭也。虽今日之茅椽蓬牖,瓦灶绳床,其晨夕风露,阶柳庭花,亦未有妨我之襟怀笔墨者。虽我未学,下笔无文,又何妨用假语村言,敷演出一段故事来,亦可使闺阁昭传,复可悦世之目,破人愁闷,不亦宜乎?

2. 一日,正当嗟悼之际,俄见一僧一道远远而来,生得骨骼不凡,丰神迥别,说说笑笑,来至峰下,坐于石边,高谈阔论:先是说些云山雾海、神仙玄幻之事,后便说到红尘中荣华富贵。此石听了，不觉打动凡心，也想要到人间去享一享这荣华富贵，但自恨粗蠢，不得已，便口吐人言，向那僧道说道："大师，弟子蠢物，不能见礼了！适闻二位谈那人世间荣耀繁华，心切慕之。弟子质虽粗蠢，性却稍通，况见二师仙形道体，定非凡品，必有补天济世之材，利物济人之德。如萌发一点慈心，携带弟子得入红尘，在那富贵场中，温柔乡里受享几年，自当永佩洪恩，万劫不忘也！"

3. 此事说来好笑，竟是千古未闻的罕事。只因西方灵河岸上三生石畔，有绛珠草一株，时有赤瑕宫神瑛侍者，日以甘露灌溉，这绛珠草始得久延岁月。后来既受天地精华，复得雨露滋养，遂得脱却草胎木质，得换人形，仅修成个女体，终日游于离恨天外，饥则食蜜青果为膳，渴则饮灌愁海水为汤。只因尚未酬报灌溉之德，故其五内便郁结着一段缠绵不尽之意。恰近日这神瑛侍者凡心偶炽，乘此昌明太平朝世，意欲下凡造历幻缘，已在警幻仙子案前挂了号。警幻亦曾问及，灌溉之情未偿，趁此倒可了结的。那绛珠仙子道："他是甘露之惠，我并无此水可还。他既下世为人，我也去下世为人，但把我一生所有的眼泪还他，也偿还得过他了。"因此一事，就勾出多少风流冤家来。

4. 这里雨村且翻弄书籍解闷。忽听得窗外有女子嗽声，雨村遂起身往窗外一看，原来是一个丫鬟，在那里撷花，生得仪容不俗，眉目清明，虽无十分姿色，却亦有动人之处。雨村不觉看得呆了。那甄家丫鬟撷了花，方欲走时，猛抬头见窗内有人，敝巾旧服，虽是贫窘，然生得腰圆背厚，面阔口方，更兼剑眉星眼，直鼻权腮。这丫鬟忙转身回避，心下乃想："这人生的这样雄壮，却又这样褴褛，想他定是我家主人常说的什么贾雨村了，每有意帮助周济，只是没甚机会。我家并无这样贫窘亲友，想定是此人无疑了。怪道又说他必非久困之人。"如此想来，不免又回头两次。雨村见他回了头，便自为这女子心中有意于他，便狂喜不尽，自为此女子必是个巨眼英雄，风尘中之知己也。

5. 众人见黛玉年貌虽小，其举止言谈不俗，身体面庞虽怯弱不胜，却有一段自然的风流态度，便知他有不足之症。因问："常服何药，如何不急为疗治？"黛玉道："我自来是如此，从会吃饮食时便吃药，到今日未断，请了多少名医修方配药，皆不见效。那一年我三岁时，听得说来了一个癞头和尚，说要化我去出家，父母固是不从。他又说：既舍不得他，只怕他的病一生也不能好的了。若要好时，除非从此以后总不许见哭声，除父母之外，凡有外姓亲友之人，一概不见，方可平安了此一世。'疯疯癫癫，说了这些不经之谈，也没人理他。如今还是吃人参养荣丸。"贾母道："正好，我这里正配丸药呢。叫他们多配一料就是了。"

6. 不想如今忽然来了一个薛宝钗,年纪虽大不多,然品格端方,容貌美丽,人人都说黛玉不及。那宝钗却又行为豁达,随分从时,不比黛玉孤高自许,目无下尘,故深得下人之心,就是小丫头们亦多和宝钗亲近。

参考读物

Hawkes, David. Trans. *The Story of the Stone* [M]. London:Penguin Books Ltd,1986.

冯庆华.红译艺坛:《红楼梦》翻译艺术研究[M].上海:上海外语教育出版社,2006.

江帆.《红楼梦》百年英译史话(一)至(五)[J].东方翻译,2011(1)—(5).

杨宪益、戴乃迭译. *A Dream of Red Mansions* [M]. 北京:外文出版社,1978—1980.

王宏印.《红楼梦》诗词曲赋英译比较研究[M].西安:陕西师范大学出版社,2001.

第十八课

《黄帝内经》

▶▶ 一、内容简介

《黄帝内经》(以下简称《内经》),即《素问》与《灵枢》之合称,为我国现存最早之医学典籍,反映了我国古代的医学成就,奠定了我国医学发展的基础,成为我国医药之祖、医家之宗。唐人王冰在《黄帝内经素问注·序》中说:"其文简,其意博,其理奥,其趣深;天地之象分,阴阳之候列,变化之由表,死生之兆彰;不谋而遐迩自同,勿约而幽明斯契;稽其言有征,验之事不忒。"

《内经》之名始见于西汉末年刘歆所著的《七略》,后载于东汉班固所著的《汉书·艺文志》。其冠以"黄帝"之名,乃是受当时托古学风的影响,意在表明其论之道正源远。《素问》的成书年代历来有不同的说法。其名始见于东汉张仲景撰写的《伤寒论》序言中。《灵枢》作为《黄帝内经》之分册,其名出现较晚,始见于中唐时期王冰的《黄帝内经素问注·序》。关于其命名之含义,历来说法不一。

从现存《素问》所述来看,其内容大致可以分为如下三个部分。第一部分为除运气七篇和两个附篇外的全部内容,是《素问》成编时的基本内容。一般认为这部分内容非一时一人之作,但对其成编时间说法不一。第二部分为运气七篇。《素问》至隋唐时期已残缺第七卷,唐人王冰在整理《素问》时,自称得其先师秘藏,补入了这部分内容。第三部分为《素问》遗篇,即"刺法论"和"本病论"。这两篇内容在王冰校注《素问》时尚缺,仅保存了两篇篇名,并注明"亡"。宋人林亿等校正《素问》时发现有此二篇之流传本,认为其为伪作。但就其内容来看,与"运气七篇大论"属同一学术体系,对"运气七篇大论"内容有一定的补充意义,所以现一般将其作为《素问》之附篇。

《灵枢》的内容十分丰富。它以阴阳五行学说为指导，全面论述了人体的生理、病理、诊断、治疗、摄生等问题，并叙述了脏腑、精神、气、血、津液的功能和病理变化，强调了人与自然的密切联系及人体内部协调统一的整体观念，而其最突出的特点则是更翔实地阐述了经络理论和针法。与此相关的内容占了《灵枢》的五分之四左右。因此，《灵枢》是总结汉代以前我国经络学和针刺技术的最重要著述，为针灸学的发展奠定了基础。此外，《内经》中还记述了大量古代天文、气象、物候等学科的知识，为各有关学科的研究提供了重要的史料。

二、翻译传播

根据记载，中国与西方世界的交往可以追溯到汉代（武斌，1998：345—355），但中西方之间真正意义上的文化交流则始于元明之际。随着中西方之间商业往来的开展，传教士也循迹而至。他们在努力向中国人民宣扬基督教义的同时，也不断地向西方传递有关中国历史、文化、社会等方面的各种信息。作为中国医药宝典的《内经》，有关其思想理论的信息也间接地被传递到了西方世界。

但中国医药与《内经》思想真正传入西方，还是18世纪以后的事情。随着西方文艺复兴及工业革命的完成，西方资产阶级完成了其原始资本积累，开始将贪恋的目光投向世界的其他地区。于是，大批西方的殖民者和冒险家们以种种名义奔向世界各地开辟殖民地。这些以坚船利炮为先导的西方殖民主义者在明清时期已陆续来到亚洲，先后征服了印度等古老国家，并在那里建立了所谓的贸易公司。其中最为臭名昭著的就是设立在印度的"荷兰东印度公司"，该公司为了牟取暴利，大肆贩卖鸦片到中国，给中国人民带来了空前的灾难，并引发了西方列强直接侵略中国的鸦片战争。

伴随着西方殖民者而来的，除了殖民、鸦片、掠夺和杀戮外，还有一些西方医学家和植物学家。他们出于职业的原因，对异域文化和医药产生了浓厚的兴趣。如当时供职于"荷兰东印度公司"的几名荷兰医生，在印度和日本接触到了中国医药，并设法找到了一些资料。回国之后，他们根据自己的发现和观察并结合所收集到的资料，对中国医药进行了初步的研究分析，并撰文著书，介绍中国医药的基本理论和实践。当然这些介绍都是非常简单的，而且带有很大的猜测性。但对于西方读者来讲，这仍然是闻所未闻的故事。这些故事在19世纪的西方曾经引发了关于中国医药的第一次热潮。（李照国，2009：146—149）。

在19世纪上叶，虽然中国医药学，特别是针灸学，曾经在西方风靡一时，但有关《内经》的思想并未在西方得到系统的介绍。因为那时的西方人对中国医药知识还是一知半解，甚至完全属道听途说，还没有人能真正了解中国医药的真谛，也还没有人能够完整地掌握以《内经》为代表的中国医药体系。

直到20世纪初，法国驻中国外交官苏理（George Soulie de Morant, 1878—1955）的出现，才改变了中国医药在西方的境况。苏理在中国医药，特别是针灸在西方的再度复兴中发挥了重要的作用。苏理于1907—1927年在中国任外交官，学会了中文，并从一位姓杨的针灸师那里学会了针灸。回国后不久辞去外交职务，专门从事针灸的临床实践和宣传推广工作，并于1934年出版了《真正的中国针刺术》一书，在法国与欧洲产生了深远的影响。在苏理的影响下，一些西方学者开始关注中国医药及其典籍的翻译问题，并将《针灸大成》等中医典籍翻译成西方文字出版。但有关《内经》的翻译，却迟迟无人问津，因为这实在是一项常人难以想象的艰巨任务。直到1945年2月，美国人Ilza Veith 在勒克菲勒基金会的赞助下，在约翰·霍布金斯大学的医学史研究所开始研究翻译《内经》，并以此作为自己的博士论文。第二年勒克菲勒基金会再次提供经费，支持她的这项翻译研究。

经过艰苦的努力，Veith 将《内经》中的《素问》部分81章中的前32章翻译成英文出版，其中有三分之一的内容是对《素问》理论和思想体系的研究评介。尽管只翻译了《素问》的前32章，不足《内经》全文的五分之一，但这亦是破天荒之举，足以震惊世界中医界和西方汉学界，给中国医药的西传发挥了重要作用。

早在Veith之前，《内经》的一些内容和篇章已经以这样或那样的形式介绍到了西方世界。如 Alfred Forke 1923 年在伦敦出版的《中国人的世界观念》(The World-Conception of the Chinese)一书的第250—252页，曾引用了《内经》的部分内容；Percy M. Dawson 在1923年出版的《医学史年鉴》(Annals of Medical History)第七版59—64页所发表的《素问——中国医学的基础》一文中，引用了《内经》的部分内容；William R. Morse 在1934年纽约出版的《中国医学》第75页引用了《内经》的部分内容(Veith, 2002:XVII)。但这些介绍或翻译只能算是只言片语之介或零敲碎打之译，还不足以反映《内经》思想和体系的全貌。

Veith 翻译的《素问》前32章以 Yellow Emperor's Classic of Internal Medicine(黄帝内经)之名出版，容易给人造成《内经》全译本的印象。但事实上却只翻译了《内经》极少的一部分内容。尽管如此,她的翻译仍然具有划时代的意义,因为这是历史上第一次将《内经》的某些章节连贯而完整地翻译成英文,且由西方人自己完成。这足以使西方人有机会了解《内经》的基本思想和学术体系的概貌,且为后来的翻译作了十分有益的探索。

第二次世界大战之后,中西方的文化交流得到了空前的加强。冷战时期虽然由于意识形态的原因,中西方之间的交往受到了极大的阻滞,但有关中国文化、中国经籍和中国医药的研究和探索,在西方却一刻也没有停止过。在这一历史时期,西方一些学者开始努力研究《内经》,试图揭开中国医药文化之谜。《内经》的英文译本、法文译本、德文译本等先后在西方出版问世。20 世纪末 21 世纪初,《内经》的思想在西方得到了进一步的传播和弘扬,又有一些译本在西方陆续出版。有些是西方学者自己翻译的,如德国慕尼黑大学文树德教授(Paul. U. Unchuld)不仅研究中医药与中国文化,而且出版了《素问》研究著作。有些是华裔学者翻译的,如美国华裔学者 Maoshing Ni 和加拿大华裔学者吕聪明等就曾先后在西方翻译出版《内经》。此外旅美华人吴连胜、吴奇父子也翻译了《内经》,其译本 1997 年由中国科学技术出版社出版。

中国大陆学者很早就开始尝试翻译《内经》。19 世纪 30 年代,中国学者王吉民先生与伍连德先生出版了他们用英文撰写的巨著《中国医学史》(History of Chinese Medicine),其中就摘译了部分《内经》的内容。19 世纪 50 年代,中国学者黄雯曾将《内经》的一些重要章节译成英文在《中华医学杂志》上连载(李照国,1993:6)。进入 21 世纪,《内经》在中国大陆的翻译有了新的进展。如朱明将中医院校《内经》讲义中所摘录的部分《内经》原文翻译成英文,由外文出版社出版。李照国翻译的《内经》作为"汉英大中华文库"之一部先后于 2005 年和 2008 年由世界图书出版公司出版。

这些不同地域、不同时期、不同译者所英译的《内经》,无论是全译、简译还是摘译,都不同程度地向西方读者展示了《内经》的基本思想和理论体系。当然,就翻译的"信"、"达"、"雅"而言,可谓各有千秋。总体上来看,西方译者在语言的运用方面比中国译者要自然流畅,而中国译者在对原文的理解和把握方面要比西方译者高出一等。

▶▶ 三、翻译对比

- 原文:

昔在黄帝,生而神灵,弱而能言,幼而徇齐,长而敦敏,成而登天。

乃问于天师曰:"余闻上古之人,春秋皆度百岁,而动作不衰;今时之人,年半百而动作皆衰者,时世异耶? 人将失之耶?"

岐伯对曰:上古之人,其知道者,法于阴阳,和于术数,食饮有节,起居有常,不妄作劳,故能形与神俱,而尽终其天年,度百岁乃去。今时之人不然也,以酒为浆,以妄为常醉以入房,以欲竭其精,以耗散其真,不知持满,不时御神,务快其心,逆于生乐,起居无节,故半百而衰也。

夫上古圣人之教下也,皆谓之虚邪贼风,避之有时,恬淡虚无,真气从之,精神内夺,病安从来。是以志闲而少欲,心安而不惧,形劳而不倦,气从以顺,各从其欲,皆得所愿。故美其食,任其服,乐其俗,高下不相慕,其民故曰朴。是以嗜欲不能劳其目,淫邪不能惑其心,愚智贤不肖不惧于物,故合于道。所以能年皆度百岁而动作不衰者,以其德全不危也。

Ilza Veith 译文:

In ancient times when the Yellow Emperor was born he was endowed with divine talents; while yet in early infancy he could speak; while still very young he was quick of apprehension and penetrating; when he was grown up he was sincere and comprehending; when he became perfect he ascended to Heaven.[1]

The Yellow Emperor once addressed T'ien Shih[2], the divinely inspired teacher: "I have heard that in ancient times the people lived (through the years) to be over a hundred years, and yet they remained active and did not become decrepit in their activities. But nowadays people reach only half of that age and yet become decrepit and failing. Is it because the world changes from generation to generation? Or is it that mankind is becoming negligent (of the laws of nature)?"

Ch'i Po answered, "In ancient times those who understood Tao (the way of self cultivation) patterned themselves upon the Yin and the Yang (the two principals in nature) and they lived in harmony with the arts of divination.[3] There was temperance in eating and drinking. Their hours of rising and retiring were regular and not disorderly and wild. By these means the ancients kept their bodies united with their souls so as to fulfill their allotted span completely, measuring unto a hundred years before they passed away. Nowadays people are not like this; they use wine as beverage and they adopt recklessness as usual behavior. They enter the chamber (of love) in an intoxicated condition;[4] their passions exhaust their vital forces; their cravings dissipate their true (essence); they do not know how to find contentment within themselves; they are not skilled in the control of their spirits. They devote all their attention to the amusement of their minds, thus cutting themselves off from the joys of long (life). Their rising and retiring is without regularity. For these reasons they reach only one half of the hundred years and then they degenerate."

"In the most ancient times the teachings of the sages (圣人) were followed by those beneath them; they said that weakness and noxious influences and injurious minds should be avoided at specific times. They [the sages] were tranquilly content in nothingness and the true vital force accompanied them always; their vital (original) spirit was preserved within; thus, how could illness come to them? They exercised restraint of their wills and reduced their desires; their hearts were at peace and without any fear; their bodies toiled and yet did not become weary. Their spirit followed in harmony and obedience; everything was satisfactory to their wishes and they could achieve whatever they wished. Any kind of food was beautiful (to them);⁵ and any kind of clothing was satisfactory. They felt happy under any condition. To them it did not matter whether a man held a high or a low position in life. These men can be called pure at heart. No kind of desire can tempt the eyes of those pure people and their mind cannot be misled by excessiveness and evil. (In such a society) no matter whether men are wise or foolish, virtuous or bad, they are without fear of anything; they are in harmony with Tao, the Right Way. Thus they could live more than one hundred years and remain active without becoming decrepit, because their virtue was perfect and never imperiled."

[Veith 译文原注]

1. See also: Edouard Chavannes, Les Memoires historiques de Sema Ts'ien (Paris, 1885), p. 26.

2. 天师 This title when applied to formal Taoism means "Master of Heaven" and denotes the highest rank in the Taoist hierarchy. See W. Grube, Religion and Kultus der Chinesen (Leipzig, 1910), p. 115.

3. Fung Yu-lan, A History of Chinese Philosophy, tr. by Derk Bodde (Peipin, 1937), p. 26. Wang Ping says: 术数 are the great rules of the protection of life. These characters, of an ancient science combining astrology and divination. The chronomancy of the calendar repre-

sents one of the phases of these artful calculations.

4. Wang Ping explains: They were satisfied with good food as well as bad food.

Maoshing Ni 译文:

In ancient times the Yellow Emperor, Huang Di, was known to have been a child prodigy. As he grew he showed himself to be sincere, wise, honest, and compassionate. He became very learned and developed keen powers for observing nature. His people recognized him as a natural leader and chose him as their emperor.

During his reign, Huang Di discoursed on medicine, health, lifestyle, nutrition, and Taoist cosmology with his ministers Qi Bo, Lei Gong, and others. Their first discussion began with Huang Di inquiring, "I've heard that in the days of old everyone lived one hundred years without showing the usual signs of aging. In our time, however, people age prematurely, living only fifty years. Is this due to a change in the environment, or is it because people have lost the correct way of life?"

Qi Bo replied, "In the past, people practiced the Tao, the Way of Life. They understood the principle of balance, of yin and yang, as represented by the transformation of the energies of the universe. Thus, they formulated practices such as Dao-in, an exercise combining stretching, massaging, and breathing to promote energy flow, and meditation to help maintain and harmonize themselves with the universe. They ate a balanced diet at regular times, arose and retired at regular hours, avoided overstressing their bodies and minds, and refrained from overindulgence of all kinds. They maintained well-being of body and mind; thus, it is not surprising that they lived over one hundred years. These days, people have changed their way of life. They drink wine as though it were water, indulge excessively in destructive activities, drain their jing—the body's essence that is stored in the kidneys—and deplete their qi. They do not know the secret of conserving their energy and vitality. Seeking emotional excitement and momentary pleasures, people disregard the natural rhythm and order of the universe. They fail to regulate their lifestyle and diet, and sleep improperly. So it is not surprising that they look old at fifty and die soon after.

"The accomplished ones of ancient times advised people to guard themselves against zei feng, disease-causing factors. On the mental level, one should remain calm and avoid excessive desires and fantasies, recognizing and maintaining the natural purity and clarity of the mind. When internal energies are able to circulate smoothly and freely, and the energy of the mind is not scattered, but is focused and concentrated, illness and disease can be avoided. Previously, people led a calm and honest existence, detached from undue desire and ambition; they lived with an untainted conscience and without fear. They were active, but never depleted themselves. Because they lived simply, these individuals knew contentment, as reflected in their diet of basic but nourishing foods and attire that was appropriate to the season but never luxurious. Since they were happy with their position in life, they did not feel jealousy or greed. They had compassion for others and were helpful and honest, free from destructive habits. They remained unshakable and unswayed by temptations, and they were able to stay centered even when adversity arose. They treated others justly, regardless of their level of intelligence or social position."

李照国译文:

Huangdi, or Yellow Emperor [1], was born intelligent. He was eloquent from childhood. He behaved righteously when he was young. In his youth, he was honest, sincere and wise. When growing up, he became the emperor.

Huangdi asked Master Qibo, "I am told that people in ancient times all could live for one hundred years without any signs of senility. But people nowadays begin to become old at the age of fifty. Is it due to the changes of environment or the violation of the way to preserve health?"

Qibo answered, "The sages in ancient times who knew the Dao (the tenets for cultivating health) followed the rules of Yin and Yang and adjusted Shushu (the ways to cultivate health). They were moderate in eating and drinking, regular in working and resting, avoiding any overstrain[2]. That is why they could maintain a desirable harmony between the Shen (mind or spirit) and the body, enjoying a good health and a long life. People nowadays, on the contrary, just behave oppositely. They drink wine as thin rice gruel, regard wrong as right, and seek sexual pleasure after drinking. As a result, their Jingqi (Essence-Qi) is exhausted and Zhenqi (Genuine-Qi) is wasted. They seldom take measures to keep an exuberance of Jingqi (Essence-Qi) and do not know how to regulate their Shen (mind or spirit), often giving themselves to sensual pleasure. Being irregular in daily life, they begin to become old even at the age of fifty."

"When the sages in ancient times taught the people, they emphasized the importance of avoiding Xuxie (Deficiency-Evil) and Zeifeng (Thief-Wind)[3] in good time and keep the mind free from avarice.[4] In this way Zhenqi (Genuine-Qi) in the body will be in harmony, Jingshen (Essence-Spirit) will remain inside, and diseases will have no way to occur. Therefore people in ancient times all lived in peace and contentment, without any fear. They worked, but never overstrained themselves, making it smooth for Qi to flow. They all felt satisfied with their life and enjoyed their tasty food, natural clothes and naïve customs. They did not desire for high positions and lived simply and naturally. That is why improper addiction and avarice could not distract their eyes and ears, obscenity and fallacy could not tempt their mind. Neither the ignorant nor the intelligent and neither the virtuous nor the unworthy feared anything. Such a behavior quite accorded with the Dao (the tenets for cultivating health). This is the reason why they all lived over one hundred years without any signs of senility. Having followed the tenets of preserving health, they could enjoy a long life free from diseases."

[李照国译文原注]

1. Huangdi, also known as Yellow Emperor in the West, was one of the legendary kings in ancient China. He was the son of Shaodian(少典). His family name was Gongsun(公孙). He used to live by the Ji River(姬水). That was why people took Ji as another family name of him. Since Huangdi(黄帝) was born in a hill called Xuanyuan(轩辕), he was named after the hill. He founded his kingdom in Youxiong(有熊). So He was also called Youxiong(有熊). Owing to his great merits and virtues, he was supported by the heads of all tribes as the king. Since his kingdom took the color of earth as the auspicious sign, he was called Huangdi(黄帝), literally meaning Yellow Emperor, because the color of earth is yellow in the central region of China. During his reign, Huangdi(黄帝) made magnificent contributions to the civilization of the Chinese nation. That is why Huangdi(黄帝) is worshiped as the father of the Chinese nation.

2. Overstrain here actually means both sexual and physical exhaustion.

3. Xuxie(虚邪) and Zeifeng(贼风) refer to all abnormal climatic changes and exogenous

pathogenic factors. Gao Shizong(高士宗)said:"All the abnormal Qi in the four seasons can be called Xuxie(虚邪) and Zeifeng(贼风)." Usually Xieqi(邪气 Evil-Qi, or pathogenic factor) attack the human body when it has become weak. What is why Xieqi(邪气) is called Xuxie(虚邪)which literally means "weak-evil" or "deficiency-evil". Liuyin(六淫 six abnormal changes of the climate, i. e. wind, cold, summer-heat, dampness or wetness, dryness and fire) usually attacks the human body without being observed. Therefore, they are called Zeifeng(贼风)which literally means "thief-wind". Wang Bing(王冰)said, "Xieqi(邪气) attacks the human body when it has become weak, that is why it is called Xuxie(虚邪); when it secretly harms the human body, it is called Zeifeng(贼风)."

4. This sentence is also understood like this: In ancient times, people all followed the teachings of the sages who mastered the way to cultivate health and possessed supreme morality.

四、翻译赏析

（一）书名翻译赏析

翻译《内经》时,译者遇到的首要问题就是难解古文之意。历代虽有众多有关《内经》的注疏、校勘,但由于年代久远和辗转传抄,多有讹误,正确理解实非易事。《内经》书名的翻译就是典型之例。

表面看来,"黄"、"帝"、"内"、"经"四字并不难解,似乎也不难译。深加探究,其实不然。以前在国内外,不少译者都将《黄帝内经》译为 Yellow Emperor's Internal Medicine 或 Yellow Emperor's Internal Classic。"黄帝"之"帝"是 emperor 吗？似乎还不能如此简单释义。因为中国作为王权象征的 emperor,其实始于秦王嬴政。秦之前的国君皆称作"王"。"三皇五帝"属上古传说中的华夏民族首领,与大一统帝国时期的统治者有着本质的不同。所以《汉英词典》将"五帝"翻译为 five lords,而不是 five emperors;将"黄帝"音译为 Huangdi,而不是直译为 Yellow Emperor。

对"黄帝"尊号翻译之争,表面上看反映了译人对中国传统文化的不同理解和解读,究其实质,反映的则是今人对古典文化形神关系缺乏基本的了解。不少人以为将"黄帝"译为 Yellow Emperor 颇为滑稽,不合实际。"黄"与"帝"在汉语中究竟是什么意思？将"黄帝"译作 Yellow Emperor 为何不妥？要解决这些问题,就必须从中国古典哲学中寻求答案。

海外译者常常对"黄帝"的称谓感到不可思议。不知道为什么要将轩辕帝称为"黄帝"。在汉语中,"黄"与"帝"的结合有着深刻的文化与哲学基础。不明其喻,便难晓其理。根据中国古典哲学五行学说的理论,以"五行"配"五方",则"五方"之"中"与"五色"之"黄"恰相匹配。传说帝轩辕居于中原,中原之土亦为黄色,而帝轩辕又有土瑞之德,故称其为"黄帝"。在中国文化背景下,"黄帝"之"黄"的形式与它所承载的文化内涵,经过千秋万载的磨合,达到了圆满的统一。而在西方文化背景下,yellow 与 emperor 的形式和内涵之间尚未实现统一,尚不足以表现其在中国文化中所承载的深刻内涵。所以将"黄帝"直译为 Yellow Emperor,便显突兀。

表面上看来,Yellow 在英语中似乎仅仅是一个色彩概念,因此与 Emperor 搭配在一起自然缺乏必要的文化基础。很多国内译者正是基于这样的认识,认为将"黄帝"译为 Yellow Emperor 不够妥当。其实人们之所以觉得 Yellow Emperor 这种译法不够严谨,难以接受,实在是由于译文形式与内容的"两相悬隔"而造成的。假如中国文化已经比较系统而深入地传播到了西方,假如西方人对中国文化有了比较深刻的了解和认识,就像今天的中国学人对西方文化了解和掌握的那样,那么英译的中国古典文化的概念的形式与其所承载的实际内涵,就一定会在西方文化的背景下逐步实现圆满的统一。目前其形式和内容之间还没有实现统一,这一现实只能说明我们对外翻译传播中国古典文化还不够深入扎实,还有很长的路要走,而不能简单地否定某种译法,或提倡某种译法。

从目前的中西方文化交流的实际来看,国内译者对 Yellow Emperor 译法的非议很多情况下都是从自身的理解出发来考虑问题的,其实未必完全符合西方读者看待中国文化的心态。了解这一点对于客观传译国学典籍至为重要。因为译者在翻译一部典籍时,不仅仅要立足原文的主旨精神,而且要从译者的角度来解读和领会原文之意。翻译和介绍中国文化和国学典籍时,当然需要考虑海外读者的理解能力,但更应该考虑的是如何在翻译时既能照顾到读者的接受能力,又能努力保持中国文化的系统性、完整性和原质性。如果一味地从读者——其实往往是从译者自身化了"想象读者"——的角度考虑问题,削足适履便在所难免。

鉴于"黄帝"尊号在国内外的翻译实际,尤其考虑到约定俗成的原则,我们在翻译《内经》时,综合了意译和音译两种看似相反实则相成的翻译方法,将音译的 Huangdi 作为正名,以保持其内涵的原质性;将意译的 Yellow Emperor 作为副名,对正名起补充说明的作用,以利于读者理解原文的基本含义。翻译上如此处理,原因有二:一是随着中国文化对外传播和交流的不断发展,西方读者对"黄帝"这样的中国特有名称和概念的实际内涵的理解,也在逐步加深;二是在西方,Yellow Emperor 的译法较为流行,为不少人所熟知。音译加意译,自然利于西方读者更好地了解"黄帝"的真正含义。但这样一种处理方法其实并不能从根本上解决"黄帝"的翻译问题,因为它并没有给出读者一个完整的概念或足以帮助读者理解此概念具体、实际内涵的信息来。所以在音译加意译之后,我们还在文后给读者提供了一条较为详细的注解(见上文),以帮助读者准确了解"黄帝"尊号的实际内涵。

此外,"内经"之"内"很多译者将其直观地译作 internal 或 interior。其实,"内经"之"内"是中国古代书籍卷次的表示方法,类似于今天所说的"上卷"或"上册",而不是什么 internal 或 interior。"内经"自然也不是什么 internal medicine(内科学)。在国学典籍中,很多书都是以"内"或"外"命名的,如《白氏内经》、《白氏外经》、《扁鹊内经》、《扁鹊外经》等。其实除《黄帝内经》外,还有《黄帝外经》,只是后者在历史的长河中不幸亡佚了。近年来已有出版社出版了据说是新发现的《黄帝外经》,但还没有得到学界的公认。

(二) 语言特点与翻译赏析

1. 语言古奥

由于《内经》的思想形成于远古,体系构建于春秋,编撰成书于秦汉,其文字颇具远古形质和先秦风韵,因此远在隋唐时期,这部经籍已颇不易解。再加上古时没有印刷业,文字多写于锦帛之上或刻于木竹之简。而锦帛和木竹又易于损坏,不易保存。因此,经籍常常因此而字迹不清或文辞含混,如《素问·脉要精微论》篇有"反四时者,有余为精,不足为消"(If the conditions of the pulse are contrary to the changes of yin and yang in the four seasons, superabundance indicates excess while insufficiency indicates consumption)之说,其中"精"字颇不易解。

唐人王冰(公元710—804)注解《内经》时,将此处之"精"解为"精气"(essential qi)。明人张介宾(公元1563—1640)在注《类经》时,则认为此处之"精"实指"邪气"(pathogenic factor)。明清之际学人张志聪(1616—1674)在《素问集注》中则蹊径另辟,以为此处之"精"为肾藏之精(essence stored in the kidney)。日本人丹波元简(公元1755—1810)在《素问识》中,则疑其为错简,因为"精"、"消"二字其义不明。其后各家皆有见解,但何者为正,何者为误,至今仍需慎加剖析。

《内经》语言之古奥难解,由此可见一斑。海外译者往往很难辨析《内经》的字词结构及其喻义特点,翻译时便难免猜测揣度,甚至张冠李戴。例如,美国人 Ilza Veith 将"反四时者,有余为精,不足为消"译为 those who act contrary to the laws of the four seasons and live in excess have insufficient secretions and dissipate their duties,便属望文生义之举。

就词语而言,古汉语中单纯词最为常见,复合词较为少见,《内经》也是如此。《内经》中的单纯词有时也由两个汉字组合而成,但却不是复合词。这一点非常独特,如果稍加疏忽,就可能误解其意。《内经》中的此类单纯词大致包括联绵词、叠音词、偏义复词和单纯复音词类。

1.1 联绵词

一般来讲,这类单纯词中的两个汉字只是代表两个音节,因此不能按照有关字形的表层之意去解读。事实上,这样的联绵词是一个整体,只能表达一个意思,而不是两个字的表层意思之和。在《内经》中,这样的联绵词又可以分作两类,即双声联绵词(如"密默"、"凛冽"、"恍惚"等)和叠韵联绵词(如"招尤"、"逡巡"、"从容"等)。

对这样的联绵词若缺乏认识,则必然影响对《内经》经文的理解和释义。如《素问·五脏生成篇》"徇蒙招尤,目冥耳聋,下实上虚,过在足少阳、厥阴"(dizziness, tremor, dim vision and deafness are caused by excess in the lower and deficiency in the upper due to disorder of the meridians of Foot-Shaoyang and Foot-Jueyin)一句中有"招尤"(tremor)一词,就是一个叠韵联绵词。唐人王冰在注解《素问》时忽略了叠韵联绵词这一修辞现象,对这个词语作了不太贴切的解释,以为"招"是"掉"(shaking)之意、"尤"是"甚"(severe)之意。根据东汉人许慎(约58—约147年)所著的《说文解字》及后世学人的研究和分析,这里的"招尤"其实就是"招摇"(tremor)之异,属叠韵联绵词。

Veith 在翻译此句时将"徇蒙招尤"译作 lack of discernment causes evil,即将"招尤"理解为动宾结构,显属误解。

1.2 叠音词

所谓叠音词,即由两个音节相同的字所构成的词语。这类词语仍然属于单纯词,如《素问·脉要精微论篇》中"浑浑革革,至如涌泉,病进而危;弊弊绵绵,其去如弦绝者死"(large and rapid pulse that beats like gushing of a spring indicates critical progress of a disease; weak and indistinct pulse that beats a musical string on the verge of breaking indicates impending death)中的"浑浑"、"革革"、"弊弊"、"绵绵"等就是叠音单纯词。"浑浑"指脉大(large pulse),"革革"指脉急(rapid pulse),"弊弊"指脉微(indistinct pulse),"绵绵"指

脉弱(weak pulse)。Veith 将这句话译为：

When the pulse of the pulse is turbid and the color disturbed like a bubbling well, it is a sign that disease has entered the body, the color has become corrupted and the constitution delicate. And when the constitution is delicate it will be broken up like the strings of a lute and die. Therefore, it is desirable to understand the force of the five viscera.

仔细推究便可发现,译文中对有关词语的理解颇显表化,如将"浑浑"译作 turbid,而"革革"、"弊弊"、"绵绵"等叠音词译文皆无体现。其他概念的翻译也很值得商榷,如将"病进"(progress of disease)译作 disease has entered the body,即属字面之译。此外,"浑浑"、"革革"、"弊弊"、"绵绵"等都描述的是脉动之象,译文却和 constitution(体质)无端地加以关联,似有凭空杜撰之嫌。

对于这样的叠音词,翻译时应根据具体的语言环境去理解,而不能按照有关字的本义去解读。

1.3 偏义复词

所谓偏义复词,就是由意义相反的两个字构成的词。但该词的含义却不是两个字意义之和,而是只取其一。《内经》中常见的偏义复词包括"逆从"、"死生"、"虚实"等。如《素问·上古天真论篇》"辩列星辰,逆从阴阳"(to differentiate the order of constellations and to follow the law of yin and yang)中,"逆从"只表示"从"(abide by),而不表示"逆"(deviate from)。

但"逆从"一词在《内经》并不总是偏义复词,有时也是并列词组。如在《素问·平人气象论篇》"脉有逆从四时"(Pulse either corresponds to or differs from climatic changes in the four seasons)一句中,"逆从"就表示的是"逆"与"从"两层含义,而不是只"逆"不从或只"从"不"逆"。

"死生"也是《内经》中常见的一个偏义复词。如在《素问·阴阳别论篇》"别于阳者,知病忌时;别于阴者,知死生之期"(Differentiation of yang enables one to know where the disease is located while differentiation of yin enables one to know when death will occur)一句中,"死生"就是一个偏义复词,只指"死期",不含"生期"。再如《素问·三部九候论篇》说:"戴阳者太阳已绝,此决死生之要,不可不察也"(Patient with the manifestations of floating yang indicates exhaustion of taiyang, which is a critical sign of death and should not be overlooked),此句中的"死生"也是偏义复词,只表示"死期",不含有"生期"。

要对《内经》中诸如"死生"这样的偏义复词之内涵作出准确的判断并不是一件容易的事情,需要根据诸多因素进行综合分析。如《素问·移精变气论篇》"余欲临病人,观死生,决嫌疑"(I want to inspect patients to decide favorable and unfavorable prognosis so as to make correct diagnosis)中的"死生"一词,学界多以为是偏义复词,单指"死期"。但据笔者观之,此处之"死生"却应包括"死"与"生"两个方面,即良与不良之预后。这从上下文之论述即可明了一二。

Veith 将这句话译作"I should like to be near a sick person and to observe when death strikes. The sudden end of life fills me with curiosity and doubts,"对"生死"的理解、对"嫌疑"的释义均失之偏颇。

这样的例子在《内经》中并非个别。如《素问·脉要精微论篇》说:"观五脏有余不足,六腑强弱,形之盛衰,以此参伍,决死生之分。"(A synthetic analysis of the conditions of the five zang-organs, which may be either deficiency or excess, the six fu-organs, which may be either hypoactive or hyperactive, and the body, which may be either strong or weak, will enable one to know whether the disease in question is curable or incurable.)此句中的"死生"也是既指"死",又指"生",Veith 将其译作 to decide upon the share of life and death,Maoshing Ni 将其译作 determine the life and death of the patient,均较为符合原文之意。

对于《内经》中诸如"逆从"、"生死"这样一些独特的偏义复词,翻译时只有根据上下文意慎加辨析,方可准确把握实际内涵,才能避免按字释义之误。

1.4 单纯复音词

这类复音词由两个单独的汉字构成,但两个汉字各自的含义在该复音词中并不存在。也就是说,该复音词不能拆开理解。若拆开解读,便是望文生义,曲解原文。

《内经》中的"祝由"一词便是典型之例,如《素问·移精变气篇》说:"余闻古之治病,惟其移精变气,可祝由而已。"(I have heard that in ancient times diseases were cured by sorcerers through transforming essence and changing qi.)隋唐学人杨上善(589—681)在注解"祝由"时,以为古人治病,"祝为去病之所由",即认为"祝由"是"祝说病由"。唐人王冰在解读这句话时也以为如此。

其实按照《说文》等经籍解,"祝由"是一个单纯的复音词,意即通过诅咒消除疾病,不能将"祝由"拆开分解。类似"祝由"这样的复音单纯词在《内经》中还有不少,如表示穴位名称的"天窗"、"扶突"、"委中"等皆是如此。其他的如药石名谓、疾病名称等，亦是如此。翻译时，此等词语皆不可拆分理解。若强加拆分，虽则可以训得大意，却难免穿凿附会、曲解文义。

Veith 将这句话翻译为：I understand that in olden times the treatment of diseases consisted merely of the transmittal of the Essence and the transformation of the life-giving principle. One could invoke the gods and this was the way to treat.

Veith 的译文比较透迤晦涩，尤其是将"变气"译作 life-giving principle，显得语义不明。但将"祝由"译作 invoke the gods，似乎在一定程度上揭示了其基本内涵。

Maoshing Ni 将这句话翻译为：I have heard that in ancient times, when the sages treated, all they had to do was employ methods to guide and change the emotional and spiritual state of a person and redirect the energy flow. The sages utilized a method called zhu yuo, prayer, ceremony, and shamanism, which healed all conditions.

Maoshing Ni 之译显属意释，所以译文较为冗长，但基本揭示了原文的实际内涵，尤其是将"祝由"音译为 zhu yuo（应为 zhu you），附加文内注解，是比较可取的。

2. 用词讲究

《内经》语言极其优美。无论理论阐发、是非论辩还是客观陈述，都字斟句酌，且以常见胜、以平见奇、以陈见新。

2.1 贴切准确

《内经》词语的运用可谓精雕细琢，恰到好处，因景设喻，因意遣词，错落有致，妙得其趣。

如谈到"清浊"问题时，《素问·阴阳应象大论篇》说："故清阳出上窍，浊阴出下窍；清阳发腠理，浊阴走五脏，清阳实四支，浊阴归六腑。"（Thus the lucid yang ascends to flow through the orifices in the upper part of the body while the turbid yin descends to be discharged from the orifices in the lower part of the body; the lucid yang penetrates through the muscular interstices while the turbid yin moves into the five zang-organs; the lucid yang fortifies the four limbs while the turbid yin nourishes the six fu-organs.）。此文之述，对仗工整，平仄相应，文词呼应，妙趣横生。其中"出"、"发"、"走"、"实"、"归"五字皆为普通词语，但与"清阳"、"浊阴"相配，神机顿生，细微而贴切地表达了二者之不同走向、作用特点和循行大势。纵观上下文意之布陈，其字词的选择可谓恰如其分、贴切之极。

Veith 将这句话翻译为：The pure and lucid element of light is manifest in the upper orifices and the turbid element of darkness is manifest in the lower orifices. Yang, the element of light, originates in the pores. Yin, the element of darkness, moves within the five viscera. Yang, the lucid element of life, is truly represented by the four extremities; and Yang, the turbid element of darkness, restores the power of the six treasuries of nature.

Veith 的译文，除"走"之外，基本没有能够揭示"出"、"发"、"实"、"归"等四字的基本内涵，原文的实际含义自然无法再现于译文。同时对一些基本概念的理解和翻译，也大有商榷之处。例如，将"清阳"（lucid yang）译作 the pure and lucid element of light，将"浊阴"（turbid yin）译作 the turbid element of darkness，喻意未明；将"腠理"译作 pores，释义偏狭；将"六腑"（six fu-organs）译作 six treasuries of nature，显属误译。

再如《素问·脉要精微论篇》说："夫精明者，所以视万物，别黑白，审长短；以长为短，以白为黑，如是则精衰矣。"（The eyes function to observe things, distinguish white from black and differentiate long from short. If the eyes take long as short and white as black, it is a sign that essence is declining.）其中的"视"、"别"、"审"三个动词的使用自然而贴切，形象而准确地描绘了眼睛的基本功能，即观察事物、分辨黑白、审视长短。翻译时只有对其别加分析，慎加转换，方能较为准确地表达原文之意。但这样的细细分析和谨慎转换，有时似乎并不易为。如 Veith 将此句经文译作：

But those who are skilful and clever in examination observe every living creature. They distinguish black and white; they examine whether the pulse is short or long. When they mistake a long pulse for a short one and when they mistake white for black or commit similar errors, then it is a sign that their skill has deteriorated.

将原文与译文详加比较便可发现，译文和原文可谓南辕北辙。原文中的"精明"指的是眼睛，而译者却将其误以为是 those who are skilful and clever in examination。如此一来，其他部分的翻译自然是"离题万里"了。

Maoshing Ni 将这句话译作：

Healthy organs will manifest a healthy luster. Without this expression of the five colors, the jing/essence of the organs is departing and coming to the surface. These colors give the physician the basis for a prognosis. The lustrous colors indicate a better prognosis than the dull colors. However, even the lustrous colors must not be obvious. When obvious, even the healthy colors can indicate an extreme consequence.

与原文相比,这个译文也使人读来如坠云海雾山之感,不知其所云者何。

又如《素问·离合真邪论》篇"必先扪而循之,切而散之,推而按之,弹而怒之,抓而下之,通而取之,外引其门,以闭其神"(Feel and press the acupoint first in order to disperse meridian qi. Then push, press and flick the acupoint so as to dilate the meridian. Finally nail the acupoint and insert the needle into it. When qi has arrived, the needle should be removed. After the needle is withdrawn, the needled region should be immediately pressed to prevent leakage of qi.)一句,连用"扪"、"切"、"推"、"弹"、"抓"、"通"六个动词,表达了针刺前后医者所采取的一系列连续动作。Veith 的译文如下:

One must first feel with the hand and trace the system of the body. One should interrupt the sufficiencies and distribute them evenly, one should apply binding and massage. One should attack the sick part and allow it to swell, one should pull it and make it subside, one should distribute it and get hold of the evil.

这个译文开句与原文还较为吻合,但很快便偏离主题,另行其说了。翻译这句经文时,译者必须明确这一系列的动作都是和"穴位"、"经络"和"针刺"手法密切相关的,必须围绕这个三点一线的主题来释义。若偏离了这一主题,便难循其意。

2.2 鲜明生动

《内经》作者在描写人体生理功能、病理变化以及自然现象和天人关系时,用词往往精细而生动,使有关概念内涵深刻、语义鲜明、形象生动,读来引人入胜。

如《素问·藏气法时论》篇谈到心病的发展时说:"心病者,日中慧,夜半甚,平旦静。"(Heart disease tends to be improved in the noon, worsened at middle night and stable in the morning.)文中使用了"慧"、"甚"、"静"三个形容词,将心病的特点和临床表现刻画得可谓淋漓尽致。特别是"慧"字的运用,有出神入化之功,形象地刻画了病人因病情减轻而产生的爽快之感。Veith 将这句话译为:

Those who suffer from a sick heart are animated and quick-witted at noon, around midnight their spirits are heightened, and in the early morning they are peaceful and quiet.

译文将"慧"译作 animated and quick-witted,将"甚"译作 their spirits are heightened,颇不合原文之意。"慧"的意思是"病人感觉清爽",与"智慧"(wit)没有关系;"甚"的意思自然是"病情加重",译作 their spirits are heightened 便不知所云了。

又如《素问·离合真邪论》篇谈到自然界与人体经脉的关系时说:"天地温和,则经水安静;天寒地冻,则经水凝泣;天暑地热,则经水沸溢。"该段文字用词颇为讲究。其中"天地温和"、"天寒地冻"、"天暑地热"对仗工整,前后呼应,层层递进,环环紧扣。而"安静"、"凝泣"、"沸溢"则形象地描述了"经水"在不同季节和气候情况下的形态变化。Veith 将这段精辟的论述翻译如下:

When Heaven and Earth are warm and gentle, then the main arteries of the water are peaceful and quiet. When Heaven is cold and the Earth is icy (frozen), then the main arteries of water are stiffened and frozen. When Heaven is very hot and the Earth is heated, the arteries of water boil over.

这个译文基本上还是达意的,但就文趣而言,显然过于质直。所谓"天地温和",即 when it is warm;所谓"天寒地冻",即 when it is cold;所谓"天暑地热",即 when it is hot。原文中的"天"和"地"实际上指的就是自然或气候,不必逐字照译。

2.3 音韵和谐

古人著文,非常重视音韵节奏,所以南宋人陈骙(1128—1203)在其所著的《文则》一书中说:"夫乐奏而不和,乐不可闻;文作而不协,文不可诵。"《内经》的文体也是如此,不但注意"文协",而且注意平仄。虽然《内经》并非骈文,但字里行间却时时激荡着优美的旋律与和合的韵律。

如《素问·调经论篇》"其生于阳者,得之风雨寒暑;其生于阴者,得之饮食居处"一句中,"风雨寒暑"和"饮食居处"的平仄对仗颇合律诗要求,其平仄格式为"平仄平仄,仄平仄平"。这种优美的韵律,译文往往很难再现。

美籍华人吴氏父子将此句译为:The infections from yang are due to the invasion of wind, rain, cold and wetness, and those from yin are due to the intemperance of taking food and drink, abnormal daily life.

Maoshing Ni 将此句译为:A yin condition typically arises from improper diet, a lack of regularity in lifestyle, excess sex or lack of harmonious emotions. A yang condition is typically brought on by exposure to rain, wind, cold, or summer heat.

两则译文均在一定程度上传达了原文之意,但原文之韵律对仗却没有体现。由于中西语言和文化的差异,此般缺憾自然是可以理解的。此外,对一些具体概念的翻译,两则译文皆有未尽之意。如这里的"阴"和"阳",实际上指的是"阴经"(yin meridian)和"阳经"(yang meridian),直接音译作 yin 和 yang,意思不甚明确。所以若将"其生于阳者"与"其生于阴者"译作 diseases involving the yang meridians 和 diseases involving the yin meridians,似乎方较为妥当。

再如《素问·四气调神人论》篇说:"秋三月,此谓容平;天气以急,地气以明,早卧早起,与鸡俱兴;使志安宁,以缓秋刑;收敛神气,使秋气平;无外其志,使肺气清。"此段文字对仗工整,韵脚前后一致,颇有诗家风韵。Veith 将此段韵味十足的文字翻译如下:

The three months of Fall are called the period of tranquility of one's conduct. The atmosphere of Heaven is quick and the atmosphere of the Earth is clear. People should retire early at night and rise early (in the morning) with [the crowing of] the rooster. They should have their minds at peace in order to lessen the punishment of Fall. Soul and spirit should be gathered together in order to make the breath of Fall tranquil; and to keep their lungs pure they should not give vent to their desires.

在这个译文中,由于可以理解的原因,原文之神形气韵自然荡然无存。一些基本概念的理解和表达,也略嫌不足。如"容平"(full maturity of all things in nature)指自然界万物形态稳定,不再继续生长,译作 tranquility of one's conduct 便费解了;"天气以急"(wind blows violently)指天空的风气劲急,译作"The atmosphere of Heaven is quick",似乎未明其要;"收敛神气"(moderate mental activity)指思维活动适中,译作"soul and spirit should be gathered together"显然喻意不明;"使秋气平"(adapt to the changes of weather in autumn)指的是适应秋季的气候变化,译为 in order to make the breath of Fall tranquil 便有些不知所云了。

又如《素问·四气调神大论篇》"水冰地坼,无扰乎阳,早卧晚起,必待日光"一句,前后押韵,一韵到底,读来朗朗上口,如词文诗语一般。Veith 将其翻译如下:

Water freezes and the Earth cracks open. One should not disturb one's Yang. People should retire early at night and rise late in the morning and they should wait for the rising of the sun.

这则译文基本揭示了原文的实际内涵,语义还是比较明确的,只是在音韵和节奏上稍逊于原文。这也是翻译中国古典文献时无法突破的一个瓶颈。这个问题的存在自然与中国语言和文字的独有神韵密不可分。

3. 讲究修辞

《内经》各篇,行文工整,讲究修辞,音韵协和,文采飞扬。如谈到养生的原理和要旨时,《素问·上古天真论篇》篇说:"志困而少欲,心安而不惧,形劳而不倦,气从以顺,各从其欲,皆得所愿。"(People in ancient times lived in peace and contentment, without any avarice and fear. They worked, but never exhausted themselves, making it smooth for qi to flow in its own way. Everything was satisfactory to their wishes and that was why they could achieve whatever they wished.)

整段文字,文简趣深,气韵相调,精妙至诚。若将其翻译成英语,则很难在译文中保持如此典雅的形质神韵。纵观海内外现有的几种《内经》译本,能使译文与原文形神相应、音韵相合者,几乎没有。这是英译《内经》时译者不得不面对的一大现实难题。

《内经》语言精美卓绝,修辞手法灵活多样,且常常互参并举,为其理论体系的构建和理法方药的推演开辟了广阔的思辨空间,成为《内经》学术思想体系不可分割的一个重要组成部分,同时也为中国修辞学嗣后的发展奠定了实践基础。这从庄子的《养生主》到孟子的《公孙丑章句》,从《红楼梦》到《聊斋志异》,即可看出几分端倪。

(三)修辞特点与翻译赏析

《内经》全书23万余言,文简趣深,气韵相调。其修辞手法,精妙绝异,几达至善,几近至美。除现今较为流行的比喻、比拟、借代、对偶等手法外,还广泛使用了诸如联珠、辟复、互文、讳饰等卓异修辞之法。

1. 比喻

比喻有明喻和隐喻之分。明喻一般由本体、喻体和喻词组成,常用的喻词有"如"、"若"、"犹"、"譬"、"似"、"像"等。而隐喻则常常以判断句的方式出现,实际上却体现了比喻之法,只是这种比喻不似明喻那么直接,所以称为隐喻。

《内经》常用明喻和隐喻的方法来阐述医理、医法。这其实与中国古代学者认识事物和分析事物的基本方法有着密切的关系。在中国古代,人们在进行理论探讨或思想论辩时,常常借助于比喻之法来阐明事物的原理,揭示问题的本质。这种论述的方式在诸子百家著作中,可谓屡见不鲜。《内经》中属于明喻的例子很多,如:

例1:目裹微肿,<u>如卧蚕起之状</u>,曰水。(《素问·平人气象论》)

这句话的意思是说,眼睑微肿,如卧蚕之状,即为水病。将眼睑之肿比喻为"卧蚕",可谓形象之至。Veith 将其译为"When within the eye there is a minute swelling, as though a dormant silkworm were beginning to take shape, it is said to have been caused through water"。美籍华人吴连胜、吴奇氏父子将其译为"When the eyelid is swelling like the silkworm lying torpid, it is also the disease associated with water"。两者均采用"化比喻为比喻"之法翻译"卧蚕",大致符合原文之意。但就整句话的理解和翻译来看,二者均似未尽其善。如所谓"曰水",就是"水病"(edema)的意思,不是什么 caused through water 或 associated with water。

例2:夫善用针者,取其疾也,<u>犹拔刺也</u>,<u>犹雪污也</u>,<u>犹解结也</u>,<u>犹决闭也</u>。(《灵枢·九针十二原》)

在论述针刺治疗疾病的神奇疗效时,原文以"犹"为喻词,一连使用了四个比喻,说明了针刺治病的原理。吴氏父子将其译为"A physician who is good at acupuncture can cure the disease, even it is a protracted disease, just like pulling a sting, removing a stain, untie a knot or clear away the silt in the river flow"。译文的意思是清楚的,但句式结构似乎不够简洁明了。若调整为"Those who are good at acupuncture treat diseases just as simple as pulling a sting, removing a stain, untying a knot or clearing away silt in a river",似乎更为紧凑一些。

例3:天之道也,<u>如迎浮云</u>,<u>若视深渊</u>。(《素问·六微旨大论》)

本例通过比喻之法,将"天道"(law of nature)的幽深和神秘进行了形象的描述,认为对于常人而言,"天道"犹如浮云一样捉摸不定,恰似深渊一样幽不可探。吴氏父子将其译为"How profound is the principle of heaven: It is like the floating cloud above, and the deep abyss below."这个译文与原文在语义和形式上还是比较接近的。但若将"天道"译作 law of nature,可能更符合原文之意。

《内经》隐喻的例子亦很多,如:

例4:太阳为<u>开</u>,阳明为<u>阖</u>,少阳为<u>枢</u>。(《素问·阴阳离合论》)

在这句话中,以"为"作隐喻词,一共使用了三个隐喻。Veith 将其译作"The Great Yang acts as opening factor, the 'sunlight' acts as covering factor, and the lesser Yang acts as axis or central point"。将"为"译作 act as,可谓达旨。"太阳"、"阳明"和"少阳"现多音译为 taiyang, yangming, shaoyang。也有的将其分别译作 greater yang, bright yang, lesser yang,但使用范围远不及音译者广泛。此外,"开"、"阖"和"枢"现一般多译作 opening, closing, pivoting。

例5:阴阳者,血气之<u>男女</u>也。(《素问·阴阳应象大论》)

本例貌似判断句,实际上却是隐喻,即以"男女"比喻"血气"的阴阳属性。若对此判断不明,则必然释义含混。Veith 将其译为"Yin and Yang [the two elements in nature] create desires and vigor in men and women",可谓南辕北辙。另一位海外译者 Maoshing Ni 将其译为"the masculine and feminine principles, the qi and the blood, all reflect the interplay of yin and yang",释义不明。吴氏父子将其译为"For human being, those who draw support from Yang energy abundantly are men and are of vital energy, those who draw support from Yin energy abundantly are women and are of blood, so the Yin and Yang are the man and woman of energy and blood",更是毫厘之失。

实际上这句话的意思是:以阴阳来区分血气的属性,则血为阴,气为阳。所以这句话的恰当释义应该是"If yin and yang are used to differentiate the nature of blood and qi, blood pertains to yin while qi to yang."

例6:胃者,水谷之<u>海</u>,六腑之大<u>源</u>也。(《素问·五脏别论》)

本例也是一个看似判断、实则隐喻的句子,即将"胃"比做饮食之"海"和"六腑"之"源"。Veith 将其译作"The stomach acts as a place of accumulation for water and grain and as a source of supply for the six bowels."这个译文基本揭示了原文的隐喻之意。但在有关概念的翻译上,却颇值商榷。如将"六腑"译作 six bowels,语义即显局促。事实上,bowel 只是六腑之一,而不是全部。"六腑"现一般多译作 six fu-organs 或 six fu-viscera。另外,"水谷之海"现一般多直译为 sea of water and grain。

2. 借喻

所谓借喻，即以彼作此，只言喻体，不言本体。此一修辞手法虽然新颖，但若不解其本体之实，便难晓其实际所指。

例7：开鬼门，洁净府，精以时服，五阳已布，疏涤五脏。（《素问·汤液醪醴论》）

在本例中，"开鬼门"、"洁净府"就是借喻，借"鬼门"和"净府"来比喻"汗孔"和"膀胱"。不了解这个借喻，便难明其实。Veith 在翻译这句话时，因不解其喻，便信笔曲意旁解。其译文如下：

One should restore their bodies and open the anus so that the bowels can be cleansed, and so that the secretions come at the proper time and serve the five viscera which belong to Yang, the principle of life. One should put in order the five viscera which were remiss and cleanse and purify them.

在这个译文中，译者将"鬼门"（sweating pores）理解为 anus（肛门），将"净府"（bladder）理解为 bowels（肠道），乃指鹿为马之误。所谓"开鬼门"，即 inducing sweating；所谓"洁净府"，即 promoting urine discharge。其他内容的理解和翻译也颇为南辕北辙，不合原意。如"精以时服"指"水精得以正常运行"（normal flow of water essence），不是 the secretions come at the proper time；"五阳已布"指"五脏的阳气得以敷布"（distribution of yang from the five zang-organs），而不是什么 serve the five viscera which belong to Yang，因为以阴阳分"脏腑"，则"五脏"从来都属阴而不属阳；"疏涤五脏"指"五脏郁积得以疏通涤除"（removing stagnation in the five zang-organs），而不是 put in order the five viscera which were remiss and cleanse and purify them。

例8：观权衡规矩，而知病所主。（《素问·阴阳应象大论》）

在本例中，"权"（the sliding weight of a steelyard）指秤锤，"衡"（steelyard）指秤杆，"规"（compasses）指圆规，"矩"（carpenter's square）指曲尺。《内经》用"权"、"衡"、"规"、"矩"比喻四时脉象。这里所谓的"观权衡规矩"，就是诊察四时脉象的常变（carefully examining the normal states and variations of the pulse in the four seasons）。Veith 在翻译时疏

忽了这里的借喻关系,所以对原文作了别样解译。其译文如下:

One should examine irregularities which must be adjusted according to custom and usage, and then the location where the disease prevails will become known.

将"权衡规矩"理解为 custom and usage(习俗和用法),实属奇谈怪论了。

例9:论言治寒以热,治热以寒,而方士不能废<u>绳墨</u>而更其道也。(《素问·至真要大论》)

"绳墨"指木工测量木材时所使用的线绳和墨斗,本例借以比喻规则和原则。吴氏父子将这句话译为"It was stated in the treatise that one should treat cold disease with the hot medicine, treat hot disease with the cold medicine and a physician must not annul this rule to treat in some other ways."译文虽然略嫌透迤,但基本意思还是明确的。

3. 比拟

比拟又有拟人和拟物之分。所谓拟人,就是将自然事物按照人的情态予以刻画描述,从而使所描述对象显得生动活泼。所谓拟物,就是以物拟物的修辞方式。拟人和拟物这两种修辞手法在《内经》中都比较常见,这也是《内经》语言显得生动活泼的原因之一。

例10:肝恶风,心恶热,肺恶寒,肾恶燥,脾恶湿,此五脏气所恶也。(《灵枢·九针论》)

"恶"(音 wù),是"厌恶"、"憎恶"的意思,常用来表示人的情态感受。这里用"恶"表述五脏的生理特点,就属拟人之用。这里的"恶"可以译为 detest 或 dislike。吴氏父子在翻译这句话时,即采用了这一译法,其译文如下:

The liver detests the wind, the heart detests the heat, the lung detests the cold, the kidney detests the dryness, the spleen detests the wetness. These are the five detestations of the viscera to the various energies.

译文中的 wind, heat, cold, dryness, wetness 之前似不必加定冠词,因其属泛指。此外,"湿"译作 wetness 在程度上有太过之虞,现一般多译为 dampness。"五脏气"即"五脏","气"暗含"功能"之意,译作 five zang-organs 或 five viscera 即可,不必硬译为 the viscera to the various energies。

例11：气有余则制己所胜而侮所不胜，其不及则己所胜侮而乘之，己所胜轻而侮之。（《素问·五运行大论》）

"侮"是"侮辱"、"欺侮"的意思，常用以描绘人的不当之为。本例中用"侮"描述五行运动中因气有余而引起的"恃强凌弱"的现象。这句话的意思是说"五运之气太过，不仅加重克制它所能克制的气，而且还欺侮本来克制它自己的气。但若五运之气不及，则原属于自己所克制的气，却轻视自己反而加以侵犯"（If the motion is excessive, it will control the one inferior to it and subjugate the one superior to it; if the motion is insufficient, it will be subjugated by the one normally inferior to it）。有些较为流行的注解本对这句话的解释似乎有误。如山东中医学院和河北中医学院所编写的《黄帝内经素问校释》（人民卫生出版社，1982年版）对这句话恰好作了相反的解释。在一些流行的英语译本中，这句话的翻译也常常似是而非。吴氏父子将其译作：

When the element's motion arrives at the time when it should not arrive, it shows the energy is excessive, not only it will invade the element's energy which it can subjugate (such as wood subjugates earth), but will also subjugate reversely the element which can overcome itself (such as wood subjugates metal reversely). When the element's motion is not arriving when it should arrive, it shows the energy is insufficient, when it is insufficient, it will not only be subjugated by the element which can overcome itself (such as wood being subjugated by the metal), but also will be subjugated reversely by the element which can not overcome itself (such as earth subjugates wood reversely).

原文颇为简洁，译文却显得繁琐晦涩，且不易理解。

例12：谷味酸，先走肝，谷味苦，先走心，谷味甘，先走脾，谷味辛，先走肺，谷味咸，先走肾。（《灵枢·五味》）

用"走"来描述五味的趋向，颇有拟人之味。所谓"走肝"、"走心"等，就是"入肝"、"入心"的意思。这里的"走"可以译为 enter，吴氏父子之译就是如此。其译文如下：

The sour taste tends to enter into the liver first; the bitter taste tends to enter into the heart first; the sweet taste tends to enter into the spleen first; the acrid taste tends to enter into the lung first; the salty taste tends to enter into the kidney first.

译文与原文之意基本吻合。但 enter 宜取其及物之用,删去 into 似乎更为妥当。

4. 对偶

对偶是汉语特有的修辞方式,这种修辞方式可使文句形式上工整、结构上匀称、视觉上醒目、听觉上悦耳,有很强的感染力。这种修辞格式在六朝时发展到极致,从而形成了重视声韵和谐、辞藻华丽的骈体文体。《内经》中对偶修辞法的运用则比较灵活多样,不似六朝骈体那样讲究辞藻。

例13:拘于鬼神者,不可与言至德;恶于针石者,不可于言至巧。(《素问·五脏别论》)

本例是一则典型的对偶句式,字数相同,结构一致,表述一体。这里的"拘"是"拘守"的意思,所谓"拘于鬼神者"(those who are superstitious and believe that diseases are caused by ghosts or spirits)就是迷信鬼神的意思,以为疾病是由鬼神作祟而引起的;"至德"(abstruse theory of medicine)指"至深的道理",所谓"不可与言至德"(it is improper to talk about the abstruse theory of medicine with them),就是不能与之讨论至深的医学道理;"至巧"(excellent therapeutic methods)指精巧的医疗技术,所谓"不可与言至巧"(it is improper to discuss excellent therapeutic methods with them),就是不可以与之讨论精巧的医疗技术。

海外一些翻译人员不了解此句之寓意,翻译时按字释义,往往使译文文理浑漫不清。Veith 将这句话翻译为"Those who would restrain the demons and the gods (good and evil spirits) cannot attain virtue by speaking about it; and those who dislike acupuncture cannot achieve ingenious results by speaking about them." 比较原文和译文,未尽之意不言自明矣。

例14:草生五色,五色之变,不可胜视;草生五味,五味之美,不可胜极。(《素问·六节藏象论》)

本例既使用了对偶,也使用了联珠的修辞格式。关于联珠修辞格,下文将详加介绍。这里所谓"不可胜视"(unable to observe all)指"看也看不尽"的意思;所谓"不可胜极"(unable to taste all)指"尝也尝不尽"。海外译者对此之理解常有悖于原意。Veith 将其译为"Grass and herbs bring forth the five colors; nothing that can be seen excels the variations of these five colors. Grass and herbs also produce the five flavors; nothing excels the deliciousness of these five flavors."整个译文的意思还是比较清楚的,但对"不可胜视"和"不可胜极"的翻译,却不太符合原文之意,因之颇值商榷。

Ni 将其翻译为"In the plant kingdom there are the five colors. Within the five colors there are variations in tone. The plants have five flavors. Though distinct, there are also variations of the flavors."比较原文,译文的意思似乎更加难以琢磨。

例 15:故积阳为天,积阴为地。阴静阳躁,阳生阴长。阳杀阴藏。阳化气,阴成形。寒极生热,热极生寒。寒气生浊,热气生清。清气在下,则生飧泄;浊气在上,则生䐜胀。(《素问·阴阳应象大论》)

这段论述所采用的也是典型的对偶修辞格。除"阴静阳躁,阳生阴长。阳杀阴藏"在结构上略有出入外,其他各部分均属对偶句法。整段话的含义非常清楚,理解起来并不困难。但从海外译者的翻译实践来看,却并非如此。下面是 Veith 对这段话的翻译:

Heaven was created by an accumulation of Yang, the element of light; Earth was created by an accumulation of Yin, the element of darkness. Yang stands for peace and serenity, Yin stands for recklessness and turmoil. Yang stands for destruction and Yin stands for conservation. Yang causes evaporation and Yin gives shape to things. Extreme cold brings forth intense heat (fever) and intense heat brings forth extreme cold (chills). Cold air generates mud and corruption; hot air generates clarity and honesty. If the air upon the earth is clear, then food is produced and eaten at leisure. If the air above is foul, it causes dropsical swellings.

在这段译文中,"故积阳为天,积阴为地。阴静阳躁,阳生阴长。阳杀阴藏。阳化气,阴成形。寒极生热,热极生寒"的翻译还是比较达意的。但"寒气生浊,热气生清。清气在下,则生飧泄;浊气在上,则生䐜胀"的翻译,却颇为浑漫不清。如"寒气生浊"(coldness produces turbid yin)指寒气凝结可以产生浊阴,而不是产生什么 mud and corruption;"热气生清"(hotness ascends to produce lucid yang)指热气升腾可以产生清阳,而不是产生什么 clarity and honesty;"清气在下,则生飧泄"(failure of lucid yang to rise up causes undigested diarrhea)指清阳应升而不升则可引起飧泄,"飧泄"即完谷不化之泄泻,而不是什么 food is produced and eaten at leisure;"浊气在上"(failure of turbid yin to descend)指浊阴之气该降不降,不是什么 the air above is foul;"则生䐜胀"(abdominal distension and fullness)

指引起胀满,译作 dropsical swellings 似意犹未尽。

5. 联珠

联珠也叫顶真或顶针,就是用前一句话的结尾词作为后一句话的开首词,使两句话首尾相贯,丝丝入扣,从而加强语气。有人统计,《内经》中使用联珠修辞手法的有两百多处,这为《内经》物理与医理的论述增色不少。联珠还分直接蝉联、简介蝉联和交错蝉联等不同形式。

例16:寒气化为热,热胜则腐肉,腐肉则为脓,脓不泻则烂筋,筋烂则伤骨,骨伤则髓消。(《灵枢·痈疽》)

本例属典型的联珠修辞格,各分句首尾用词完全一致。由于中英语言的差异,中文这种独特的修辞格一般都很难在译文中得以保持。吴氏父子的译文就很能说明问题。其译文如下:

The cold-evil can turn into heat, and when heat is excessive it will corrupt the muscle, and when the muscle is corrupted, it will change into pus, when the pus is not eliminated, it will corrupt the tendon, when the tendon is corrupted, it will injure the bone, when the bone is injured, it will consume the marrow.

整个译文的意思还是比较清楚的,但结构似乎不够精练。若采用分号对有关内容进行分割处理,各部分之间的关系会更加清晰,整个句子的逻辑关系也将更加明确。

例17:东方生风,风生木,木生酸,酸生肝,肝生筋,筋生心。(《素问·五运行大论篇》)

本例亦属典型联珠修辞格,每一分句和下一分句之间首尾相贯,密切相关。本句谓语虽只用一个动词"生",但其意却各有不同,不能一概译作 generate 或 produce。"东方生风,风生木,木生酸"之"生"可以译作 generate 或 produce。但"酸生肝,肝生筋,筋生心"之"生"却不宜译作 generate 或 produce,而应译作 nourish 或 promote。

Veith 将本例翻译为"The East creates the wind; wind creates wood; wood creates the sour flavor; the sour flavor strengthens the liver; the liver nourishes the muscles; the muscles strengthen the heart."

Veith 对本例的翻译，无论从结构还是从内涵上看，都和原文比较接近，十分难得。特别是对"生"一字的翻译，更是可圈可点。虽然本例一连使用了六个"生"，以表达相关概念之间的关系，但 Veith 却使用了三个不同的英语单词进行翻译，如将"筋生心"和"酸生肝"之"生"译作 strengthen，将"肝生筋"之"生"译作 nourish，皆属可取。但将"东方生风"、"风生木"、"木生酸"之"生"一概译作 create，却颇值推敲。其实"风生木"之"生"，含有 promote 或 invigorate 或 resuscitate 之意。

例18：故清阳为天，浊阴为地。地气上为云，天气下为雨。雨处地气，云出天气。（《素问·阴阳应象大论》）

本例所体现的就是交错联珠修辞法。句首尾字"天"与第四句的句首之字相关联，第二句的尾字"地"与第三句的句首相关联。第三句的句尾字"云"与第六句的句首相关联。第四句的句尾字"雨"又与第五句的句首字相关联。也就是说，在这段话中，两组联珠修辞格交错相贯，巧妙结合，形成了一种交互关联、珠联璧合的修辞效果。

这种珠联璧合的修辞格式虽然美妙绝伦，但却难化转到译文之中。这从现行的几个《内经》英译本中，即可看出几分端倪。如 Veith 将这段话译为"The pure and lucid element of light represents Heaven and the turbid element of darkness represents Earth. When the vapors of the earth ascend they create clouds, and when the vapors of Heaven descend they create rain. Thus rain appears to be the climate of the earth and clouds appear to be the climate of Heaven."。

这个译文自然无法再现原文的交错联珠修辞法，这是可以理解的。除此之外，译文对原文的解析亦存在诸多值得商榷之处。如将"地气"和"天气"译为 climate of the earth 和 climate of Heaven，显属失当。"清阳为天"指"清阳之气升腾而为天"，"浊阴为地"指"浊阴之气下降凝聚而为地"，译作 the pure and lucid element of light represents Heaven 和 the turbid element of darkness represents Earth，与原文颇不吻合。

《内经》虽然成书于秦汉之际，但其修辞手法不但至善至美，而且灵活多样，丰富和发展了我国古代修辞学。限于篇幅，这里仅举数例以示其貌。虽然这些修辞手法在目前的翻译实践中还无法一一化转到译文之中，但对其系统而深入的了解，有利于我们完整准确地掌握《内经》的语言特点和行文风格，从而更好地理解其实际内涵并将其以较为贴切的方式传达到译文之中。

五、课后练习

（一）思考题

1. 《黄帝内经》是怎样的一部经典？
2. 《黄帝内经》的理论基础是什么？
3. 《黄帝内经》在中国文化走向世界历史进程中的作用与地位是怎样的？

（二）翻译题

1. 余闻上古有真人者，提挈天地，把握阴阳，呼吸精气，独立守神，肌肉若一，故能寿敝天地，无有终时，此其道生。中古之时有至人者，淳德全道，和于阴阳，调于四时，去世离俗，积精全神，游行天地之间，视听八达之外，此盖益其寿命而强者也；亦归于真人。其次有圣人者，处天地之和，从八风之理，适嗜欲于世俗之间，无恚嗔之心，行不欲离于世，被服章，举不欲现于俗，外不劳形于事，内无思想之患，以恬愉为务，以自得为功，形体不敝，精神不散，亦可以百数。其次有贤人者，法则天地，象似日月，辩列星辰，逆从阴阳，分别四时，将从上古合同于道，亦可使益寿而有极时。

2. 春三月，此谓发陈，天地俱生，万物以荣，夜卧早起，广步于庭，被发缓形，以使志生，生而勿杀，予而勿夺，赏而勿罚，此春气之应，养生之道也。逆之则伤肝，夏为寒变，奉长者少。夏三月，此谓蕃秀，天地气交，万物华实，夜卧早起，无厌于日，使志无怒，使华英成秀，使气得泄，若所爱在外，此夏气之应，养长之道也。逆之则伤心，秋为痎疟，奉收者少，冬至重病。秋三月，此谓容平，天气以急，地气以明，早卧早起，与鸡俱兴，使志安宁，以缓秋刑，收敛神气，使秋气平，无外其志，使肺气清，此秋气之应，养收之道也。逆之则伤肺，冬为飧泄，奉藏者少。冬三月，此谓闭脏，水冰地坼，无扰乎阳，早卧晚起，必待日光，使志若伏若匿，若有私意，若已有得，去寒就温，无泄皮肤，使气亟夺；此冬气之应，养藏之道也。逆之则伤肾，春为痿厥，奉生者少。

3. 阴阳者，天地之道也，万物之纲纪，变化之父母，生杀之本始，神明之府也，治病必求于本。故积阳为天，积阴为地。阴静阳躁，阳生阴长。阳杀阴藏。阳化气，阴成形。寒极生热，热极生寒。寒气生浊，热气生清。清气在下，则生飧泄；浊气在上，则生䐜胀。此阴阳反作，病之逆从也。故清阳为天，浊阴为地。地气上为云，天气下为雨。雨处地气，云出天气。故清阳出上窍，浊阴出下窍；清阳发腠理，浊阴走五脏；清阳实四支，浊阴归六腑。

4. 女子七岁，肾气盛，齿更发长；二七而天癸至，任脉通，太冲脉盛，月事以时下，故有子;三七,肾气平均,故真牙生而长极;四七筋骨坚,发长极,身体盛壮;五七,阳明脉衰,面始焦,发始堕;六七,三阳脉衰于上,面皆焦,发始白;七七,任脉虚,太冲脉衰少,天癸竭,地道不通,故形坏而无子也。丈夫八岁,骨气实,发长齿更。二八,肾气盛,天癸至,精气溢泻,阴阳和,故能有子;三八,肾气平均,筋骨劲强,故真牙生而长极;四八,筋骨隆盛,肌肉满壮;五八,肾气衰,发堕齿槁;六八,阳气衰竭于上,面焦,发鬓斑白;七八,肝气衰,筋不能动。八八,天癸竭,精少,肾脏衰,形体皆极,则齿发去。肾者主水,受五脏六腑之精而藏之,故五脏盛乃能泻。今五脏皆衰,筋骨解堕,天癸尽矣,故发鬓白,身体重,行步不正,而无子耳。

5. 心者,君主之官也,神明出焉。肺者,相傅之官,治节出焉。肝者,将军之官,谋虑出焉。胆者,中正之官,决断出焉。膻中者,臣使之官,喜乐出焉。脾胃者,仓廪之官,五味出焉。大肠者,传道之官,变化出焉。小肠者,受盛之官,化物出焉。肾者,作强之官,伎巧出焉。三焦者,决渎之官,水道出焉。膀胱者,州都之官,津液藏焉,气化则能出矣。凡此十二官者,不得相失也。故主明则下安,以此养生则寿,殁世不殆,以为天下则大昌。主不明则十二官危,使道闭塞而不通,形乃大伤,以此养生则殃,以为天下者,其宗大危,戒之戒之!

参考读物

Veith, Ilza. The Yellow Emperor's Classic of Internal Medicine [M]. California: California University Press, 2002.

Ni, Maoshing. The Yellow Emperor's Classic of Medicine [M]. Boston: Shambhala Publications, Inc., 1995.

Unchuld, P. U. Huang Di Nei Jing Su Wen [M]. Los Angelis and London: University of California Press, 2003.

李照国,刘希茹. 大中华文库汉英对照黄帝内经·灵枢[M]. 西安:世界图书出版公司,2008.

李照国,刘希茹. 大中华文库汉英对照黄帝内经·素问[M]. 西安:世界图书出版公司,2005.

吴连胜,吴奇译. 黄帝内经. 北京:中国科学技术出版社[M],1997.